William Metcalfe, Joseph Metcalfe

Out of the Clouds Into the Light

William Metcalfe, Joseph Metcalfe

Out of the Clouds Into the Light

ISBN/EAN: 9783337345693

Printed in Europe, USA, Canada, Australia, Japan

Cover: Foto ©Lupo / pixelio.de

More available books at **www.hansebooks.com**

OUT OF THE CLOUDS:

INTO THE LIGHT.

SEVENTEEN DISCOURSES

ON THE

LEADING DOCTRINES OF THE DAY,

IN THE

LIGHT OF BIBLE CHRISTIANITY.

BY THE LATE
REV. WM. METCALFE, M.D.

TOGETHER WITH A

MEMOIR OF THE AUTHOR,

BY HIS SON,
REV. JOSEPH METCALFE.

PHILADELPHIA:
J. B. LIPPINCOTT & CO.
1872.

KIND READER,—A work like the one before you needs little preface. The memoir of its author, by his son, will introduce you to the man.

In the sermons which follow, the man speaks for himself of the truths to which he dedicated his life.

CONTENTS.

MEMOIR OF THE REV. WILLIAM METCALFE.

CHAPTER I.

Introduction—Birth and Early Education of Wm. Metcalfe—Exemplary Youth—Literary Taste—Theological Studies—Adoption of a Vegetarian Diet—Marriage . . . 9

CHAPTER II.

History of the Origin of the "Bible-Christian Church"—Mr. Metcalfe studies under Dr. Cowherd—Death of Dr. Cowherd—Emigration to America of a Number of "Bible-Christians" with the Rev. William Metcalfe—Defection and Separation—Mr. Metcalfe opens an Academy—Organization of the "Bible-Christian Church" in Philadelphia . 15

CHAPTER III.

Allurements in Poverty—Mr. Metcalfe as a Preacher—The Doctrines he presented—Opposition of the Clergy to his Preaching—His Reply and Challenge—No Response—Removal to Kensington 21

CHAPTER IV.

The First Total-Abstinence Society and the First Tract on Entire Abstinence from all Intoxicating Liquors—The

Dietetic Reform—The Labors of Mr. Metcalfe in behalf of Vegetarianism—Mr. Metcalfe engages in Printing and Editing—Graduates as an M.D. 31

CHAPTER V.

Rebuilding and Dedication of the "Bible-Christian Church" —Correspondence with James Simpson, Esq., and Drs. Graham and Alcott—Formation of the American Vegetarian Society—Mr. Metcalfe's Visit to England—Death of Mrs. Metcalfe—The Organ of the Vegetarians—Mr. Metcalfe's Duties and Labors—Invitation to Revisit England as Pastor of the "Bible-Christian Church"—Marriage to Miss Cariss—Departure for England 36

CHAPTER VI.

Mr. Metcalfe in England—The Death of Joseph Brotherton, M.P.—Returns to his Church in Philadelphia—Death of Dr. William A. Alcott—Election of Rev. Dr. Metcalfe to the Presidency of the Vegetarian Society—Ordination of his Successor in the Ministry—Celebration of the Semi-Centennial Anniversary of his own Ordination—The Closing Days of his Life—Death—Remarks on his Life—The Funeral Sermon 41

CHAPTER VII.

Description of a Tablet to the Memory of the Rev. William Metcalfe—Testimonials—Resolutions adopted by the "Bible-Christian Church" of Philadelphia—Letter of Condolence from Christ Church, Salford, England 48

TRIBUTE OF RESPECT 49

DISCOURSES.

DISCOURSE I.
On the Being and Unity of God 53

DISCOURSE II.
On the Lord Jesus Christ 63

DISCOURSE III.
On the Trinity 75

DISCOURSE IV.
The Bible a Divine Revelation 89

DISCOURSE V.
On Creation 101

DISCOURSE VI.
On the Original State of Man 112

DISCOURSE VII.
On the Popular Doctrine of Original Sin . . . 122

DISCOURSE VIII.
On the Garden of Eden and its Trees 133

DISCOURSE IX.
On the Forbidden Fruit, and the Tempter . . . 141

DISCOURSE X.

Bible Testimony on Abstinence from the Flesh of Animals as Food 151

DISCOURSE XI.

On the Sacrifices of the Jews 184

DISCOURSE XII.

On the Ten Commandments 197

DISCOURSE XIII.

On the Resurrection of Jesus Christ, and the Divine Nature of his Resurrection-Body 206

DISCOURSE XIV.

On the Passion of the Cross, or Salvation by the Blood of Christ 215

DISCOURSE XV.

On Faith 225

DISCOURSE XVI.

Sermon Delivered on the Fiftieth Anniversary of Ordination, August 11th, 1861 236

DISCOURSE XVII.

The Jubilee—Being a Historical Sketch of the Bible-Christian Church—June 12th, 1859 247

MEMOIR

OF THE

REV. WILLIAM METCALFE.

CHAPTER I.

Introduction—Birth and Early Education of Wm. Metcalfe—Exemplary Youth—Literary Taste—Theological Studies—Adoption of a Vegetarian Diet—Marriage.

A GOOD man's life is a worthy subject of study. Besides furnishing an illustration of the powers and graces of honest virtue, it also assists to a knowledge of ourselves. Genius or talent alone may secure great distinction, but simple goodness will prove more powerful for human happiness than both combined. The conviction of this truth is growing upon the public mind; and it is hoped that these pages will aid in giving it strength.

It is not claimed that the subject of this memoir was endowed with extraordinary mental powers, or that he had attained extensive notoriety in the world. The Rev. WM. METCALFE was simply a Christian minister, unpretending and unobtrusive in deportment. He was an honest, conscientious, RELIGIOUS REFORMER; and it is his life and labors as such that this brief sketch is intended to exhibit. As his son, I sincerely and gratefully honor his character:

yet my purpose here is not to eulogize *him*, but only to furnish, in unadorned simplicity, the narrative of a well-spent life.

The Rev. William Metcalfe was the son of Jonathan and Elizabeth Metcalfe. He was born at Sproadgill, in the parish of Orton, Westmoreland, England, March 11th, 1788. His parents were in moderate circumstances, and contrived to give him a good classical education at the academy of Mr. Roberts, who was then celebrated as a philologist and the author of an English dictionary.

At the age of nineteen, he left home, with the consent of his parents, to see what he could do in the world. He soon obtained employment, engaging himself as an accountant in an establishment near Keighley, Yorkshire. As he was entirely dependent upon his own exertions, and as he found his situation agreeable, he at once considered himself settled.

His course of life at this period furnishes an admirable example to youth generally, of the importance of starting in the world with a proper moral ideal. Doubtless he had all the ardent flow of animation which is common to youth; he was inexperienced in the temptations of town life; he was among strangers, and free from the restraints of immediate parental oversight; but Providence seems to have early surrounded him with religiously-disposed associates, and he at once accepted the Christian influences, and thus secured himself in a great measure from the direct temptations of evil society. He was a constant attendant of the church services on the Sabbath day, and at length attached himself to the "New Church" of Keighley, then under the pastorship of his subsequent father-in-law, the Rev. JOSEPH WRIGHT.

His leisure hours appear to have been occupied in literary pursuits; and the Muses came in for a share of his attentions. Born and educated among the pastoral hills of Westmoreland, his poetical efforts were distinguished for their rural simplicity and amiability. In 1809 he paid, as he supposed, his farewell visit to his boyhood's home. The following lines, bearing date "Kendal, Sunday evening, May 21st, 1809," are a transcript of his feelings and his style at that time. They are headed

ON LEAVING MY NATIVE PLACE.

Farewell, good friends, companions, youthful mates!
May comfort smile within your cheering gates!
Farewell those hours that bless'd the youthful scene
When mutual kindness echoed through the green;
When gambols, harmless as the tender dove,
Endear'd our hearts, and oped the mind to love:
My Brothers, Sisters, Parents,—all adieu!
What thanks can pay the debts I owe to you?

Ye happy cots, where Peace untroubled lives,
Where Heaven-made bounty each one's want relieves;
Within whose doors all happiness I've known;
In each one welcome, frown'd upon by none:
Each guileless eye beam'd on my youthful face,
And kindly hail'd me with an artless grace:
Ah! can I from such friends, such kindness, part
Without the tribute of a grateful heart?

Peace, health, to all!—and may your hearts receive
That joy and kindness they so gladly give:—
Whate'er my fortune in this world may be,
Whate'er kind Providence may do for me,
Whate'er my lot in life's uncertain scene,
Still I'll remember what with you I've been:
This look's my last, from off this well-known peak:
My feelings dictate, but I cannot speak.

His pastor, recognizing his talents, persuaded him to apply himself to the study of Theology, with a view to the ministry. He freely gave him his assistance, and supplied him with books. Next to the word of God itself, Swedenborg became his favorite author. Mr. Metcalfe read all the works of the illuminated Scribe within his reach, with avidity and care; and acknowledged that they supplied the most nourishing food to the understanding in the whole field of theological literature. Whilst he was ready to honor truth, come from what source it might, he considered Swedenborg a powerful uprooter of doctrinal errors and a good sower of Bible seeds.

The Rev. Joseph Wright had carried on a correspondence for some years with the Rev. WILLIAM COWHERD, at one time President of the "*New Church*" Conference, and an ordaining minister of that body. In some of his letters, the Rev. Dr. Cowherd eloquently presented the doctrine of entire abstinence from all animal food and from all intoxicating drinks. He urged this abstinence as a healthful, moral, and religious duty. Mr. Metcalfe was favored with the perusal of those letters by his pastor, who had himself already yielded to the humane and Scriptural testimony adduced in regard to this discipline, although he did not make it a test of church-membership. Mr. Metcalfe examined the whole subject with great care, reviewing all the evidences, scientific and Scriptural, and finally determined to test the system by a personal experiment. Accordingly, on the 1st of September, 1809, he gave up, at once and entirely, fish, flesh, and fowl as food, and every kind of intoxicating liquors as drink; and so favorably impressed was he with his own experience that he *never* after even tasted the one or the other.

Mr. WILLIAM METCALFE married Miss SUSANNA WRIGHT, daughter of the Rev. Joseph Wright, on the 14th of January, 1810. She was some years his senior in age, earnest in the advocacy of the system of diet he had adopted, and was possessed of a cultivated mind.

It is not to be supposed that Mr. Metcalfe adopted a vegetarian life without meeting with the opposition of those whom he respected and loved. In a letter describing this period of his life, he gives the following historical testimony:—

"My friends laughed at me, and entreated me to lay aside my foolish notions of a vegetable diet. They assured me I was rapidly sinking into a consumption, and tried various other methods to induce me to return to the customary dietetic habits of society; but their efforts proved ineffectual. Some predicted my death in three or four months; and others, on hearing me attempt to defend my course, hesitated not to tell me I was certainly suffering from mental derangement, and, if I continued to live without flesh-food much longer, would unquestionably have to be shut up in some insane-asylum. All was unavailing. Instead of sinking into consumption, I gained several pounds in weight during the first few weeks of my experiment. Instead of three or four months bringing me to the silent grave, they brought me to the matrimonial altar. I dared even to get married; and I am thankful to 'Our Father in heaven' that my mental operations have, up to this day, been such that I have never even seen the *interior* of any insane-institution.

"In my wife I found an invaluable helpmeet,—a blessing which all who enter the married state do not realize. She fully coincided with me in my views on vegetable diet, and, indeed, on all other important points,—was always ready to defend them to the best of her ability,—studied to show our acquaintances, whenever they paid us a visit, that we could live in every rational enjoyment without the use of flesh for food; and, being an excellent cook, we were never at a loss 'for what we should eat, although we would not have meat.' We commenced housekeeping in January, 1810; and from that date to the present time we have never had a pound of flesh-meat in our dwelling, have never patronized either slaughter-houses or grog-shops.

"When, again, in the course of time, we were about to be blessed with an addition to our family, a renewed effort was made. We were assured it was impossible for my wife to get through her confinement without some *more strengthening food*. Friends and physician were alike decided upon that point. We were, notwithstanding, unmoved, and faithful to our vegetarian principles. Next, we were told by our kind advisers that the little stranger could not be sufficiently nourished unless the mother would eat a little meat once a day, or, if not that, drink from half a pint to a pint of ale daily. To both proposals my wife turned a deaf ear; and, thanks to a Divine and Merciful Providence, both she and the child did exceedingly well."

It may be proper to add here that the "*little stranger*," above referred to, is the author of this Memoir, that he is in the fifty-sixth year of his age; that he has never so much as *tasted* animal food nor used intoxicating drinks of any kind, and that he is hale and hearty.

CHAPTER II.

History of the Origin of the "Bible-Christian Church"—Mr. Metcalfe studies under Dr. Cowherd—Death of Dr. Cowherd—Emigration to America of a Number of "Bible-Christians" with the Rev. William Metcalfe—Defection and Separation—Mr. Metcalfe opens an Academy —Organization of the "Bible-Christian Church" in Philadelphia.

As my father's future life is much interwoven with the succeeding history of the " Bible-Christian Church," it may be satisfactory to our readers to give here a brief account of its origin.

The Rev. Dr. COWHERD was, unquestionably, the first, most earnest, practical advocate, in the present century, of those reforms now technically called Temperance, or Tee-totalism, and Vegetarianism. As early as 1807 he publicly taught them, as imperative duties, from his pulpit. He labored to induce the clergy—especially those of the "New Church," or Swedenborgians—to acquaint themselves with the principles and testimony upon which they were advanced. But his zeal for these and some strictly theological views caused him, and those who coincided with him, to be treated with great coldness and indifference by the leading ministers of that Church. They denounced him and his friends as being "restless and uncontrollable," as "advocates of fanatical opinions," and as "not strictly adhering to the views of Swedenborg." The hope of a more tolerant spirit prevailing in the "New Church" counsels was feeble. Still, the Rev. Joseph Wright made an effort, by calling a Conference of the ministers and lay delegates of the "New Church," to be held at the Rev. Dr. Cowherd's church, Salford, Manchester, June 29th, 1809. No other Conference of the "New Church" was held that year; although the Conference of the year previous contemplated that one should be held in Manchester. Invitations were sent, and the Conference met. But the only ministers present were the Rev. Joseph Wright, of Keighley, the Rev. George Senior, of Dalton, near Huddersfield, the Rev. Samuel Dean, of Hulme, and the Rev. William Cowherd, of Salford,—both the latter churches representing Manchester. There were also a number of lay delegates from different parts of the kingdom. It was now evident that the "New Church" was not disposed to meet the issues. The Conference, however, was duly organized, and remained in session four days. Its deliberations were conducted throughout in an orderly and devout manner. Every inquiry was considered with candor, earnestness, and moderation, under a spirit of true Christian harmony and peace. It was unanimously agreed that the BIBLE, as the divinely inspired record of the word of God, contains all the principles and doctrines necessary to man's salvation,—that God was in CHRIST, and that beside HIM there is no other GOD. He is, therefore, the only proper object of worship. Disclaiming any human being or creed as authority, and cordially accepting the BIBLE as the divinely inspired word, and CHRIST as their only GOD, the members of the Conference desired to be known only as "BIBLE-CHRISTIANS." Much interest prevailed throughout the session, and there was not one discordant heart or dissentient voice from first to last. Such, in brief, is the history which ultimated in the organization of the visible "BIBLE-CHRISTIAN CHURCH."

Dr. Cowherd had instituted an Academy of Sciences at Salford, over which he presided, assisted by several other reverend gentlemen in the various departments. To this academy Mr. Metcalfe went as a student, designing to prepare himself for the ministry. When he had been there about a year, the Rev. Robert Hindmarsh withdrew from the classical department of the academy, and Dr. Cowherd immediately invited Mr. Metcalfe to assume the vacancy. This was in the early part of 1811. He accepted the offer, and continued in that position about two years.

In the mean time, my father's home was in Addingham, Yorkshire. Here he had got together a small congregation as early as 1810, to whom he dispensed the doctrines of Bible-Christianity on each successive Sabbath. At the solicitation of this congregation, Mr. Metcalfe was presented, by its representative Mr. Jonathan Wright, as a candidate for the ministry, to the Rev. Dr. Cowherd. He was, accordingly, ordained by that reverend divine on Sunday, August 11th, 1811, in Christ Church, Salford.

One of his church-members in Addingham erected a handsome church-building, in which was also a commodious school-room. This was placed at his service. He therefore left his position under Dr. Cowherd, and opened a grammar-school in the place prepared for him. Here he was much appreciated, both as a minister and a teacher, and the church and school were well sustained.

Whilst engaged at Salford, my father had formed a desire to emigrate to America. Nor was he alone in this desire. In one of his letters to a friend, written shortly after his ordination, he says, "The civil and religious freedom of the people of the United States has been the topic of many an hour's conversation among the teachers of the Salford Academy and the members of the church." He speaks also of Dr. Cowherd as an enthusiastic admirer of the free institutions of America. It appears that the then existing war between the two countries caused them to suppress their thoughts of removing: abandoned they were not, for on the restoration of peace the desire again became prominent. The arrangements for emigrating were, however, once more temporarily suspended, by the death of the Rev. Dr. Cowherd. This event took place on the 29th of March, 1816, and quite a gloom was cast upon all who had connected themselves with the "Bible-Christian Church," by that bereavement.

In the early part of the spring of 1817, a company of forty-one persons, all members of the "Bible-Christian Church," embarked from Liverpool for Philadelphia. This little community comprised two ministers,—the Rev. James Clark and the Rev. William Metcalfe,—with twenty other adults and nineteen children. After a tedious voyage of eleven weeks, they all landed safely and in good health at the port of their destination, on the 15th of June.

The crowning objects of these emigrants, as they professed, were the propagation of their peculiar religious doctrines and the establishment of the "Bible-Christian Church" in this highly favored land. But, alas! how frail and fickle are human purposes! Of the twenty-two adults and their families, eleven adults and seven children only were faithful when they reached Philadelphia. The strong salt breeze of the Atlantic, or some other cause, dissolved not only their purposes, but their practical precepts; and at the first opportunity they gave way to indulgences in eating and drinking those things which their principles had forbidden. Some of these might possibly have been reclaimed, had they been able to locate near their more faithful brethren. But all were poor, depending for their daily bread upon their daily labor, and to obtain employment they were necessarily scattered far apart. Thus isolated from one another, in a strange country, and among a people who had no sympathy with their habits, but who advised them that "it would be impossible to live in this *hot climate* without animal food," it is scarcely surprising that they relaxed their interest. Their heroism to principle failed them, and the "crowning objects" of their emigration, with them, at least, were abandoned.

This apostasy was a source of great sorrow and mortification to the faithful. They too were widely separated. The Rev. James Clark and family, with two other families who were his personal friends as well as strict members of the Church, determined to locate themselves as farmers. Accordingly, they purchased some wild land in Lycoming County, Pennsylvania, and removed thither. They formed a church and Sabbath-school; but, not meeting with that encouragement from the surrounding neighborhood which Mr. Clark thought them worthy of receiving, he resolved to remove. Ardent in temperament, he could not brook coldness and indifference in others. The following spring he went to Baltimore, leaving those who had devotedly followed *his lead* into the wilderness, still there. After much buffeting about, he finally settled as a farmer in the State of Indiana. Although he remained faithful to the principles of Bible-Christianity, he made no special effort to organize a church. The Rev. James Clark died, August 31, 1826, in the forty-seventh year of his age.

The Rev. William Metcalfe remained in Philadelphia, intending, by the blessing of Providence, to support himself and family by school-teaching. He bought out the good-will and fixtures from a teacher, and rented his dwelling and school-room, in the rear of No. 10 North Front street. In this arrangement he purposed also to fulfill his ministerial duties, by preaching on the Sabbath-day, like the apostle of old, "in his own hired house," to as many as were willing to listen to his testimony. The meetings of the "Bible-Christian Church" were held in his own school-room; and there were present at the first administration of the Holy Supper five adults, including the minister and his wife.

The day-school was opened under the most flattering prospects, and my father's most sanguine expectations were more than realized. His academy was patronized by some of the wealthiest families of the city, and my mother's services were called into requisition by a class of young ladies. In purchasing the good-will and fixtures of the academy, only a portion of the money was to be paid at the time,—the balance having to be paid within the year. The rental for his house and school-room was considered, at that time, to be somewhat exorbitant; but he was enabled to meet all his engagements, and he began to think himself comfortably established. Just at this time, however, the yellow fever broke out in the immediate neighborhood of his residence, in the fall of 1818. His school was deserted by his pupils, and he was compelled to keep it closed several weeks. Two or three of his pupils died with the plague; and, on re-opening, so many of them had been placed in other schools, that for several weeks after he numbered only nine scholars. This visitation was not the end of his troubles. The fever again appeared in the summer and fall of 1819, and yet again in 1820. My father was not prepared for these heavy drawbacks. He was in actual poverty and want. The proximity of his academy to this yearly contagious visitant rendered it unsafe to send pupils to him for instruction, and he was entirely dependent upon his school for a livelihood.

CHAPTER III.

Allurements in Poverty—Mr. Metcalfe as a Preacher—The Doctrines he presented—Opposition of the Clergy to his Preaching—His Reply and Challenge—No Response—Removal to Kensington.

DARK and lowering as were the affairs of Mr. Metcalfe at this time, he had nevertheless secured the friendship of many influential persons. But their solicitude for him only increased his troubles, and he might have exclaimed with propriety, even in his poverty, "Save me from my friends!" Offers of an alluring character were made to him; but they were so conditioned with objectionable features that they aggravated, rather than ameliorated, his condition. It was urged upon him that if he would cease to present temperance and abstinence from flesh-food as religious duties, and renounce his scheme to build up the " Bible-Christian Church," he would be certain of support. One offer was an academy, with a regular, comfortable salary, under the patronage of a religious denomination, located a few miles from the city; and another was the pastorship of an established congregation, insuring him a respectable living, if he would conform to such stipulations. These and other offers somewhat similar were doubtless made from honest and benevolent motives. They were all, however, respectfully declined. In truth, they tended rather to increase his estimation of Bible-Christianity, and to make him labor even more earnestly in its vineyard.

Now, it is not surprising that Mr. Metcalfe was approached in the manner just described. His talents would have been an invaluable help to any ordinary religious denomination, either as a preacher or teacher, if he could have cramped himself to the creed. At this time he was in the vigor of manhood,—just over thirty years of age,—tall and commanding in person, mild and sociable in manners. As a preacher, it is true, he was not what would be called an orator; but his delivery was easy, plain, distinct, and impressive. His action was moderate and graceful. He was never boisterous, never sensational, and seldom allowed his imagination to display its powers in the pulpit. His sermons were suggestive and instructive, always including some teaching on practical, every-day duties. He sought all fields for the illustration of Bible truths, especially availing himself of the lights of modern science and of ancient history in the elucidation of his subjects. Owing, perhaps, to the peculiarity of his religious views and his earnest desire to leave a clear impression on the minds of his hearers, his style of pulpit-speaking was that of a teacher more than that of a preacher.

In this description of Mr. Metcalfe's preaching, I have limited myself to a simple statement of his personal appearance and general style. However unadapted he might be for a *reformer*, he would most certainly have become a popular pastor, had he gone with a popular current. This he would *not* do, though tempted at a time when want and suffering were inmates of his dwelling and contagious disease surrounded his household.

Under these peculiarly trying circumstances, Mr. Metcalfe industriously engaged himself in sowing the seeds of those moral and religious reforms the cultivation of which constituted the great work of his life. He advertised the Sabbath-day services held in his school-room in the newspapers and by cards. Respectable audiences were collected until the plague,—when, like his school, the church also became almost a vacant place. But even then he continued to preach, and added to his labors by availing himself of every social means, and also the newspaper-press, and tracts, to diffuse a knowledge of the doctrines of Bible-Christianity.

It is well known that the churches of that day were exceedingly tenacious of their traditional doctrines; and preachers were expected to discourse with fervid zeal upon the necessity of accepting their respective creeds in their most exact literal expressions. No latitude was allowed to rationalize any doctrine; and the non-acceptance of them in the strict meaning of their words was deemed to be rank infidelity. How far Mr. Metcalfe ran counter to these views may be better understood from the following abstract of his teachings, as enunciated by him at that time in a series of discourses. Of course, this statement must necessarily be very brief, and, consequently, very imperfect.

1. The BIBLE, being written by divine inspiration, open vision, and audible dictation, contains a record of all truths necessary to man's salvation. To interpret it aright in its literal sense, a knowledge of the literature, customs, geography, arts, and philosophy of the Bible nations and times is of great value. Beyond its literal sense, there is providentially contained within it a revelation of divine and spiritual truths. These have existed within it from the time it was first written, and have been successively developed under God, precisely when needed to re-establish or re-edify the Church,—just as the discoveries of new principles or powers in creation (which have always existed therein) were timed to the demands of the age in which they were made available. Thus, the writings and

labors of St. Augustine, Fénelon, Luther, Calvin, Wesley, Swedenborg, Priestley, and others have been and are helps to devout religious minds, according to their various mental conditions. But, with all the aid of these saints, seers, and philosophers, it is not to be presumed that ALL of God's wisdom has yet been developed from the sacred pages of Revelation. According to the earnestness and need for further light, it will be manifested in greater and brighter glory forever. The Bible, therefore, is the only creed that a Scripture-founded Church ought to recognize or espouse.

2. THIS CHURCH, having no creed but the Bible, does not constitute a sect or denomination, but simply a "*Bible-Christian Church;*" and its members claim to be in perfect union and connection with the sincere and conscientious members of all the various denominations of professing Christians. This Church holds all the fundamental *doctrines*, though not all the doctrinal *opinions* or *views*, of the different sects, so far as they are founded on the obvious truths of the Bible. Thus, the antagonistic doctrines of the unity and the trinity of God, the manhood and the divinity of Christ, the predestination and freedom of man, the doctrine of faith and also that of works, with other doctrines, are presented in a light reconcilable to reason and harmonious to each other.

3. GOD IS ONE in essence and in person. Whilst the Bible nowhere says that there are *three Persons* in the Godhead, it manifestly teaches that there is a threefold combination in Deity, corresponding to that which distinguishes man,—namely, soul, body, and operative power. In the Bible there is a threefold combination evidently attributed to God, under the names of Father, Son, and Holy Ghost. The Father is the Inmost or Essential Divine Spirit, which is infinite love; the Son is the Great

Wisdom, or Word of God, effluxed by, and everywhere combining with, the Father; and the Holy Spirit is the Divine Proceeding or Emanating Energy and Power of God.

4. "God was in Christ." The Lord "gave not his Spirit by *measure* to Jesus Christ,"—"the Word made flesh,"—but dwelt in Him, in heaven, and in the universe at one and the same time,—One Undivided God. He assumed the spirit of man, which through sin had become partially separated from its appropriate degree of connection with the Divine Spirit, so that he might meet the Powers of Darkness on their own plain, combat with them, and, by overcoming, redeem mankind to spiritual freedom, and thereby enable the race to become reunited with the Great Omnipotent of heaven and earth.

5. Providence is the government of divine love and wisdom, and has for its end the salvation of man, and the formation of a heaven out of the human family. It is universal and particular; and its laws are those of Appointment and Permission.

6. Man is endowed with Freedom of Will to choose good or evil. By virtue of this free will in spiritual things, he can be conjoined to the Lord, and the Lord to him. Thus, he has the capacity of being reformed, regenerated, and finally saved.

7. At death, man puts off the material body, which, being no longer needful, is *never* again reassumed. "Flesh and blood cannot enter the kingdom of heaven." Man's spirit can never die: after death he rises in a spiritual body into the spiritual world, in which he continues to live forever,—in heaven, if he has lived a sincerely religious and good life on earth; or in hell, if his ruling thoughts, affections, and life have been evil. "Like associates with like," of its own free will.

8. THE SECOND ADVENT, or coming of the Lord, is a coming, not in Person in the clouds of *our* atmosphere, but in the power and spirit of the Lord's own Divine Truth. It is now, and ever has been, coming to every willing mind that attains to the knowledge of Heavenly Truth. The world will never be destroyed. "One generation passeth away, and another cometh; but *the earth abideth forever.*"

9. CHRISTIAN DISCIPLINE consists in obedience to the appointed or eternal laws of the Lord, as revealed in his Word and Works. These, unquestionably, enjoin worship and love to the Lord supremely; honesty, truthfulness, and affection towards all men; and purity of heart, understanding, and life in the individual. Besides the ordinary virtues of Christian professors, the appointed laws revealed in the Divine Word also require abstinence from the flesh of animals as food, from all intoxicating liquors as beverages, and from war, capital punishment, and slavery.

10. THE RELIGIOUS CEREMONIES of the "Bible-Christian Church" are two,—viz.: *Baptism*, by which persons are admitted to church-membership; and the *Holy Supper*, which, in the elements of bread and wine, symbolizes the preparation made by the Lord for the strengthening and refreshment of the souls of his people by his divine truth and love. Both these sacraments are open and free to all who desire to partake. The wine used in the Holy Supper is unfermented, and, consequently, unintoxicating. The observance of the Sabbath as a day of worship and religious instruction is enjoined, as is also family and private prayer.

Such, in brief, were the doctrinal views and church-organization presented to the public of Philadelphia, nearly fifty years ago, by the Rev. William Metcalfe. Considering the rigid religious dogmas which prevailed at that time, it is not surprising that he met with a storm of opposition. A religious monthly, published by an Orthodox body in this city and edited by twelve of the leading clergymen of the country, considered it necessary, as they said, "*to unmask*" such an attempt to rationalize religious doctrines. In a leading article, after speaking of "wolves in sheep's clothing," the magazine says,—

"These remarks are occasioned by the preaching of a man who professed to be a 'Bible-Christian,' and who under this disguise attacked the most plain and important doctrines of our holy religion."

The article is too lengthy to republish here; but it accuses the Bible-Christians with claiming their name from self-righteous motives: it attempts to prove the necessity for human creeds, and proclaims the doctrines of its Church, such as the *tri-personality of God*, the *sacrifice* of the Son for the atonement of the Father, *faith* in the imputation of Christ's righteousness, etc., as Scripture doctrines; and concludes with the following flourish:

"The design of these pretended reformers, notwithstanding their professions, is to impose their own creed upon mankind, and take away from us the doctrines for which martyrs bled,—doctrines which possess exclusively the features of divine revelation,—doctrines which, while they present the divine government in *awful* purity and majesty, and stamp iniquity with deeper odium than the increasing weight of eternal perdition ever could, exhibit at the same time, in the *sacrifice* of Him who is over all, God blessed forever, an *atonement* whose solidity, riches, and excellence can be measured only by the unchangeable existence, unlimited fullness and dignity, of Him who dwells in light inaccessible and full of glory."

To this article Mr. Metcalfe replied at length, in the "*Freeman's Journal.*" After noticing the principal topics of a religious character, and answering them, he concludes by adverting to the uncharitable spirit betrayed in the article, saying,—

"They ought to know that religious reformers in all ages of the world have been accused as men who 'turned the world upside-down,' as enemies to the 'traditions of the fathers,' and as authors of 'innovation.' Let them reflect that while they indulge themselves in calumniating the characters of men of whom they have no knowledge, and in declaiming against doctrines of the nature of which they are utterly ignorant, they are, in fact, betraying the weakness of their cause, and displaying to every one their want of Bible-Christian principles, which would induce them ' to do to others as they would have others do to them.' If they really wish information relative to the views and characters of Bible-Christians, let them attend their meetings, which are open to all; and we promise them a friendly welcome. If they are still dissatisfied, *we invite them to a free and candid discussion.* Truth cannot suffer by the closest investigation; nor is its progress to be arrested either by the fulminations of a body of priests or the pointless censures of an association of reverend reviewers."

The challenge thus publicly given was never accepted,—the "*Magazine*" not even deigning to notice the reply or the Church. This was one mode of attack, varied by shorter articles in the daily newspapers. Other modes were resorted to, affecting him in his profession as a teacher, which were even less creditable to their authors. Even the unsubstantiated cry of "Skeptic!" and "Infidel!" caused some to withdraw their patronage. A public charge always called forth a prompt rejoinder from Mr. Metcalfe; the latter modes were too far beneath the consideration of sensible men for him to deem worthy of notice.

Besides the labors of school-teaching, Mr. Metcalfe was employed as editor of a monthly periodical, entitled "*The Rural Magazine and Literary Evening Fireside,*" devoted, as its title indicates, to agriculture and general literature. It was published by his landlords, Messrs. R. &

C. Johnson, No. 31 Market Street, but was discontinued at the close of 1820.

On account of the repeated visits of the yellow fever to the neighborhood of our residence, my father removed, in the spring of 1821, to the northern suburb of the city, then called West Kensington. He continued his school for a time, however, in the central part of the city,—No. 7 Pear Street. In the mean time, my mother opened a school at our residence, which was numerously patronized, so that my father's aid was absolutely needed. Accordingly, he closed his school in the city, and took a building which had been erected purposely for a school-house in the neighborhood, and there opened his academy. From this time he was quite prospered in his avocation as a teacher.

The Church now began to assume some proportions of size and strength. There had been an increase in its membership, by the return of the two families that had gone out with the Rev. Mr. Clark, by emigrants from England, and by new converts. But great inconvenience was experienced from the want of a permanent place of meeting. After the school-room in Pear Street was given up by my father, the Church was unlocalized,—sometimes meeting at a public hall, sometimes in an engine-house, sometimes in a school-room, and these widely distant from one another. The only remedy for this unstable condition was in the Church being itself the owner of a place of meeting. This it resolved to do, poor as were its members; and on May 21st, 1823, the lot of ground was purchased on ground-rent which is now held in fee-simple by the Church, situated in North Third Street above Girard Avenue. A frame building, which had been used as a Lancasterian school, in Coates Street, was purchased and removed to the lot. It was rejuvenated with paint and other alterations, and fitted up in a plain and suitable style for the church-services. It was publicly opened and dedicated, by the Rev. William Metcalfe, to the worship of the Creator, Redeemer, and Saviour of men, on Sunday, December 21st of the same year.

Connected with the Church in its migratory experiences was a Sunday-school, conducted and supported by the church-members. This also, with the Church, had at length found a resting-place and a home, although it was but an humble frame. The building, however, was indicative of the character of the congregation who gathered under its shelter,—plain, honest, and unostentatious. To secure even such a religious home within little more than six months from the time of the inception of the idea, demanded from each individual member great personal devotion, and evinces the fact that, though poor in worldly wealth, they were rich in heavenly zeal. Their pastor, like themselves, labored hard during the whole week, not alone for the support of his family, but also to collect a congregation and to be prepared to give instruction on the Sabbath-day in the truths of Bible-Christianity. And these truths, practically presented, necessarily came into deadly hostility to the popular sentiments and the perverted appetites of the community around him: yet they were nevertheless religiously reverential and pure in doctrine and in life. Shortly after the church had been opened, an organ was purchased; and the younger members composing the choir were so earnest in their duties that the Church became somewhat noted for its superior musical talent.

CHAPTER IV.

The First Total-Abstinence Society and the First Tract on Entire Abstinence from all Intoxicating Liquors—The Dietetic Reform—The Labors of Mr. Metcalfe in behalf of Vegetarianism—Mr. Metcalfe engages in Printing and Editing—Graduates as an M.D.

DURING the years 1820 and 1821, a series of tracts, entitled "*Letters on Religious Subjects*," was republished under the supervision of Mr. Metcalfe. They were explanatory of the leading doctrines of the "Bible-Christian Church," and were mostly written by the Rev. Dr. Cowherd. They were somewhat altered, so as to adapt them to the wants of the people of this country.

It has already been stated that the "Bible-Christian Church," as early as 1809, taught and enforced the principle that *abstinence from all intoxicating beverages is a necessary duty*. So strictly was this principle carried out, that the wine used for sacramental purposes was expressly made in such a manner as to remain unfermented and, consequently, unintoxicating. Strictly speaking, therefore, it was the *first* temperance society, based upon the total-abstinence principle, in modern times. Among the tracts published by Mr. Metcalfe at this period was one in regard to "*The Duty of Abstinence from all Intoxicating Drinks.*" The vice of drinking intoxicating liquors in those days was one of the most common customs of society. In the transaction of business, in social gatherings of old or young, male or female, or miscellaneously mixed,—whether met for moral purposes or for mere pleasure,—to partake of this liquid poison was considered absolutely essential. Even the clergy were as much addicted to this habit as any other class or profession. The little band of Bible-Christians set their faces sternly against this common custom, and zealously sowed the seeds of those temperance organizations which began to appear some ten or twelve years afterwards. The tract alluded to says,—

> "If this vice of intemperance is to be patronized, it is quite in vain to erect places of worship, or to expect any thing but disappointment in attempting to diffuse religious knowledge. There remains only one effectual way of counteracting this evil, and that is, for all ministers of the gospel and all sincere reformers to strike at the root of the gigantic tree of intemperance,—not alone by preaching, but by setting an example of *entire abstinence from this baneful liquor*. In order to adopt any system, it is desirable to see the practicability of it. In this case it is quite easy. There only wants a beginning in the performance. The *accursed beverages* ought NEVER *to gain admittance to our dwellings*, and, if possible, we should not even hear or see their names."

This was the language, word for word; and the tract sustained its position with sound reason and considerable learning. A large edition was printed and gratuitously distributed. It was, we believe, the FIRST TOTAL-ABSTINENCE TRACT published in this country. When the principles of temperance became more operative in the community, Mr. Metcalfe freely contributed his aid and influence in the organization of societies and in the support of lecturers.

But he was early convinced that the DIETETIC REFORM would be of a much slower growth than that of temperance. The evil of drunkenness so openly manifests itself in the fearful blight which falls upon its victims, that but little effort was needed, he supposed, to call forth those who would see and proclaim its wickedness. But eating the flesh of animals—though really as criminal, as debasing, and as barbarous as that or any other known evil—does not manifest itself in the same heinousness OUTWARDLY: therefore its opponents, he was assured, would not be so numerous nor so popular. He was satisfied, however, that there is a desolation wrought in the soul by the sin of flesh-eating *more fearful* than any outward ghastliness, but which cannot be understood, because of the long and unlimited prevalence of the custom. Hence a constant and self-sacrificing devotion was needful on the part of those who were enlightened in the principles of Vegetarianism, to awaken the public mind to its enormity. Mr. Metcalfe gave his time, talent, and means, unstintedly, to present to the world this cause simply as a moral reform. In 1821, he published a tract on the subject of "*Abstinence from the Flesh of Animals,*" which was freely and extensively distributed. He resorted to the columns of the newspapers to excite public attention to the subject. Articles were published in the "*Saturday Evening Post,*" "*The Philadelphia Gazette,*" "*The American Sentinel,*" "*The United States Gazette,*" and other papers, from his pen, at various intervals, to excite public attention to the consideration of this humane reform. He also instituted correspondence with any inquiring mind, upon the least appearance of interest in the principles which he had so deeply at heart.

During the first ten or twelve years, his labors in this direction appear to have been entirely unproductive of any promising results. In 1830, Dr. Sylvester Graham was employed as a temperance-lecturer, and was introduced to some of the members of the "Bible-Christian Church." He was at this time earnestly studying human physiology, as furnishing testimony upon the subject which was the theme of his public lectures. He had arrived at some conclusions in regard to the dietetic character of man, by this study. The mode of life adopted by his Bible-Christian friends was made known to him; and this most probably caused him to make a more searching investigation as to the scientific grounds for such a course, and finally led him to adopt its teachings and to become its champion. As soon as my father became aware of his position, he addressed a letter of encouragement to him, and also one to Dr. William A. Alcott, who had likewise publicly declared his conviction that a vegetarian diet was the most proper for mankind. This correspondence with them was continued through life, with much interest to all. The basis of the dietetic reform was freely discussed, and projects suggested for the propagation of its principles. In 1835, Dr. Alcott commenced the "*Moral Reformer*," a monthly periodical, which was afterwards substituted by the "*Library of Health.*" In 1838–39, the "*Graham Journal*" was also published, in Boston, and physiological societies were organized in several of the New England towns and in Philadelphia, principally among the Bible-Christians. The inquiry began to be agitated as to "The Bible Testimony on Abstinence from the Flesh of Animals;" and a sermon with this title was preached and published by the Rev. William Metcalfe. It had an extensive circulation throughout the United States, and was generously reviewed, *pro* and *con*, by the newspaper press generally.

It would be almost impossible to enumerate all the varied projects in which Mr. Metcalfe engaged to promote the cause of Vegetarianism. Suffice it to say that, next to the Church, it had his most anxious thoughts and his most constant labor.

But he was overtasking his strength by his close and constant application. School-teaching itself, at the time he was engaged in it, was a health-destroying profession. Then, the school-rooms were generally low, ill-ventilated apartments; and his was greatly crowded. During fully one-half the year he was employed with a day and an evening school, from eight o'clock in the morning until ten at night; Saturday was devoted mainly to preparation for his Sunday duties; so that he had no time for relaxation or bodily exercise. It is not surprising that he found his health failing, from his close confinement and labor in a vitiated atmosphere.

After following the avocation of a school-teacher for more than twenty years, as a change, he engaged, in 1832, with the writer of this in the letter-press printing. We published a weekly newspaper, entitled " *The Independent Democrat,*"—my father being editor and pressman. It was political in its character, but a large portion of its space was devoted to moral and literary articles. In 1838, a daily newspaper was printed at our office, called " *The Morning Star.*" The principal object of the projectors of this paper was to secure the nomination and election of General HARRISON to the Presidency of the United States; and we were assured by many of the leading advocates throughout the country that the undertaking would be amply sustained. The patronage it had was not sufficient, and the promises of the politicians were not fulfilled. It finally ceased in 1841, and we were involved in great pecuniary embarrassment. Although General Harrison was no party to the promises which had led us to undertake the publication, yet, being personally acquainted with my father, he volunteered, after his election, to assure him that we should be repaid. His death, a month after his inauguration, put an end to this prospect. Excepting the subordinate position of measurer in the custom-house,—which my father held about two years,—and a position in the post-office by the writer, no recompense was ever made.

My father, meanwhile, carried on the printing-business himself, issuing from his office " *The Temperance Advo-*

cale." This was also an unprofitable undertaking ; and he resolved to direct his attention to another channel for support.

He had always entertained the idea that the union of the medical and ministerial duties was eminently proper and desirable. With this view, he attended a course of lectures in the college, as early as 1820-21, but was compelled to abandon his intention for want of means. In 1845, with the advice and assistance of his son-in-law, Dr. Henry Taylor, he recommenced the study of medicine, under the homœopathic system. After private study, he entered the college, and graduated as an M.D. in 1852.

CHAPTER V.

Rebuilding and Dedication of the "Bible-Christian Church"—Correspondence with James Simpson, Esq., and Drs. Graham and Alcott—Formation of the American Vegetarian Society—Mr. Metcalfe's Visit to England—Death of Mrs. Metcalfe—The Organ of the Vegetarians—Mr. Metcalfe's Duties and Labors—Invitation to Revisit England as Pastor of the "Bible-Christian Church"—Marriage to Miss Cariss—Departure for England.

In 1844, the frame building in which the Bible-Christians held their meetings began to bear evident marks of decay. Its repair was almost out of the question. The trustees, therefore, commenced taking the necessary measures for the erection of a more substantial edifice. The incumbrance on the ground had been extinguished; and a fund was accumulating in anticipation of requiring a new edifice. To aid this fund, the ladies of the church held a fair, which realized a handsome sum. A subscription was opened, and the members and friends of the church were liberal in their contributions: so that the trustees felt warranted in commencing the building. On the 4th of June, 1845, the work was begun: the building was roofed over, and the basement story finished, and formally opened and set apart for church services, by the Rev. William Metcalfe, on Sunday, November 2d, of the same year. Nearly two years after, the whole building was completed and furnished. The church proper, occupying the second story, was dedicated, October 10th, 1847, to the ONLY WISE GOD, our Saviour. The discourse by the pastor, the Rev. William Metcalfe, was founded upon the twentieth chapter of Exodus, and the ceremonies were interspersed with appropriate music.

About this time Mr. Metcalfe received from JAMES SIMPSON, Esq., a member of the "Bible-Christian Church" of Salford, Manchester, England, several copies of pamphlets on the subject of Vegetarianism. He also received from the same gentleman an encouraging letter as to the progress of the cause in that kingdom, stating that its advocates designed forming associations for the propagation of vegetarian principles as a moral reform. This was subsequently accomplished, and James Simpson, Esq., was elected president of the Vegetarian Society of Great Britain. Mr. Metcalfe immediately proposed the formation of a similar society here. He corresponded with Drs. Graham, Alcott, Mussey, and others, and finally an American Vegetarian Convention assembled in Clinton Hall, New York, May 15th, 1850. This meeting brought together friends of the cause who were personally strangers, but who had, nevertheless, long known each other by correspondence or repute. The Rev. WILLIAM METCALFE was elected President of the Convention. Addresses were made by Mr. Metcalfe, Drs. Graham, Alcott, and others. The formation of the Vegetarian Society was agreed to; a constitution and by-laws were presented, and also the form of a declaration of abstinence from animal food,—all of which were adopted. The Society was organized by electing Dr. WM. A. ALCOTT, President, Rev. WILLIAM METCALFE, Corresponding Secretary, and Dr. R. T. TRALL, Recording Secretary. The project of publishing a Vegetarian magazine was canvassed; and it was determined to commence such a journal, as the organ of the Society. Mr. Metcalfe was named as the editor, to be assisted by Dr. Wm. A. Alcott and others. The first number was issued in November, 1850, under the title of the "*American Vegetarian and Health Journal;*" but its regular monthly publication did not commence until 1851.

Having fully organized the Vegetarian reform, and arranged for the organ of the cause, Mr. Metcalfe determined to pay a visit to England. This resolution becoming known, he was officially appointed as a delegate from the "American Vegetarian Society" to the annual meeting of the "*Vegetarian Society of Great Britain;*" also as a delegate from the "Pennsylvania Peace Society" to the *World's Peace Convention*, and as delegate from the "Pennsylvania Temperance Society" to the *Grand Temperance Demonstration* to be made in London in the latter part of the month. He sailed from the port of New York, on Saturday, July 5th, 1851, in the steamer Arctic, and arrived in due time to take part in these several gatherings. He also visited the *Crystal Palace*, which had just been opened. But the most pleasing feature of his visit was his reception from the members of Christ Church, Salford, where forty years before he had received holy orders. They gave him a most cordial welcome; and he had the gratification of preaching twice, during his brief stay, in the building where he had received ordination. On Sunday evening, August 10th, a "tea-party," comprising the whole congregation, convened in the school-room connected with the church. It had been arranged by the ladies as a means of testifying the respect which the members of the church entertained for the Rev. Dr. Metcalfe. The tables were spread with chaste elegance, and simplicity withal. JOSEPH BROTHERTON, Esq., member of Parliament, presided on the occasion. In the course of his opening address, alluding to Mr. Metcalfe, he said, "I can assure you, I feel difficulty in expressing my feelings towards him. I hail him as a brother, and as a much-esteemed friend for his work's sake." Another asked, "What was it that rendered Mr. Metcalfe's visit a subject of such endearing interest to the friends in England? It was not wealth; it was not literary talent or eloquence merely; but it was the conviction that Mr. Metcalfe was a *living exemplar of certain great and good principles, and the earnest promoter of the practices which those principles inculcated.*" The parting "FAREWELL" was finally said; and Mr. Metcalfe returned in time to participate in the proceedings of the second annual meeting of the "American Vegetarian Society," which convened in the Chinese Lecture-Room, Philadelphia, on the 10th of September.

In 1853, Mr. Metcalfe was called upon to suffer a severe affliction, in the death of his wife. Mrs. SUSAN METCALFE died on the 3d of November, in the seventy-fourth year of her age. For nearly forty-four years she had faithfully encouraged and sustained her consort, as a minister of Christianity, in his arduous undertaking of teaching duties and doctrines of a higher character than the world was willing to receive. Her hospitality was proverbial. Social and frank in disposition, she was ever ready to cheer the right, and to reprove in kindness those who were disposed to go astray. Her removal was mourned by the whole Church as that of a beloved mother.

Meanwhile, Mr. Metcalfe was not only the editor of the "*American Vegetarian*," but all the duties connected with its publication were performed by him gratuitously. He was proof-reader, book-keeper, folder, and mail-packer,—besides being personally responsible to the printer for his work. He had advanced money from his own resources, and at considerable embarrassment, in order to have the regular appearance of the "*Vegetarian*" secured. His statement was laid before the annual meeting of the Vegetarian Society in 1854, and the whole subject was referred to a special committee, with full power to use their own judgment in regard to its continuance. After canvassing the matter, the committee deemed it advisable to suspend its publication for a season,—hoping, if no other arrangement could be made, to be able to secure for the Society a hearing before the public through some other journal. Mr. Metcalfe being shortly after called upon to labor in another direction, no attempt was made by the others of the committee to resume its publication; and the volume of 1854 closed the "*American Vegetarian.*"

The "other direction" in which Mr. Metcalfe was called was England. The Rev. J. B. STRETTLES, officiating minister of Christ Church, Salford, Manchester, died in the early part of 1855. Mr. Metcalfe received an invitation to visit that church, if only for a short period, until a suitable person could be obtained to occupy the pulpit made vacant by the death of its late occupant. This invitation Mr. Metcalfe presented to a meeting of the members of his church, and solicited leave of absence to fulfill the request of the bereaved church. The Rev. Joseph Wright, his brother-in-law, who had been ordained by the Rev. Dr. Cowherd, was a resident of Philadelphia and an active member of the church; to him he purposed to confide its pastoral duties, if the church should grant his request. The proposition, being urged with such an evident desire to aid the sister church, was granted, the Rev. Joseph Wright consenting to take upon himself the duties of the ministry. Mr. Metcalfe had recently been married to Miss MARY CARISS, a lady who had been nurtured and raised in the principles and discipline of the "Bible-Christian Church," and who was a faithful member. In the latter part of July he and his wife embarked for Liverpool from Philadelphia. They arrived safely, and were immediately waited upon by members of the church and cordially welcomed.

CHAPTER VI.

Mr. Metcalfe in England—The Death of Joseph Brotherton, M.P.—Returns to his Church in Philadelphia—Death of Dr. William A. Alcott—Election of Rev. Dr. Metcalfe to the Presidency of the Vegetarian Society—Ordination of his Successor in the Ministry—Celebration of the Semi-Centennial Anniversary of his own Ordination—The Closing Days of his Life—Death—Remarks on his Life—The Funeral Sermon.

THE Rev. Dr. Metcalfe was immediately installed into his pastoral duties, establishing a free and friendly intimacy with all the members of the church. Again he was cordially greeted by his old friend, Joseph Brotherton, M P., who, as the early minister of the Salford church, was still looked to by its members as their chief adviser in all difficulties. James Simpson, Esq., President of the Vegetarian Society, also gave him hearty welcome, and soon had him engaged in the Vegetarian cause as a lecturer. He visited in this capacity not only many of the towns of

England, but, in company with Mr. Simpson, he also addressed meetings in Edinburgh, Glasgow, and several smaller towns of Scotland. He was peculiarly gratified with the attention which was given by the large numbers of the intelligent and sedate people of Scotland to the cause of Vegetarianism and Temperance. In fact, all his labors here appear to have been of an encouraging character.

But the prominent purpose which he ever kept in view was that of supplying a worthy successor to the pulpit of Christ Church, Salford. He assumed the duty of imparting a systematic course of instruction to a class of young men in Bible-Christian Theology. Of this class he expressed himself as quite sanguine,—its members evincing superior intelligence and pious devotion in their studies. He was the more earnest in this endeavor, as the church in Philadelphia, which, under Divine Providence, he had been instrumental in building up, was urging his speedy return.

Whilst thus busily engaged, he was startled by the sudden death of his old and endeared friend the Rev. JOSEPH BROTHERTON. Without any symptoms of previous sickness, he quietly and quickly passed from this transitory state to the eternal world, on the morning of January 8th, 1857. This was the most severe bereavement that the Salford church had experienced since the death of the Rev. Dr. Cowherd. Mr. Brotherton was highly esteemed by the community at large. He had represented Salford in Parliament for more than twenty years, and was otherwise connected with its municipal government, as well as being an active member of several of its benevolent, literary, and scientific associations. The mournful duty devolved upon the Rev. Dr. Metcalfe of performing the last sad rites over the lifeless remains of his beloved friend.

On Sunday, January 18th, he delivered a discourse "On the Death of the late J. Brotherton, Esq., M.P.," in Christ Church, Salford. Besides the mourning family and church-members, there were in attendance members of Parliament, the town-officials, and a large concourse of citizens By request of the church-deacons, the address was published in pamphlet form.

The time was now rapidly approaching when Mr. Metcalfe would be at liberty to return to Philadelphia, according to the terms of the agreement. But the congregation were now, since their bereavement, more than ever desirous of retaining him with them permanently. The church in Philadelphia, however, pressed their claims upon him, so that he declined to prolong his stay much beyond the period fixed. Mr. Metcalfe and his wife made their final arrangements for departure; and, in the early part of August, they bade an affectionate farewell to their many kind and dearly-beloved friends in England. They reached the port of New York on the 24th of the same month, where they were received by a committee of the church. They arrived at their own home on the evening of the following day, where tea had been prepared for them and the church members generally. The meeting and greetings on both sides were most cordial and happy. Mr. Metcalfe resumed his ministerial duties on Sunday, September 7th, and preached to a large congregation. He was also called upon by his old patients to recommence his medical practice; and his labors in the cause of Temperance and Vegetarianism were assumed as readily as though no interruption had taken place.

As life sinks apace, we are called upon to mourn the departure of friend after friend, in quicker succession than we appeared to do in our earlier years. This was Mr. Metcalfe's experience. Another friend and colaborer in the cause of Vegetarianism had been summoned by the hand of Death from this world of shadows. Dr. William A. Alcott, who had toiled so unwearyingly in the prosecution of philanthropic labors, and who had written so many instructive books of a practical character, died on the 29th of March, 1859, in the sixty-second year of his age,— thirty-one of which had been more or less zealously devoted to the propagation and practice of Vegetarianism. At the annual meeting of the Vegetarian Society, held September 21st, Dr. METCALFE was unanimously elected president, which position had been so ably filled by Dr. Alcott from the time of its organization. On assuming the chair, Dr. Metcalfe delivered a fitting eulogy upon the life, labors, and character of his deceased predecessor.

My beloved father had frequently, during many years past, expressed great anxiety respecting his successor to the ministry in the Church. On Sunday morning, September 4th, 1859, he had the great gratification of engaging in the solemn service of an ordination. His son, the writer of this brief memoir, was presented to him by the senior deacons of the church, Jonathan Wright and Elijah Rothwell, as a person whom the members of the church unanimously desired to have introduced into the ministry. After proper examination, the candidate was duly ordained a minister of the word of God, by the venerable hands of the ordaining minister, and the appropriate ceremonies and charges.

Another occasion which he considered himself as highly favored in being privileged to enjoy, was the semi-centennial celebration of his own ordination. In the providence of God, this was granted to the Rev. William Metcalfe, on Sunday, August 11th, 1861. After preaching an appropriate sermon on the afternoon of that day, the congregation adjourned to the school room of the church. Here, around long tables bountifully supplied with vegetarian fare and profusely decorated with flowers, they constituted themselves into a large family tea-party,—the Rev. Dr. Metcalfe, as the "father in Israel," presiding. Resolutions of a grateful and congratulatory character were presented to their venerable minister, besides some other tokens of esteem and affection. A copy of his discourse on that occasion was solicited, which was published by the committee. Thus my father continued to labor in the service of the Lord, and, as he himself remarked, "It was his joy,—and most his joy when most laborious."

And now we approach the close of this long life of incessant activity. Since his return from England, my father had enjoyed general good health. He had been troubled somewhat during the past year with a polypus in his nose: still, he had not been interrupted in any of his ministerial or other duties. Even on the Sabbath before his death he preached with all his accustomed vigor and animation. He appeared to be hoarse, as if from a severe cold: yet his delivery was as distinct as ever. Faithfully and earnestly did he lay before his flock, morning and afternoon of that day, the commandments of the Lord. That night he was taken ill with hemorrhage of the lungs, and on the following morning, when the writer called to see him, he expressed serious doubts of his ultimate recovery. Still he retained the buoyancy and cheerfulness of his disposition; and on the succeeding morning he was so much improved that he thought it possible he might again recover. He continued to gain strength, and was sitting up during most of the day. On Thursday he had been visited by all his children, and his blessing had been bestowed upon them with more than usual serenity. Some remained and took tea with him. All but one had departed, when, about eight o'clock, he prepared to retire for the night. And now, like Jacob of old, "when he had made an end of commanding his children," my beloved father literally "gathered up his feet into the bed, and yielded up the spirit, and was gathered unto his people." His removal at last was, therefore, very sudden, and was doubtless caused by a renewal of the hemorrhage. The Rev. William Metcalfe died on Thursday evening, October 16th, 1862, in the seventy-fifth year of his age. The silver cord was loosened, the golden bowl was broken, and the wheel of action stood still in the exhausted cistern of the mortal life of this truly good man; but the soul soared away to the eternal kingdom of its Lord, to join its friends, not lost, but gone before, and to become a more efficient laborer in the cause of humanity, in which it was so much interested.

The whole life of the Rev. William Metcalfe was one of unremitting labor for the good of others, and for the establishment of the vital principles of Christianity in the souls of his fellow-men. The specific work of his life was that of sowing the seeds and cultivating the principles of TEMPERANCE and VEGETARIANISM and permanently establishing the "BIBLE-CHRISTIAN CHURCH" in this country. These were no small labors for one man's life; and yet the Rev. William Metcalfe was the PRIMARY AGENCY, under Divine Providence, for the development and organization of these moral and religious reforms in this hemisphere of the world. He was not, it is true, a noisy, blustering, passionate reformer. Such displays are generally evidences of weakness, rather than of power and intelligence. He who quietly resists the current of the times, who stands up steadily against its corruptions and vices, and who, from a firm conviction of principle and with a confident reliance on Divine assistance, will not be carried away by faction, opposition, or temptation,—he is the strongest and most practical reformer. The Rev. William

Metcalfe thus stood and labored for Total Abstinence, for Vegetarianism, and for Bible-Christianity, when there were NONE but the few gathered friends around him, who had as yet raised a voice in behalf of either.

No man ever shrunk from publicity more than the Rev. Dr. Metcalfe; but his ardent zeal for truth impelled him to antagonisms, even at the expense of his feelings and of his own personal ease and comfort. He was deeply reverential, and all his religious sentiments were strong and pure,—thus uniting in himself the character of the saint to that of the reformer. As a pastor and preacher he was prompt and faithful to all his charges. During his entire fifty-two years' ministry, whatever might be his outward difficulties or embarrassments, with but very few exceptions he was to be found in the pulpit every Sabbath-day morning and afternoon, and sometimes also in the evening. His general health was so uniform that the exceptions occasioned by sickness did not number more than five or six Sabbaths. The other exceptions were during the periods when he was crossing the ocean; and even then he officiated as often as the opportunity presented itself.

The Rev. William Metcalfe was beloved by his entire congregation as a fond father, and an extensive circle of acquaintances were sincerely attached to him in the bonds of personal friendship. He retained the buoyancy and cheerfulness of his disposition to the last; and the pleasant humor and affectionate tenderness of his social intercourse, even on the day of his decease, were in beautiful harmony with his life of temperance and piety. His remains were interred in the burial-ground attached to the church which had been built under his auspices. The services were performed by the Rev. E. A. BEAMAN, who also preached an eloquent and consolatory funeral sermon, on the following Sabbath, to a large congregation.

CHAPTER VII.

Description of a Tablet to the Memory of the Rev. William Metcalfe—Testimonials—Resolutions adopted by the "Bible-Christian Church" of Philadelphia—Letter of Condolence from Christ Church, Salford, England.

A TABLET has been erected in the church, immediately behind the pulpit which he adorned so long. It is of white Italian marble, placed in a recess having a black-marbled background, thus forming a border to the tablet of four or five inches. The top of the tablet is semicircular, having in it a raised Bible, with rays diverging from it, and over which are the following words:— "THY WORD IS A LIGHT UNTO MY PATH." Underneath the semicircle is a scroll, bearing the following inscriptions:—" In Memory of our Beloved Pastor, the REV. WILLIAM METCALFE, M.D., Founder of the first 'Bible-Christian Church' in America: who departed this life October 16th, 1862, in the seventy-fifth year of his age. He was a faithful, enlightened, and exemplary minister of the Word of God for fifty-two years. 'God is not the God of the dead, but of the living.'—Matt. xxii. 32."

The periodicals of the day, in noticing the death of the Rev. William Metcalfe, paid tribute to his many virtues as a minister of religion and as a moral reformer. Numerous letters were also received by the family, from public and private sources, containing eloquent eulogies on his life and character. Testimonials from the "Bible-Christian Church" in Philadelphia, and also from Christ Church, Salford, England, are herewith appended.

TRIBUTE OF RESPECT.

The congregation worshiping in the "BIBLE-CHRISTIAN CHURCH," North Third Street, above Girard Avenue, Philadelphia, assembled in special meeting on the afternoon of Sunday, October 26th, 1862. Addresses were delivered in regard to the bereavement which the Church had experienced, and, among other proceedings, the following Preamble and Resolutions were presented by Mr. ELIJAH ROTHWELL, which were unanimously adopted, and ordered to be engrossed on the Church Journal:

"*Whereas*, In the dispensation of our heavenly Father, our beloved Pastor, the REV. WILLIAM METCALFE, M.D., has been removed by death from the scene of his labors in the external Church, to perform higher services in the Spiritual Church of the LORD; and *whereas* we have long enjoyed the privilege of his fatherly counsel, and have been intimately acquainted with his many personal virtues and his great sacrifices for the cause of Scripture-founded Christianity; and *whereas* we earnestly desire and deem it our duty to place on record a true delineation of his character: be it, therefore, hereby

"*Resolved*, That we behold in the character of our late venerable Pastor that purity of life, that humility of disposition, that equanimity of temper, and that peaceful demeanor, which constitute the necessary qualifications of a true apostle of our LORD AND SAVIOUR JESUS CHRIST.

"*Resolved*, That in the domestic circle we saw in the Rev. Dr. Metcalfe a devoted husband and a loving father. In social life he was kind and tender-hearted, and, consequently, was respected and beloved by all who knew him. His love of usefulness caused him to be active in aiding and assisting in all social and moral reforms; and his name, we are assured, is embalmed in unnumbered hearts, who will transmit the memory of his virtues and usefulness to future generations.

"*Resolved*, That in his ministerial duties the Rev. William Metcalfe was faithful and devoted to the service of his GREAT EXEMPLAR AND TEACHER,—fearlessly opposing the vicious habits and customs of society with all the ability of his talents and life,—bearing unfaltering testimony of more than fifty-two years to truth, justice, and mercy, and performing punctually, even to the last Sabbath of his life on earth, the sacred duties of his mission as a preacher of Bible-Christianity.

"*Resolved*, That a committee be appointed to cause a suitable monument to be erected over the remains of our beloved Pastor, as a token of affection on behalf of the Church of which he was, under Divine Providence, the founder in this country, and for which he so long labored.

"JONATHAN WRIGHT, *President.*

"EMANUEL HEY, *Secretary pro tem.*"

Address from the Members of the "Bible-Christian Church," Salford, to their Brethren in Philadelphia, United States.

CHRISTIAN FRIENDS:

By letters from friends on your side of the Atlantic, and from public prints received through the same channels, we are put in possession of the knowledge that your church has recently endured a most distressing bereavement in the death of your faithful friend and pastor, the Rev. WILLIAM METCALFE. Bound to you by the endearing ties of long service in the holiest things, associated in your recollections with the happiest and most interesting events of your own and your children's lives, and in perhaps a more sacred way with your troubles and losses, his removal hence cannot fail to be a cause of deep sorrow to all your little flock. The child whom he had baptized and who had lived long enough to recognize the benevolent expression of his countenance, reflecting the light within,—the young man or maiden whom he has received into the bosom of the Church, and to whom, under God, he has ministered the bread of life and the living waters of comfort and peace,—the devout servant of the Lord, who has waited on his ministrations and profited by the detail of his heavenly experiences and emotions and his intimate acquaintance with the divine truth,—each and all must feel conscious of a void which cannot easily be supplied,—a loss which is all but irreparable. In presence of such a calamity, we desire to offer you our warmest sympathies, and the assurance of our unabated attachment to yourselves and the principles we hold in common. Our hearts unite in "weeping with them that weep," because of the loss to the world in our dear friend's death, and particularly for the loss the "Bible-Christian Church" has sustained thereby. Our own loss and our own sorrow are only second to yours in this afflicting dispensation of Divine Providence; but we desire to encourage and to strengthen you as the Lord has taught us. Whilst acknowledging in sadness that "no chastening seemeth for the present joyous, but grievous," we also hope that this chastisement will "afterwards yield the peaceable fruits of righteousness to them that are exercised thereby." May our heavenly Father so teach you and us that we may find that godly exercise in our present grief, which shall yield us the peaceable fruits of righteousness! May we learn even now to say, The Lord is gracious and merciful; his ways are good and right! He is the Father of the fatherless, the Husband of the widow, the Friend of the friendless. In each of these relationships we humbly pray that He may now be manifested to you, "carrying your little ones in his arms as on eagle's wings," consoling the widowed Church with the assurance of his protection and love, and supplying by the direct influences of his Spirit the need created by the death of your revered minister.

Our great comfort is that whatever is true or good cannot perish. Its vitality is in the charge of Him who is the truth and who alone is perfectly good. We have, therefore, no fear that the principles of Bible-Christianity can die. Though they may wane for a season through lack of zeal or the want of faithful men, yet must they spring again, like seeds long buried in the earth, when the needs of mankind lead them to remove the crust of errors and evils that has overlaid the good and the true.

We sorrow not as those without hope, but as looking and waiting ourselves for the great deliverance, when to die will be gain, inasmuch as we shall be with the Lord. This hope, we doubt not, abides with you, and our prayer to God on your behalf is, that it may abound more and more until the day when faith shall be lost in sight.

* * * * * * * * * * * * *

Praying that our heavenly Father may aid and comfort you at all times, but especially at the present time of need, that He will enlarge you and give you increased proofs of his regard for you,

    We are,
        Christian friends,
            Yours affectionately,
                  JAMES CLARK, Minister,
                  ROBERT MILNER,
                  EDWIN COLLIER,
                      Committee of Correspondence.

OUT OF THE CLOUDS:

INTO THE LIGHT.

DISCOURSE I.

ON THE BEING AND UNITY OF GOD.

Zechariah xiv. 9.

We propose delivering a course of Theological instruction on the leading principles of the Bible-Christian Church, and we take as an introductory to such a series of religious Discourses, and as an important leading doctrine of our Church, *The Being and Unity or Oneness of God* as our morning's subject.

We have made this selection from a thorough conviction that the idea we entertain in regard to God enters into our every thought, and qualifies every idea relating to Religious doctrines, to the Church and to Worship. Above all other subjects Theological principles should occupy a prominent place in the human mind, and among the most important of these is the idea we entertain respecting the *Being, Unity,* and *attributes of God.* If this primary subject be erroneously understood, all the doctrines deduced from it, participating of its nature, will, as a natural consequence, be also erroneous. As is the *fountain,* so also will be the *streams* flowing from it. For that which is *supreme* or *inmost* constitutes the very Essential principle of all that is derived from it; and the Essential or inmost principle, like the soul in the material body, gives form and appearance after its own peculiar image and nature; and even when the mind takes into contemplation the truths of *Creation* or of *Revelation*, its erroneous opinion relative to the Divine Being, as the medium through which it beholds all such truths, gives to them also a tinge, a coloring, or appearance, in harmony with its own peculiar nature. Our young friends, therefore, and our hearers generally, will see how very necessary it is that our most earnest attention should be directed to the acquisition of a correct knowledge of the subject before us.

The man who professes to believe that it is his duty to worship God, must, if he act rationally, do it on the conviction that there is such a Being. "He that cometh to God must believe that He is" a Being infinite, eternal, unoriginated, and self-existent; the Cause of all other beings,—on whom all being depends, and by whose Goodness, Wisdom, Power, and Providence all other beings exist, live, and are supplied with the means of continued existence and life, or rather are recipients of life from Him. From the beauty, order, and regularity manifested in the works of Creation, we may not merely infer the Being of a God of such a character, but we may prove it by a logical demonstration: we cannot calmly contemplate the spangled heavens—that shining frame—and not be convinced that such a magnificent display of grandeur, order, and sublimity is evidently the effect of One Almighty Being. There is intelligence, there is wisdom impressed upon the *design itself*, and this is evidence of the existence and the wisdom of the Designer. When we reflect on the numerous planetary orbs in our solar system, on the regularity and order with which they perform their revolutions round the sun, as their common parent and centre, while each at the same time performs a rotary motion on its own axis by which the days and nights are formed, and the periods fixed for labor and rest; these are all so many indubitable tokens of infinite intelligence which can exist only in a First Cause, and that First Cause is God, the Infinite, Unoriginated, Self-existent, Eternal, and Living *One*.

Whatever may be the condition of man, the Bible teaches him to hope for better things. We are not to rest satisfied with any present attainment, but to press forward to a higher mark. Moral and mental acquirements have no absolute stopping-place; whenever they are stayed in their onward progress, we may trace the cause to *an enemy* attempting to turn aside the purposes of God. As Bible-Christians we receive this Book as a divine composition, containing a Revelation *of* God, and *from* God. But objectors say this Book takes for granted two disputable points: first the existence of God, as its revealer, and next the existence of the human spirit, capable of receiving his inspiration. It is true these facts are taken for granted by believers in the Bible as a Divine production. But there must be a point from which to start in our inquiries respecting its character. The necessity of a Divine Revelation implies man's natural ignorance of these two things; and the gift of such a revelation proves their reality. If man did not know there was a God, and if he were unacquainted with the spiritualities of his own nature, the circumstance of such a Revelation being made to him is a proof of both,—a proof which is independent of any precise statement contained in that Revelation. But a Divine Revelation has been made, therefore God and the human soul exist. The question then arises, Could this knowledge ever have entered the world without Revelation? Ideas of God and of the human soul exist. They have prevailed during all historical time, and among all civilized people, and even many savage tribes are not entirely without them. A universal impression prevails respecting the existence of both. There is an influx universal into the souls of men, teaching both the Being and the Unity of God. Even the Atheists of modern civil life, though they say "there is no God," are not entirely without these impressions; the facts which they indicate may be contrary to their speculations, but not so to their experience. If any of them insist that they have no such experience, we of course believe what they say, but we maintain they have not observed their experiences correctly; or, even if they have, their case does not disprove what every one else acknowledges to be true. If they have no possession of gold, that is no evidence that all other persons are destitute of that precious metal. The blind man may truly say he does not see, but it does not follow that all other men are therefore deprived of sight. He, then, who insists that he has no experience as to the universality of impressions respecting the Being of a God, only tells us of an exceptional case. But the impression and consequent idea of the existence of God prevails among mankind, and has always done so. *Cicero* says, "There is no nation so wild and savage, no man so rude and uncultivated, whose mind is not imbued with the opinion that there is a God. Many have wrong sentiments concerning Him, but all think there is a Divine Power." *Lord Brougham*, in a discourse on Natural Theology, says, "There can hardly be found a tribe so dark and barbarous as to be without some kind of worship, and some belief in a God, and in a future state of existence." To these statements, however, there may be some slight exceptions. *Locke*, the author of an Essay on the Human Understanding, refers to some savage people, reported by navigators, "among whom there was found to be no notion of a God, and no religion." *Swedenborg* also remarks in his T. C. R., 274, that there were persons born in remote islands who had no knowledge at all concerning God. But these cases are so few as to be of little weight against the general argument that there is an influx universal into the souls of men, teaching the Being of a God. As, then, no period of history nor scarcely any people can be shown to have been without this impression, whence did it originate? How did the first men obtain this knowledge? How did the idea of God originate with primitive men? Various opinions have prevailed in relation to these questions. They may be divided, however, into three general classes, among each of which there is great diversity of sentiment.

First, the Atheists: they assert that there is no such a being as God! Some of these say that the idea of God is the offspring of ignorance, and others among them that it is the invention of fear, or a device of the clergy.

Second, the Deists: they admit that there is a God, but deny that the Sacred Scriptures are any revelation from Him. Among them, some maintain that the idea of God's existence is impressed upon us by what they call the hand of nature; others of them, that the existence of a God is a philosophical idea; and others, that it is derived from feeling and natural logic.

Third, the Religionists: they believe in God's existence, and receive the Bible as a Divine communication from Him. With some of these, there is no very definite opinion about the origin of this idea; others again insist, among whom are Bible-Christians, that the idea of a God is the sole issue and end of Divine Revelation.

It is not our purpose at this time to dwell on either the Atheistic or the Deistic opinions, but rather to refer to the light which Revelation sheds on our subject. We therefore come at once to the idea entertained by professors of religion, and particularly to that of Bible-Christians, on this topic. It seems plain to us that the knowledge of God's existence must have originally sprung out of his Revelation of the truth to man. No other view can adequately account for its antiquity, its universality, or its permanence. "Now we all know that the *idea* of God exists; and this, upon the principle we have laid down, is a proof that GOD exists. No man is conscious of having originated this idea in himself. All now know that it is the result of *instruction;* there must, then, have been a first instructor. There may be, there doubtless is, an internal influx operating upon the mind of every one, inclining it to the favorable reception of the idea of a God, when it is *presented;* still, without the *presentation* that influence could have no ground nor mental plane on which to act. The primeval idea can be accounted for upon no other principle than that of God having revealed Himself to the human mind. We maintain therefore that the idea of the existence of God has come into the world by means of Revelation. We do not mean to say that that Revelation was the Bible precisely as we have it, because the idea of God's existence prevailed for many ages before the Bible became a written Revelation." But the first portions of the Bible contain a history of the religious condition of the earliest inhabitants of the world, and from it we learn that God made Himself known to them; and that they acknowledged his existence.

Immediately after the creation of man, God is represented as having spoken to him. This, of course, was in itself Revelation. Thus the oldest history extant, apart from the fact of its being itself a revelation, declares that the first *idea* which man had of God's existence was communicated from God Himself. It is therefore historically certain that all the ideas concerning GOD which have ever existed in the world must have originally sprung from God's having, at different times, revealed or manifested Himself to men;—not that the *perversions* of Revelation came from Him; but even *they* prove that there was some primary truth to *pervert*. But while it is conceded that the idea of the Being of a God, since its first promulgation, has been propagated by means of *instruction*, more or less imperfect, the perpetuation of it has been assisted by other means. The wonderful fact of its continuance and universality cannot be accounted for on the ground of mere *teaching*. This human effort, carried on by the faithful teachers, members of his Church, has always been *assisted* by a Divine provision. As we have already said, there has always been an influx from God into the souls of men, inducing them to receive favorably the idea that there is a God. Without this influx human effort would have been fruitless. That there is an influx of this nature is well known. The Bible teaches it; and experience confirms it. "A man can receive nothing except it be given him from heaven." Again, "Every good and perfect gift is from above, and cometh down from the Father of lights." The order of the descent of this influx is for the superior to flow into the inferior: for God, who is the Supreme Spirit, to cause an influx of Himself into the human soul; from the soul into the mind, and from the mind into the nervous and muscular organs which constitute the body; and into each of these according to its peculiar adaptability. The knowledge of the being of a God, since it was first revealed, has been universally taught,—taught, it must be confessed, in numerous cases, with strange additions, and marvelous omissions and perversions; but still the idea of a Supreme existence—Omnipresent, Omniscient, and Omnipotent—has been at the foundation of them all.

The truth, having been once introduced to the human mind, and continued by external teaching, has been met by a spiritual influx, inspiring the idea with a living character, and so providing for the continuation of the teaching, by perpetuating the belief. Everywhere may be seen testimonies of his Being, and the imprint of his Benevolence and other attributes is legibly enstamped on Universal Creation. It may be also clearly perceived that there can be but *One Great First Cause* of all things. *Unity* of purpose is visible in all the diversified objects throughout Creation; everything indicates the existence of one intelligent, indivisible, and independent Being; and yet the order and harmony manifested in all things conclusively show there cannot possibly be more than *one* such intelligent and Omnipresent BEING.*

---

* While we are zealous for the Unity or Oneness of the Divine Being, we would not that any of our hearers should confound us with those known in the religious world as *Unitarians*. No two views concerning the Godhead can be more at variance. The Unitarians consider *Jesus Christ* to have had no existence till his birth into the world; they suppose Him to have been a *mere man* like themselves, the natural son of Joseph and Mary, and consequently as having no claims, by birth or descent, superior to those of any other moral human being. Whereas the members of the Bible-Christian Church believe and maintain that *God was in Christ;* that He is "The True God and Eternal Life;" "God over all, blessed forever;" that "in Him dwells all the fullness of the Godhead bodily."

These truths we shall demonstrate in our Discourse on The Lord

It is from this great *First Cause,* "*the one living and true God,*" that all Creation subsists, and by whom all created substances were originally produced. A little reflection will satisfy the minds of our hearers that it is impossible any substance could ever spring up *out of nothing; from nothing,* nothing can come. All things that exist, therefore, must necessarily have been produced from God, the Creator of all; and produced in a way and order that effectually preserves the most perfect and complete distinction between the Great Creator and the creatures of his hand. But we are not left to vain conjecture on the subject before us.

In Divine Revelation He has given the most absolute and unmistakable declarations both of his Being and Unity. The Bible says, "Hear, O Israel, the Lord our God is one Lord." "Thus saith the Lord, the King of Israel, I am the *First,* and I am the Last, and beside me there is no God." "Thou shalt have no other Gods before me." "I am the Lord thy God, and thou shalt know no God but me." "In the beginning God created the heavens and the earth." "I am the Lord that maketh all things, that stretcheth forth the heavens *alone,* that spreadeth abroad the earth *by myself.*" "I have made the earth, and created *man* upon it; I, even my own hands, have stretched out the heavens, and all their hosts have I commanded." "There is ONE GOD, and there is none else." Is it not therefore obvious to our hearers, that it is entirely at variance with both enlightened reason and Divine Revelation to say with "*the fool, there is no God,*" or with some professors of religion that there are *more Gods than one?*

---

and Saviour Jesus Christ. We have mentioned them here only to prevent any misapprehension on the part of our hearers.

From what has been said, we trust our hearers will see the weighty importance of having a just and clear idea of the Being and Unity of God, as constituting the first article of true religion. They will perceive the necessity and use of Revelation to help us to the attainment of a proper idea of God and his attributes. Thus aided, it will be seen that Creation, or what is called Nature, and all its parts, must have had a cause or beginning; and that all things owe their being to God. HE must have existed from eternity as *One, Indivisible, Independent, Omnipotent, Omniscient, and Omnipresent* GOD. It will also have been perceived that the imprint of his Being and of his Divine Attributes is enstamped on Universal Creation; and that in harmony with these there is an *influx universal* ever flowing into the souls of men, inducing the idea of the Being and Unity of God. We have shown, also, that there is no people throughout the world possessed of religion and intellectual intelligence that does not confess the Being of a God, and that He is One. And we have directed your attention to the Scripture testimony with respect to the Being and Oneness of God.

> Almighty God! thou First and Last!
>   How wonderful, how great art Thou!
> The present, future, and the past
>   To Thee are one eternal *now*.
> Thou Infinite! no finite thought
>   Could e'er approach thy high abode;
> But as Revealed, to vision brought,
>   We see Thee One!—We know Thee God!

And now our fervent prayer to that glorious Being is, that all that has been said in harmony with his Divine Will may be deeply impressed upon your minds, take root in your thoughts, and bring forth fruit unto eternal life. Amen.

DISCOURSE II.

ON THE LORD JESUS CHRIST.

John x. 30.

In our recent Discourse on the Being and Unity of God, we attempted to make you acquainted with the views of the Bible-Christian Church respecting that important subject. From what was then said, it is presumed we may justly conclude, without offering violence to the truth, that there is a God, and that He is One. Every individual in the enjoyment of his rational powers must admit it would be the height of folly to acquiesce in the creed of the *Atheist*, and say "*there is no God;*" and that it would be nothing less at variance with the truth to suppose for a moment that there are *more Gods than one*. The characteristics of a God are indelibly enstamped upon all creation, and interwoven throughout the whole moral and intellectual nature of humanity. We purpose, this morning, bespeaking your serious and Christian attention to the importance of a knowledge of the TRUE GOD; and as this knowledge is of the utmost importance to the everlasting interests of every one of us, anything that has a tendency to answer satisfactorily the question, "*Who is the Lord,*" or *the true God?* will doubtless be received by every one of our hearers with joy and gladness of heart. It is not sufficient for all the purposes of religion and life to know simply that God is, and that *God is One;* but it is also expedient to know as correctly as possible *who* is the great object claiming our best affections, and *who* demands the warmest gratitude and thanksgivings of our hearts.

In commencing our subject, therefore, we would ask, in the language of the Bible, "*Who is the Lord?*" "*What think ye of Christ?*" These questions are short and simple, and the only true answers to them are equally so. In solving these queries, we would state, according to our view of the Bible testimony, that the glorified JESUS CHRIST is the only Lord. Some one may perhaps say, Is HE the ONLY LORD? We answer, Bible-Christians believe He is the ONLY LORD,—"THE ONLY WISE GOD, OUR SAVIOUR," in "*whom dwelleth all the fullness of the Godhead bodily;*" that "*He and the Father are One.*" In making these declarations, it may be thought necessary that we should enter into some more full explanation of so important a doctrine as that respecting the Supreme Divinity of Jesus Christ, and attempt to show how the doctrine is to be understood. This we will make an effort to do, and afterwards proceed to the scriptural proof of our proposition, so that no doubts may remain upon the minds of our hearers as to the truth of the Bible-Christian doctrine. The Infinite and Eternal GOD, the Creator and FATHER of all in Heaven and throughout the universe, is, in the Scriptures of the Old Testament, revealed to us by his name JEHOVAH,—translated Lord; and we are informed, in that revelation which He has been pleased to give of Himself, that He did, at sundry times and in divers manners, through the instrumentality of *Moses*, the *Patriarchs* and *Prophets*, manifest Himself and reveal his will to his church and people; that his appearance was always to instruct them in things belonging to their peace, and to point out to them the path of wisdom and of true holiness. But such was the proneness of fallen human nature to folly and wickedness, that mankind from the fall continued to go still farther and farther from the sphere of the Divine Presence; wickedness and folly attended their idolatrous and destructive progress, until their spiritual "beauty and comeliness" as the Lord's people were exchanged for that direful and distressing state described by the prophet, viz., "The whole head is sick, and the whole heart faint; from the sole of the foot even unto the head there is no soundness in it, but wounds, and bruises, and putrefying sores." The mental and moral degeneracy of the people, indeed, increased so rapidly in regard to spiritual things that "Wickedness burned as an oven, and the foolishness of men was so great" that, notwithstanding the Divine manifestations, many began to say in their hearts, "*There is no God.*" In order, then, to reach this low state of human mentality and effectually redeem mankind from this deadly infatuation and folly, JEHOVAH, our Creator and Heavenly Father, whose goodness and mercy had followed sinning mankind in all their declining ways and spiritual degeneracies, in his love and in his pity, became our *Redeemer* and *Saviour*. He visited his people, and, in the person of JESUS CHRIST, brought LIFE and immortality to light where darkness only had reigned; for "GOD was then manifested in the flesh,"—"God was in CHRIST" to restore man to the condition he had lost by his sinfulness, and to open again that way of life, and heaven, and happiness which, through the transgressions of man, had become closed. On this account, and for this specific purpose, "GOD was in CHRIST, reconciling the world to Himself." When, however, we announce that JESUS CHRIST is the "ONLY TRUE GOD and ETERNAL LIFE,—the supreme object of all Christian worship,—we would guard and caution our hearers, and especially our young hearers, against imagining that we confine the name JESUS CHRIST to the finite and material *form* assumed from the mother; for with respect to the material body, JESUS CHRIST was subject to hunger and thirst, and to all other infirmities to which nature must forever be subject; but, to *reach* and *redeem* man, He also assumed, through the same medium, the fallen, sinful human spirit that needed to be redeemed,—the affections and thoughts of man's sinful soul. It was in this assumed spirit of man that He experienced *temptation,*— for God cannot be tempted; that He met and conquered the powers of darkness, "led captivity captive," and redeemed this *assumed spirit* or nature *of man* from all its impurities, filled it with its appropriate degree of his own Glory, and reunited it with the Essential Divine Spirit (the Love and Wisdom of the Great Infinite, which stood into Christ unfinitedly, and became, as it were, soul in HIM). In this manner He opened a new way of access to mankind for their salvation. He came that He might be able to *reach* and to *save all* men. A careful distinction, then, must ever be made between that which in reality is JESUS CHRIST, the LORD of GLORY, his genuine Manhood, and that material, organized body of flesh and blood which was needed in this outer world during the process of redemption, but which, when that work was accomplished, was put off and dissipated in the sepulchre, and finally deflagrated at the ascension,—for "Flesh and blood," we are expressly told in the sacred volume, "cannot enter into the kingdom of heaven." It was in this assumed human, then, that THE LORD GOD of Israel, as JESUS CHRIST, visited, and taught, and redeemed his people. The term JESUS CHRIST, in the New Testament, has a similar signification to that of the LORD God, so frequently mentioned in the Old. The term JEHOVAH, or LORD, implies the Divine Love; and the term GOD, the Divine Wisdom.

This Love and Wisdom, when manifested in the fleshly tabernacle of JESUS, for the redemption and salvation of man, is the true JESUS CHRIST,—the name JESUS denoting the *Divine Love;* and CHRIST, the *Messiah,* the *Anointed,* the *Divine Wisdom,* which, as the Word, *was made flesh,* or rather made manifest in the flesh, and we *beheld his glory.* We have made these remarks in order to prevent any confusion arising in the minds of our hearers respecting the highly important principle we have this morning announced,—that JESUS CHRIST is the "*Only true God and Eternal Life,*" and that none of our hearers may suppose that we call that GOD which in reality is *not even* MAN; for flesh and blood, considered literally, according to the common acceptation of the terms, cannot be *man:* these only form the material investment or organized body, in which and by which *man,* as an immortal being or soul, is known, is seen, exists, and materializes his living purposes in this outward world of nature. It is the *Will* and *Understanding* which together *form* the human MIND, in which are contained a vast store of affections, thoughts, perceptions, and intellectual powers, which all together make up what the Bible calls the living soul; and the *living soul* is the real MAN. Justly, therefore, has the poet, Dr. Watts, said, "The mind is the measure of the man." We say, then, as Bible-Christians, that JEHOVAH GOD, mentioned in the Old Testament, and JESUS CHRIST, mentioned in the New, are only different *names* expressive of the self-same DIVINE BEING,—the different names being properly adapted to express the difference between the nature of the *Jewish* Dispensation and that of *Christianity,* and to indicate the true character and quality of each. When we maintain that JESUS CHRIST is the only true GOD and LORD of heaven and earth, we wish to be distinctly understood that we make not the most distant allusion to the mere body of flesh and blood which was crucified on Mount Calvary, but we speak of the *Love* and *Wisdom* which stood unfinitedly into the assumed *manhood* of JESUS CHRIST, and gave the power of performing all the mighty works and teaching all the heavenly principles ascribed to Him in the Gospel. Therefore, according to the doctrines of the Bible-Christian Church, the work of human redemption did not consist in JESUS CHRIST coming into the world to offer Himself as a sacrifice in the place of sinful man, with a view of appeasing the wrath of the Father, of satisfying his vindictive justice, and, by such a process, of atoning for the sins of the world; for, in the first place, there is no such odious passion as wrath in the Divine Being, nor is He possessed of any such attribute as vindictive justice. "God is Love, —the same yesterday, to-day, and forever;" He changeth not. In the next place, it is contrary to every principle of justice, divine or human, that the *innocent* should suffer for the crimes of the guilty. "The fathers shall not be put to death for the children; neither shall the children be put to death for the fathers; but every man shall be put to death for his own sin." And, in the next place, there is NO DIVINE BEING distinct from the glorified LORD JESUS CHRIST to whom to make atonement. "*I and the Father are one.*" But redemption, being a work purely Divine, consisted in the actual assumption of the fallen spirit or nature of man, and therein subduing the powers of sin and darkness, introducing order and purity where sin had reigned, bringing into subjection the powers of hell, and glorifying the manhood or human nature assumed at the incarnation as the *medium* or *mediator* between the otherwise invisible and unknown God and his creature man. "God was in Christ reconciling [or atoning] the world to Himself." With this brief explanation, we now proceed to the Bible testimony illustrative of the truth of the doctrine that the glorified JESUS CHRIST is the only true God and Eternal Life.

If we can prove from the Scriptures that the same attributes, powers, and properties are ascribed to JESUS CHRIST which belong only to the ETERNAL GOD, then, upon the just acknowledgment that GOD is ONE, we may safely say that JESUS CHRIST is The *Only Wise God*, The Creator, The Redeemer, The Regenerator and Saviour, The Omnipotent, Omniscient, and Omnipresent Giver of every good, and the Possessor of all those Divine Attributes which the sacred volume ascribes unto GOD Most High.

We shall now consider the language of Scripture with regard to,—

   I. The Creator.
  II. The Redeemer.
 III. The Regenerator.

I. Who is the Creator? We read: "In the beginning God created the heavens and the earth." "In the beginning was the Word, and the Word was with God, and the Word was God. All things were made by Him [Christ], and without Him was not anything made that was made." "He was in the world, and the world was made by Him." And now, beloved, let us look at this testimony. We have stated, *God is Love;* God is *Wisdom:* these are the two principal attributes which constitute GODHEAD. By these, in the beginning, was the world created. In the beginning was the Word. The Word was made flesh. Who was made flesh? JESUS CHRIST, the living Word. All things were made by HIM. He, then, is our *Creator*, and HE, in consequence, is our GOD. The Psalmist says of the LORD GOD as CREATOR, "The heavens are thine; the earth also is thine; as for the world and the fullness thereof, Thou hast founded them." But the apostle says of JESUS CHRIST, "By Him were all things created that are in heaven, and that are in earth, visible and invisible, whether they be thrones, or dominions, or principalities, or powers: all things were created *by* Him and *for* Him." Now, we wish you to reflect more particularly on the words, "all things were created *by Him* and *for Him.*" When the angels and glorified spirits of the just are referred to as praising GOD the CREATOR because of his Divine glory, they exclaim, "Thou hast created all things, and for thy pleasure they are and were created." At what a beautiful illustration of our Bible-Christian doctrine, then, are we now arrived! He *by whom* and *for whom* all things were created is GOD. But all things were created *by* and *for* JESUS CHRIST; therefore JESUS CHRIST is GOD; and as we have already shown there is but ONE GOD, so we trust our hearers will see JESUS CHRIST must be the One *only* GOD. We will merely refer to one more text from each Testament, relating to Creation. The Psalmist says of Jehovah, "Of old thou hast laid the foundations of the earth, and the heavens are the work of thy hands." The apostle says, "Christ, in the beginning, laid the foundations of the earth, and the heavens are the work of his hands." Comment, here, we deem unnecessary.

II. Who is The Redeemer? Redemption is a work purely Divine; no created being could redeem man. If we turn to our Bibles, we shall find the Psalmist saying, "Thou hast redeemed me, O LORD of TRUTH." Again he says, of Israel, "They remembered the HIGH GOD was their *Redeemer.*" In Isaiah we read, "Fear not,—I have *redeemed* thee; thou art mine;" "The year of my *Redeemed* is come." In his love and in his pity He *redeemed* them and was their Saviour. We find, also, the same ALMIGHTY BEING, the LORD GOD of ISRAEL, is represented as the *Saviour* of his people. "I, the LORD, am the *Holy One* of *Israel*, thy *Saviour;* I am the LORD, and beside me there is no *Saviour.*" From these, and numerous other passages which might be cited, it is abundantly evident that the *Redeemer* and *Saviour* of mankind is the LORD GOD ALMIGHTY. But, according to the Gospel, JESUS CHRIST is our *Redeemer* and *Saviour;* therefore He alone is GOD. "For JESUS will *save* his people from their sins." "This is CHRIST, the *Saviour* of the world." And JESUS CHRIST Himself, in order to comfort and encourage his afflicted people, says, "Come unto ME, all ye that labor and are heavy laden, and *I* will give you rest. Take MY yoke upon you, and learn of ME, and ye shall find *rest* unto your souls." Does it not clearly appear, from this, that JESUS CHRIST is our *Redeemer* and *Saviour?* Is it not evident that none but GOD could *redeem?* but if JESUS CHRIST did *redeem*, must He not be "GOD over all, blessed forever"?

III. Who is The Regenerator? The Supreme God is also said, in the Old Testament, to be the *regenerator* of mankind. "I will take away the stony heart, and will put a new spirit within you, and give you a heart of flesh." But in the *Gospel* JESUS CHRIST is represented as the *regenerator* of all men. "If any man be in CHRIST JESUS, he is a *new* creature." "As many as received HIM, to them gave HE power to become the *sons of God*, even to them that believe *on his name*, who are *born*, not of blood, nor of the will of the flesh, nor of the will of man, but of God."

We trust our hearers will see, from all these scriptural quotations, that Creation, Redemption, Salvation, and

Regeneration are described as the work of the LORD (Jehovah) GOD of Israel. But the operations of Creation, Redemption, Salvation, and Regeneration are attributed also to JESUS CHRIST in the Gospel; and as there is but ONE GOD, it therefore follows that JESUS CHRIST—if the Gospel be true—is the ONE ONLY GOD.

We might proceed according to this order, and show from the authority of the Bible that Omnipotence, Omniscience, Omnipresence, and Immutability — attributes which belong only to the Supreme GOD—are all ascribed to the glorified LORD and SAVIOUR, JESUS CHRIST. It is not, however, thought needful, at present, to adduce other Bible proofs in relation to these attributes. Suffice it to state, we have endeavored briefly to prove that JESUS CHRIST is the ONE ONLY GOD of heaven and earth; OUR CREATOR,—"All things were made by Him;" OUR REDEEMER and SAVIOUR;—"There is no other name under heaven whereby men can be saved;" OUR REGENERATOR, —"He guides us into all truth." As to HIS OMNIPOTENCE.—"Every knee shall bow to Him, every tongue confess that JESUS is the LORD." His eye now rests upon us all and searches our hearts. He therefore is OMNISCIENT and OMNIPRESENT; for He is everywhere. We may feel his power within us now, nerving our minds to this important duty of developing the doctrines of his Holy Word, building up the walls of his Zion, strengthening our feeble efforts, and whispering to our souls, " Fear not, *I* am with you; be not dismayed, *I* am your GOD: for as *I* live, to me every knee shall bow, and every tongue confess that I am CHRIST the LORD." In the book of Revelation, a glorious being, whom John knew to be the LORD JESUS CHRIST, reveals Himself to this beloved disciple. "And when I saw him," says John, " I fell at his feet as dead. And He laid his right hand upon me, saying unto me, Fear not; I am the *First* and the *Last;* I am He that liveth and was dead; and behold I am alive for evermore,"—or, if correctly and literally translated, "*The Living One.*" How magnificent are these declarations! They convey to the mind, in the most powerful manner, the idea of the Supreme, the Sole and Exclusive Divinity in Him who utters them. Can anything be before the *First,* or beyond the *Last?* He, then, who is entitled to declare this of Himself must be the *All-in-All,* —the *Originator* and *Sustainer* of all things,—the Supreme and Only God, who is from everlasting to everlasting. But these are the declarations of the glorified JESUS CHRIST, as seen and heard by John in spiritual vision, and commanded to be proclaimed to the Church for the information of its members from generation to generation.

JESUS calls Himself, also, "The Alpha and Omega, the Beginning and the Ending, who is, and who was, and who is to come,—the Almighty." In this language there is an obvious assumption of the Attributes of Jehovah. The meaning of the word Jehovah is, *Was*, *Is*, and *Is to Be*,— *i.e.,* The *self-existent God.* And when Jesus declares He is the Living One, and that He and the Father are One, it is nothing less than an assumption of Deity. Either, therefore, John was deceived, and JESUS CHRIST deceived him, or JESUS CHRIST is the VERY GOD, the LORD of GLORY. After a careful study of the Scripture testimony, we are fully persuaded there is no medium between treating JESUS CHRIST as an *impostor* and *worshiping* HIM as GOD. If He were not God, He deceived the apostles and his primitive followers, and they have deceived us; and the Gospel, in such a case, is no other than a cunningly-devised fable. But we know, from a long, anxious, and prayerful investigation, that JESUS CHRIST is "The true

God and Eternal Life," and we can never let go this great Bible truth.

In conclusion: If HE who created the universe, and who giveth life, perpetual support, and everything useful and necessary for the good of all the inhabitants of its unnumbered worlds,—if HE who from pure love and mercy followed man from his fall in all his devious wanderings after he turned himself from his CREATOR to the delusive pleasures of sin, and followed him in order that He might redeem and *save*,—is the proper object of worship, then that object is the LORD JESUS CHRIST. Again: If HE on whose name the primitive Christians called, in whose name the apostles and their fellow-laborers baptized the nations and performed the miracles which they wrought in confirmation of their testimony, into whose hands, in the solemn hour of death, they commended their departing spirits, and of whom one of them has expressly said, "THIS IS THE TRUE GOD AND ETERNAL LIFE,"—if *He* to whom the innumerable company of the heavenly host direct their increasing acts of adoration and praise as to HIM who alone is worthy, is Jesus Christ, then is JESUS CHRIST the only LORD GOD and our SAVIOUR,—the only proper object of Christian worship, adoration, thanksgiving, and praise. And to HIM, therefore, be glory, now and forever. Amen.

DISCOURSE III.

ON THE TRINITY.

I. John v. 7.—" There are three that bear record in heaven, the Father, the Word, and the Holy Ghost: and these three are one."

In two former discourses we have addressed you on the *Being and Unity of God*, and on THE LORD JESUS CHRIST as the *true* GOD and ETERNAL LIFE. We purpose this morning to show that the doctrines of the Divine Unity and the Divinity of Jesus Christ, together with that of a Divine Trinity, are all strictly consistent with the truths of Christianity, when the nature of each one is properly explained and clearly understood.

To proceed in this inquiry, however, it appears necessary to state what the opinions of Christians generally are respecting the doctrine of a Divine Trinity, and, as far as possible, to ascertain whether these opinions are founded in error or in truth. If they are founded in truth, they ought to be received with thankfulness and rejoicing; but, on the other hand, if in error, they should be rejected and banished from our minds. Now, the prevailing doctrine among the various denominations of Christians upon this important subject, with one or two exceptions, is, that the Divine Trinity consists of *three separate* and *distinct* Persons,—that each Divine Person is by himself GOD and LORD; but that these *three*, although separate and distinct from each other, *form* but One Infinite and Eternal GOD.

In these addresses, our object as Bible-Christians is, not to rush on with the tide of popular opinion, nor to receive any doctrine of religion upon the mere authority of a writer or speaker; we shall investigate this matter, and, taking the example of the Bereans of old time, shall search diligently the Scriptures to see whether these things are so. And whenever we are so fortunate as to discover truth, no sinister motives, no considerations on earth, should be allowed to stand between us and the reception of so precious a treasure. That a Trinity of Persons is not scriptural, is, to us, evident from this single consideration, that the Bible cannot teach two opposite doctrines; and if, as we have already seen, the Bible sets forth the *Unity* of GOD, it is plain that a plurality of Divine Persons is inadmissible.

It is argued by those in favor of the idea of a Trinity of Divine Persons, that the Scriptures reveal the *fact*. They say, "Of the *mode* of the fact" the Scriptures "offer no explanation. And where the Bible is silent, it becomes us to be silent also. The *fact*, and not the *manner* of it, being that which is revealed, is the proper and only object of our faith." There is something of plausibility in this mode of arguing, and it is by resorting to such arguments as these that so many of the human family have been lulled to mental ease, and prevented from examining into subjects which are highly important and vitally connected with their best interests.

We are repeatedly told that the doctrine of a Trinity of Divine Persons is a fact,—and that the Bible reveals this *fact*. We would simply ask, Where? If one man tells us the Bible reveals this *fact*, and another says it does *not* reveal it, what is to be done in this case? The simple *assertion* of one man is as good as that of another; both are equally to be regarded as mere *assertions*, which in the absence of *proof* must sink into nothingness. The only proper method to pursue in this case, is, to go at once to the Bible itself, and see how far the assertion is borne out by the truths it reveals. We think we can show that this *fact*, as it is called, respecting *three Divine Persons* in the *Godhead*, is nowhere declared or revealed in the Bible; and that this doctrine, popular as it is, is entirely founded upon inference and assumption; and if, upon investigation, this assumption is found to be wrong from beginning to end, the whole fabric built upon it must necessarily fall to the ground. It is reasonable to suppose that a correct knowledge of GOD is a matter of the highest importance to the believer in Christianity; and if it really be a *fact* that GOD exists in *three Persons*, is it not reasonable to suppose that *this fact* would, at least, have been mentioned *once?*—that it would have been once directly stated in language that could not have been mistaken? We now speak of the *fact*, and not of the *mode;* for if the *fact* only had been *revealed*, then there would have been a cause for our assenting to it, although we did not comprehend the *mode*. But, upon examination of the Sacred Scriptures, we find that they are wholly silent as to the existence of this supposed *fact;* and where they are silent, it becomes us to be silent also. Now, we hesitate not to declare that, from the first of Genesis to the last of Revelation, there is not one single passage which states that in the One GOD there are three distinct, Divine Persons. The whole of this *tripersonal* doctrine is built on assumption—on mere inference and conjecture, without a single positive declaration of the Bible for its support. But as regards the doctrine of the Divine Unity, there is, as we have shown, no want of Scripture evidence. Are we not warranted, therefore, in concluding that the Lord our God, both in Essence and in Person, is infinitely and eternally ONE? Are we not justified in saying that the idea of *three Divine Persons* in the *Godhead* is not a scriptural doctrine? We proceed to a more particular examination of some of those passages supposed to favor this doctrine.

In the very first verse of the book of Genesis some commentators imagine there is evidence of a *Trinity of Persons* in the Godhead, because, in the original Hebrew, *Elohim* (God) is said to have created the heavens and the earth; and this word, they contend, is a plural noun, and has reference to the *three Persons* of the *Trinity*. To this it may be answered that, though its termination *im* is similar in *form* to many plural Hebrew words, yet it is always singular in its meaning. Not fewer than two thousand five hundred times the verbs and other parts of speech dependent on the word *Elohim*, and which, according to the laws of universal grammar, ought to agree with it in number, are invariably in the singular number. Besides, *Elohim* is often used in cases where the most devoted advocate of *three Persons* in the *Trinity* must allow that no *trinity*, nor even plurality, is referred to. It cannot, therefore, be admitted that *im* forms the plural of this word. Many other Hebrew nouns have this termination which are confessedly nouns singular: thus, *Mitsray*IM, Egypt; *Shamay*IM, heaven; *paan*IM *gnalpaan*IM, face to face; *teraph*IM, an image. The *teraph*IM which Michal prepared and put into the bed to represent David was simply an *image* of a *man*—of ONE MAN, and no more. The golden calf made for the apostate Israelites by Aaron, which was certainly one single thing, is called the *Elohim*. *Dagon*, the idol of the Philistines, was named their *Elohim*, yet the image was *one*. *Moses*, who certainly was but *one person*, was declared to be as Elohim before Pharaoh. So that if the word *Elohim* has any reference to a *trinity*, it could be to no other kind of *trinity* than that which existed in *Moses*, and which, moreover, exists in every individual human being. But again: it is well known to our hearers, many passages of the Old Testament are quoted or referred to in the Gospel. As an example: "Hear, O Israel, the Lord thy Elohim [God] is one Lord." But this is given by the Lord, and by the Evangelists writing by inspiration from him, by the common Greek word for GOD—THEOS, which, like the corresponding word in English, is *singular*. The same is the case throughout the *Septuagint*, or Greek version of the Old Testament, *Elohim* being everywhere rendered by *Theos*. Indeed, the most accomplished masters of the Hebrew language — many of whom were strongly attached to the *tri-personal* doctrine, including the great reformer CALVIN himself—have allowed that it is futile to attempt to deduce the doctrine of *three Persons* in the Trinity from this word Elohim. The scholastic definition of the word *person* is an individual who is a *thinking, rational, intelligent* being. According to this definition, only three kinds of beings can properly be called *persons*,—these are *men, angels*, GOD. Applied to the first of these orders of beings, *i.e.* men, *three persons* are *three men*. To the second, *three persons* are *three angels*. Applied to GOD, *what are three persons?* Are they not three Gods? Is it not incomprehensibility itself to say that *three Divine Persons* are but *One God?* Well may they who maintain this proposition have recourse to the plea of *mystery*,—well may they say human reason is unable to understand it. But where is the sanction for this plea in the Sacred Scriptures? Where is it declared that the doctrine of a *Trinity* is incomprehensible? Where is it affirmed that the *Trinity* is a *mystery?* Produce one passage, and we will allow such persons to make the *mystery* as *mysterious* as they please; but they cannot find for it a single text throughout the Bible. The key to the Trinity of the Sacred Scriptures, however, will shortly be shown to be in the declaration of man's being created in the *image* and *likeness* of GOD. Again, v. 26, "God said, *Let us* make man in *our* image, after our likeness." An eminent tri-personalist writer says, "This is the substance of all that can be said on this text,—viz., it is a Consultation of God the Father, the Son, and the Holy Ghost." We reply that consultations are held only for one purpose,—that of getting a better idea of a subject by the parties laying their heads together than each possessed separately: thus, a consultation of *physicians* sometimes takes place usefully for such a purpose; but we know no reason why persons should consult together, especially *Divine persons*, except, indeed, the common principle that *two heads are better than one*. But how could such a purpose be applicable to the One Infinite Intelligent Being?

The word *let* is very improperly introduced into this text, because there is no authority for it in the original. The word translated *let us make* is in the *first person plural*, *We*,—i.e., *we will make man in our image*. This plural pronoun ought always, in Sacred Scripture, to be interpreted with the idea of *one single Divine Person* in the GODHEAD,—particularly if we consider it to refer to the fact that the Divine attributes of *love, wisdom*, and *power* were all exerted in the creation of man. Because of this, the plural form, "*we will make man in our image*," is used. It therefore follows, "*so* GOD *created man in* HIS OWN *image*." But to enter into a critical disquisition on a point or points of Hebrew grammar would be out of place here. We therefore come at once to the text recorded in Matthew xxviii. 19: "*Go ye therefore and teach all nations, baptizing them in the name of the*

Father, and of the Son, and of the Holy Ghost." Here the terms Father, Son, and Holy Ghost are supposed to mean three distinct *persons;* but a little attention to our Lord Jesus Christ's explanation of these terms will show that no such distinct personalities are meant. In John xiv. He speaks frequently of the Father, of Himself, and of the Holy Spirit—the Spirit of Truth, which He calls the Comforter; but He in no part makes the most distant allusion to any plurality or distinction of Persons. In one of his conversations with his disciples, Jesus says, "If ye had known me, ye should have known my Father also; and from henceforth ye know Him and have seen Him." From this we find that a correct knowledge of Jesus Christ is indispensable to a knowledge of the *Father,* and that where the one is not obtained the other cannot be: "If ye had known *me,* ye should have known my *Father* also." Philip, in answer to these remarks of Jesus Christ, put to Him a direct request, saying, "Lord, show us the Father, and it sufficeth us." But what was our Lord's reply to this? The request, and the Lord's reply to that request, must be carefully considered; and if they are, the supposed distinction of *Persons* in the Godhead will be dissipated. Philip's request was, "Show us the Father." The Lord's reply was, "Have I been so long time with you, and yet hast thou not known ME, Philip? He that hath seen ME hath seen the FATHER; and how sayest thou, then, Show us the Father? Believest thou not that I am *in* the Father, and the Father in ME? The words that I speak unto you *I* speak not of myself; but the Father that *dwelleth in me,* He doeth the works." Is there anything like plurality of Persons found in this reply? Is not the very reverse distinctly declared? *Jesus Christ* says, emphatically, the *Father dwelleth* in Him; and, when speaking of *Himself* and the *Father,* he says, *I* and the FATHER are ONE. In whatever sense the terms Father and Son are to be understood, it is clear they do not denote distinction nor plurality of Persons; for if distinction and separation be implied, how could the Father *dwell in* the Son? —how could the Father and the Son be *One?* But it may be said, if Father and Son do not imply plurality of Persons, what is the meaning of the terms? This we will explain presently. In the mean time, it is sufficient for our purpose to show that no plurality of Persons is meant; and if this be so, the doctrine of a Trinity of distinct Persons, so far as this text is concerned, falls to the ground.

Another passage supposed to favor a Trinity of Persons in God is this (Matthew iii. 16, 17): "*Jesus, when He was baptized, went up straightway out of the water; and, lo, the heavens were opened unto Him, and He saw the Spirit of God descending as a dove, and lighting upon Him; and, lo, a voice from heaven, saying, This is my beloved Son, in whom I am well pleased.*" This passage is thought to establish completely the doctrine of a *Trinity* of three Divine Persons; but, whatever may be the inference drawn from this testimony, it is very clear that no separate Persons are mentioned. The voice from heaven is supposed to be the voice of *the Father;* admitting this, although *Jesus* says of the *Father*, "*Ye have never heard his voice at any time, nor seen his shape,*" yet, is that any proof of distinct Persons? Not the least; for what did the voice say? —"This is my beloved Son, *in* whom *I* am well pleased." This is in agreement with what the LORD repeatedly declares: "I am IN the FATHER, and the FATHER IN ME: the FATHER that *dwelleth* IN *me, He doeth the works:*" "I AND THE FATHER ARE ONE." With respect to the HOLY GHOST, or Spirit of God, it is supposed to be a distinct Person from both the Father and the Son; but the distinct personality of the Holy Ghost, or Spirit, can never be substantiated, because it is said, "Jesus *breathed* on his disciples, and said, Receive ye the *Holy Ghost.*" The words in the original literally mean *Holy Breath* or *Spirit;* it was this that influenced the apostles,—it was this which the Lord required them to receive; and as this *Holy Breath,* or *Spirit,* or *Influence,* came from JESUS, and was received by the disciples, we consider this as no small proof of the *Supreme Divinity* of JESUS CHRIST, and that in Him, as the apostle says, "dwelleth all the fullness of the Godhead bodily." Does it not clearly appear, then, from these scriptures, that nothing more than *assumption* can be deduced *for* the tri-personal doctrine of the Trinity?

Another passage from which the doctrine of a Trinity of Divine Persons is sometimes attempted to be inferred, is that we have chosen for our text, recorded in I. John v. 7, where it is thus written: "For there are three that bear record in heaven, the Father, the Word, and the Holy Ghost: and these three are one." Many commentators, and among others Dr. Adam Clarke, have declared this to be a spurious passage; they say it was never written by the apostle. We think there are good reasons for believing the passage is not spurious, but that it was really and originally written by JOHN. Now, assuming it to be genuine, in what way does it support a Trinity of distinct Persons? There is nothing whatever said of Persons; and the apparent distinction and separation close in the perfect Unit,—"These three are one." If it be asked, *How* are these three one? we will not evade the question by saying, "The *fact* only, and not the *mode,* is revealed, and therefore we cannot tell;" but we trust to be able to show that the *mode* as well as the *fact* is the subject of Revelation, and that both declare and set forth the Unity of God, in Essence and in Person; and yet that this doctrine does not militate against the true Bible doctrine of a Divine Trinity.

When we reflect that in no one instance do the Sacred Scriptures declare a Trinity of Divine Persons, and that they frequently announce that God is One in person, may we not be allowed to say that the doctrine of three Persons separate and distinct in the Godhead is a groundless fallacy and contrary to the testimony of the Bible? The very idea of a Trinity of Persons is incompatible with that of a *Trinity in Unity*. *Unity* can mean but *one*,— *one only*. A Trinity, then, of three distinct *ones* cannot be a *Trinity in Unity;* it would be a *Trinity in Unanimity*,—a Trinity of three *unanimous* GODS acting in unison with each other for the accomplishment of a certain end. This is the doctrine on this subject, with two or three exceptions, of all the various denominations of what are called Evangelical Christians; and perhaps there is no doctrine that is more *fatal* to the true interests of Christianity. It destroys in the soul the correct idea of God, and fills the mind with confusion, mystery, and absurdity. The doctrine of the Bible, the unerring Book of Divine Revelation, respecting the Supreme object of Worship, is that He is ONE. This is the foundation of all *true religion;* and the humble and sincere worship of this *Almighty One* is the spring of all human joy, the source of all spiritual wisdom, and the foundation of all our hopes and expectations beyond this transitory scene of mundane things.

We have seen, then, that God is One, in Essence and in Person, and that the glorified *Lord* and *Saviour, Jesus Christ*, is the TRUE GOD and ETERNAL LIFE. We proceed to offer a few additional observations, illustrative of the sacred doctrine of the Trinity as it is presented in the Volume of Inspiration. In making these remarks, it will be obvious to our hearers that no *denial* of *a Trinity* is intended. The question we are discussing is not whether the doctrine of a Trinity be true, but whether the *Trinity* implies Trinity of Persons or a Trinity that is to be viewed in some other light,—a Trinity of Divine Attributes. So far as the *word* Trinity is concerned, the *Unitarians* and their brethren, the *Universalists*, are very forward to tell us that this word *Trinity* is not to be found in the Bible. This is undeniably true; but neither is the phrase *mere man*, which they are so fond of applying to JESUS CHRIST, to be found in that sacred book. It is not, however, whether the word Trinity be found in the Bible, but whether the *doctrine* conveyed under that term is to be therein found; this is the subject of our inquiry, and this is what must be determined. The word Trinity simply means *three*,—not *three persons*, but THREE; and a Trinity in Unity denotes a *triune* or *threefold* order existing in *one entire whole*, both as to appearance and form; this is the kind of Trinity which exists in the Divine Being, and it is properly named the Divine Trinity in Unity. Every constituent of which this triune is composed has a distinct name to designate its Divine quality and use; and in the New Testament these names are *Father, Son*, and *Holy Spirit*,—these are *the three* that *bear record in heaven;* these form the fullness and perfection of the *One* undivided, indivisible, infinite, and eternal GOD. In this LORD GOD there are three *Essential Attributes:* the *Father* is the Inmost Essential DIVINE SPIRIT, or Divine LOVE, in whom we live, and move, and have our being; the *Son* is the Infinite Human Spirit,—the Great Wisdom of God, co-extensive with the Father; and the Holy Spirit is the Divine Operating and Sanctifying Spirit or emanated sphere of the Divine. This Triune GOD is the Great First Cause of all created life,—is that by which perpetual existence and subsistence can alone be kept up. From this primary cause of all existence *we* derive every blessing, temporal and eternal. To this cause we can trace all the true joys, the heavenly blessings, and the numerous phenomena of life; the plenty and fruitfulness of the earth; the very air we breathe, and even the power of breathing it. He is the life in all things, the very staff and support of all human and angelic existence, and the bread of heaven.

We cannot fail to see that there is no word in human language so well adapted to express the unlimited goodness of this Divine Being as that of FATHER. He is the origin of our existence, the source to which we must all look for support, the *Father* of us all,—*Our Father in the heavens.* The Divine *Wisdom, Logos,* or *Son,* is the proximate sphere of the Father or Divine Love, and the Light and Glory of the Infinite. The Divine *Logos,* or *Word,* is that by which the Lord God of Israel visited and redeemed his people. The Lord, as the Divine Wisdom, manifested Himself in the person of JESUS CHRIST, and therefore Jesus is called the Son of God, IN whom the Father *dwells.* When our hearers understand that by the term *Father* is meant the Triune God with respect to his Divine Love, and that by the Son is meant the same Being as to his Divine Attribute of Wisdom, and by the Holy Spirit, the Spirit of Truth, then will they perceive the force and beauty of the expressions in the Gospel where JESUS says, "If ye had known ME, ye would have known MY FATHER also;" "The Father DWELLETH IN ME;" "The Father, that DWELLETH IN ME, He doeth the works;" "He that seeth ME seeth the Father;" "*I* and the Father are one." They will then also clearly understand the declarations of the apostles relative to this subject,—"In Jesus Christ DWELLETH ALL the FULLNESS of the GODHEAD

BODILY;" "GOD was in CHRIST, reconciling the world unto Himself;" "Great is the mystery of Godliness,—GOD MANIFEST IN THE FLESH;" "Of HIS FULLNESS have we all received, and grace for grace." All these will be seen in their true light when it is known that the terms *Father* and *Son*, when applied to GOD, denote the *Love* and *Wisdom* of the one undivided and Eternal GOD, just as *Will* and *Understanding*, when applied to finite man, denote *one mind;* or as *soul* and body constitute *one person*. From these observations, it will be seen that the *Trinity* of the Bible is not a Trinity of separate and distinct Persons in GOD, but a Trinity of Essential Attributes as the same are revealed to angels and to men. These attributes are *Love, Wisdom*, and *Sanctifying Operation*, which, in the corresponding language of the Sacred Scriptures, are called Father, Son, and Holy Spirit. These are the *three* that bear record in heaven, and these three are *One*, because they form in the complex the fullness and perfection of the *One Infinite*, undivided, and Eternal GOD. By this view of the doctrine of the Trinity, all the passages of the Sacred Scriptures relative to it may be understood,—those in which the Lord speaks of his *inferiority* to the Father, as well as those in which He speaks of his *equality* and *Oneness*. Thus, when Jesus says, "*My Father* is greater than *I*," we are taught that *Divine Love*, being the inmost of the Divine Nature (like soul in man), is superior and comparatively greater than the *Divine Wisdom*, in and by which the *Love* is ever manifested and brought forth to light. Again, "The Son can do nothing of Himself." This is most true. Neither can the Father do anything of Himself; for Divine *Love* effects nothing but by means of Divine *Wisdom*, and Divine *Wisdom* of itself can effect nothing unless the Divine *Love*, as its soul and energy, gives the power. By thus viewing the great doctrine of the Trinity in the light of the Sacred Scriptures, as consisting of a threefold combination of Divine *Attributes* instead of *Persons*, the whole of this supposed mysterious doctrine will be seen as in the clearness of the light of a meridian sun; we shall see how the *three* are *One*, and realize the blessings of the *light* of *Life*. Such is the Bible-Christian view of the Divine Trinity; and, thus seen, the doctrine forms the chief corner-stone in the Christian Church.

When this glorious truth shall be universally acknowledged, then will the happy day have come when "the knowledge of the Lord shall cover the earth as the waters cover the deep." "In that day there shall be One Lord, and his name One." Amen.

DISCOURSE IV.

THE BIBLE A DIVINE REVELATION.

John vi. 63.

When we speak of Revelation, we understand the supernatural communication of certain spiritual information, given by the Lord to mankind, which they could not obtain by any of the common processes of the human understanding; and, yet, with which it was important that they should be acquainted. Still, when communicated, it was in such a form and nature, that those among men disposed to *believe* might see and comprehend it, while others desiring to do so might find a plea for their disbelief. Religion itself was produced by *Revelation;* and man, as a religious being, depends on Revelation for the principles of his faith and for his very existence. " Where there is no vision, the people perish." Revelation appears to have been given before the Scriptures which are now extant were revealed. Of this, the Sacred Scriptures themselves furnish the evidence: they plainly state that it was coeval with the first men : " God called their name *Adam;*" and there are many instances recorded in which He spoke to them, and many precepts and laws which He gave them. These *Revelations* were to them the Word of God. There seems to be a great misapprehension in the religious world, in modern times, on this subject. It is a very general impression that a *revelation* implies a *written* communication of the Divine Will. But the Divine communications imparted to men, when they enjoyed communion with GOD, expressed by GOD's walking in the garden of Eden with them, were as much a *revelation* to them as is the *written Word* of the Lord to us. The state of mankind was indeed more perfect when they could receive instruction by this *intuitive revelation*. It was not until man had nearly closed his mind, through sin, against the inflowing of *intelligence* and *love* from his Creator, and had begun in a measure to destroy the perceptive faculty in his soul, that a *written Word* was given. The state of men in the beginning was not such as to require the *Word* in documentary form. Their minds and hearts were clear and pure. They *loved goodness* with a supreme delight, and the genius of *love* is to rule the whole mind and bring its possessor into conjunction with the object loved. The first *written Revelation* was probably effected through the instrumentality of Enoch, who collected the principles communicated to men in Paradise, and arranged them in *doctrinal* form; and this is referred to in that remarkable passage which says, "*He walked with God; and was not; for God took him.*" By "his walking with GOD," is denoted his *co-operation* with the Divine Providence in the means by which *revealed truth* was to be preserved; and by "he was not" is meant that nothing of his mind as an individual, or his character as a man, was in the principles of the *Divine truths* so collected, because "*God took him,*" *i.e.* took him under his special guidance and directed him in the performance of the work. The name ENOCH means to *instruct* or *initiate*. Ancient tradition represents him as the *first author*. Visions and prophecies are ascribed to him, which he is said to have arranged into a book. The Arabians call him *Edris*,—*i.e.* the learned. The Evangelist Jude, also, evidently regards him as a prophetical teacher; v. 14, he says, "*Enoch* also, the seventh from Adam, *prophesied* of these, saying, 'Behold, the Lord cometh, with ten thousand of his saints.'" Other scriptures are also mentioned in the Bible as having been given to men, under the title of the "Wars of *Jehovah*," "The Book of *Jasher*," etc., which are now lost. When the state of the human mind sank so low that those former *Revelations* ceased to have the beneficent and instructive effect of a *Revelation* to them, God, in his Infinite Mercy, condescended *to speak* to *Moses* and the *Prophets*, and through them to bestow on mankind *that Revelation* which we now possess in the pages of the *Bible*.

Had not the Lord given a written revelation of Himself, man, in his downward course, would have lost all knowledge of a *Supreme Being*. We read that even *Abraham*, at the period of *his call*, had so far lost a correct knowledge of the true God as to have become an *idolater; Joshua* reminded the Israelites of this in his last charge to that people, and said, "Your fathers dwelt on the other side of the flood in old time, even *Terah* the father of *Abraham*, and the father of *Nachor, and they served other gods.*" And when JEHOVAH, the God of Israel, made Himself known to *Abraham*, it was by the title *Shaddai*, Almighty, a name by which one of his idols was called, and not by his name as known in the *Adamic* or *Noachic* ages. "I appeared to Abraham, Isaac, and Jacob," said the LORD to *Moses*, "by the name of *El Shaddai*, GOD ALMIGHTY, but by my name JEHOVAH was I not known to them." So, again, the Israelites, during their continuance in Egypt, very generally lost the knowledge of the name, the nature, and the very existence of the *true God;* this is plain from the circumstance that when God appeared to *Moses*, and commissioned him to bring the Israelites out of their captivity unto the promised land, *Moses* replied, "Behold, when I come unto the children of Israel, and shall say unto them, The GOD of your fathers hath sent me unto you; and they shall say unto me, *What is his name? what shall I say unto them?*" The same principle holds good everywhere, and in all ages. In the heathen world, where the *Word of God* is not known, scarcely any idea, and certainly no correct *idea*, of the LORD exists; and what little knowledge is still preserved there, obscure, gross, and sensual as it is, is the faint glimmering of a *revelation* probably once known there, and handed down by tradition for a time, but now lost. It is obvious, then, as our hearers will perceive, that one of the great objects of a *Revelation* is to impart to mankind a correct knowledge of GOD, and, therefore, the whole of the Inspired Scriptures revolve on this subject. That this is the case is clear from the LORD JESUS CHRIST's declaration to the lawyer, that on the two great commandments—" Hear, O Israel, the Lord our God is one Lord; and thou shalt love the Lord thy God with all thy heart, and with all thy soul, and with all thy mind, and with all thy strength; and thou shalt love thy neighbor as thyself"—hang all the law and the prophets. The testimony of the Apostle *Paul*, too, is that the all-absorbing theme of *revelation* is the development of the existence of GOD, his nature, attributes, and character. In his Epistle to the Corinthians he teaches that the *Word of the Lord* consists of the *letter* and the *spirit*, and he declares the Lord is that *spirit* (viz., the spirit of the *Word of God*), and then he adds that " we *all* with open face behold [in the *Word*], as in a glass, the *glory of the* LORD." This *truth* will appear in a still more impressive light, when it is further seen that the whole of the Scriptures point especially to the great visible manifestation of GOD in the GLORIFIED person of JESUS CHRIST: " Search the Scriptures, for in them ye think ye have eternal life; and they are they that testify of ME;" "THE TESTIMONY OF JESUS is the SPIRIT *of prophecy.*" Thus, then, it is evident that both the Sacred Scriptures and enlightened reason concur in testifying to the necessity and existence of a *Revelation,* in order that man may thereby learn to know, to love, and to worship and adore the true GOD, and through love to Him, and obedience to his revealed precepts, attain to the high destination for which he was created. It is no longer a question, therefore, whether a Revelation exists, since without it man could not be man; but the question is whether the *Bible,* which claims to be a *Revelation* from GOD, is really so. This leads to the important inquiry, What is the character of a *Revelation?* and in what do its sanctity and its divinity consist?

In regard to the sanctity and divinity of the inspired writings, and in what that sanctity and divinity consist, the words of our text plainly declare, "The words that I speak unto you, they are spirit, and they are life." This Divine declaration extends not only to the words spoken by JESUS CHRIST, as recorded in the New Testament, but likewise to what is written in the Old, since both Testaments are acknowledged to be alike the *Word* or *Speech* of the MOST HIGH, and consequently both must be alike replenished with the same Divine principles, called by our REDEEMER "*Spirit* and *Life.*" The important question, then, is, What are these principles, and in what do they consist? What is this *Spirit,* and what this *Life,* which constitute the very soul and essence of every WORD of GOD? But who can give a serious and satisfactory answer to this question without being forcibly impressed with the mental conviction that when a *Divine Speaker* declares, "The words that I speak are spirit, and are life," He must of necessity mean by the terms *spirit* and *life* a Divine spirit and a Divine life? because it is impossible to suppose that any other *spirit* and *life*, except what is *Divine*, can influence the *words* of a *Divine Speaker*, so as to constitute their essential properties. Who can give a serious and satisfactory answer to these questions without being mentally impressed as forcibly with another conviction, that the terms *spirit* and *life*, when applied by a *Divine Speaker*, involve in them *distinct* Divine principles, so that *spirit* is to be understood as expressive of one Divine principle, and *life* as expressive of another? if not so, the two terms would be a useless tautology, altogether unworthy of a *Divine Speaker!* Who, again, cannot discern, as by a mid-day light, that *spirit* and *life*, according to their *distinct* signification, and as distinctly applied by a *Divine Speaker*, must of necessity mean the same things as *Divine Wisdom* and *Divine Love*, since we are assured the Godhead is *both*,— " *God is Love, God is Light,*"—and may, therefore, be called the Divine union of both in their infinity and eternity? The conclusion, then, at which we arrive is that every part of the revealed Word, both of the *Old* and the *New Testament*, is filled with the *Divine Wisdom* and with the *Divine Love* of the LORD our GOD, in indissoluble union, this being its very inmost soul and hidden essence, whilst the letter—*i.e.* its history, its prophecy, its poetry and parables—is its external body and manifested existence. From these considerations, our hearers may clearly perceive the sanctity and divinity of the Inspired Writings, and in what that sanctity and divinity consist.

But, in pursuing this inquiry, it may be well to define a little more distinctly what the *Word of God* is. In the language of the Bible, it is called " *The Wisdom of God.*" " Therefore also said *The Wisdom of God*, I will send them prophets and apostles, and some of them they shall slay and persecute." (Luke xi. 49.) It thus appears that the Word of God is the Infinite Wisdom of God, brought down and accommodated to the perceptions of finite beings. That it is Divine, follows as a natural inference from its origin; for whatever proceeds immediately from God must possess that character. It is the dictated *Word*, or speech, of GOD. Now, in all speech, whether human or Divine, there must be three distinct principles; for without these there can be no speech. These are affection, thought, and expression. Speech, therefore, is nothing but the outward manifestation or outward expression of the *affection* and the *thought* of the *speaker;* it is a kind of embodying of those principles for the purpose of imparting them to others. Thus, when a man speaks, he, as it were, embodies his *affections* and *thoughts* in such language as is best adapted to convey them to the understandings of those with whom he is speaking. So, likewise, when the Almighty speaks, He, too, embodies his Divine *Affection* and *Thought*, or, in other words, his Divine Love and Wisdom, in such language as is best adapted to convey those Divine principles to the apprehension of his creatures, whether to angels in heaven or to men upon earth; and such speech or Word is given for their spiritual and everlasting instruction in righteousness and true holiness. This view of the subject is in harmony with what *Jesus Christ* said, when speaking to his followers, in the language of our text: "The words that I speak unto you, they are *spirit*, and they are *life;*" for by *spirit* is evidently to be understood his *Divine Wisdom*, or what He in another place calls "*the spirit of Truth;*" and by *Life* is as plainly meant his *Divine Love*, since this alone is properly *life itself*. Accordingly, in every part of the Sacred Scriptures, this union of Divine *Goodness* and *Truth*, or of the Love and Wisdom of God, is observable by the spiritually-minded, even in and through its literal expressions. Not only does rational investigation conduct us to this point, but the Scriptures also affirm the same thing. As it respects the *Divine expression*, it appears, by what the Lord says by his prophet (Hosea xii. 10), that He has always spoken by a peculiar language, or *mode of expression*. He there says, "I have spoken by the prophets, I have multiplied *visions*, I have used SIMILITUDES *by the ministry of the prophets :*" thus informing us that the language by which the Lord spake by "*the ministry of the prophets*" was that of *similitudes*, analogy, symbol, figure, or correspondence. This language of analogy is *expressive* of the relationship of created things to each other, and of all to their *Great First Cause*.

That all things in creation have relation to God is evident from the fact that all things have their origin in Him, and that they were created to carry out or express the purposes of his Divine *Love* and *Wisdom*, and, as *means*, must necessarily have relation to the *end* for which they were created ; hence his Works in nature are often called the elder Scriptures. That all things have relation to each other is too obvious to be denied. It is strikingly exhibited throughout all creation. We see it in the relationship which the mineral kingdom bears to the vegetable, and through the vegetable to the animal ; while all external objects have relation to *man*. No one will surely suppose that the *Word of God* is beneath the attention of his creatures, however exalted their intelligence may be, or that the wisdom of angels is superior to the wisdom of God as revealed in his Word. Angels, although existing in a higher sphere, are but "*the spirits of just men made perfect.*" Can we imagine, then, that angelic beings derive no instruction from the infinite wisdom of the Almighty, as manifested in the *revelations* He has given in his *Holy Word?* The Scriptures testify that the *Word of the Lord is* in heaven: "Forever, O Lord, thy Word is settled in the heavens." That the Word in the New Testament is there also, is attested by John the Revelator: he says, "I saw another angel, having the everlasting Gospel to preach to them that dwell on the earth." Why should the *Word* be forever settled in the heavens, and the everlasting Gospel be there too, if not as a means of instruction to the heavenly inhabitants? If it should be objected that the angels had the Gospel to preach *to those that dwell on the earth*, this rather confirms than militates against our position; for that which is the subject of any one's preaching must be the subject of his meditation and of his devout study.

Indeed, the true *interpretation* of the Gospel must, through the disposition or ministry of angels, come to us, for it was "an angel" who had "the everlasting Gospel to preach unto them that dwell upon the earth."

The language, then, in which the *Word of God* is written is founded on that relation and mutual dependence which are universal both in the spiritual and the natural world. No other style of expression could serve as a universal *medium* to communicate the infinite and ineffable wisdom of God to finite intelligences so as to adapt it to the peculiar degree and state of relationship of each of his finite creatures to Himself; and no one save the Infinite could really employ this language,—because nothing short of *Divine Wisdom* can embrace and comprehend these relationships in all their infinitude. Every Divine truth proceeding from the LORD descends, as it were, through the heavens to men on earth. Such, also, is the nature of the Word of the Lord. In its inmost sense it is heavenly; in its interior sense it is spiritual; in its last or lowest sense it is natural, and, to us, in that sense in its fullness and efficacy.

From what we have said respecting the *character* of the Word, it will naturally be expected that the views of Bible-Christians respecting the nature of *Inspiration* differ in some degree from those generally current. It is popularly believed that the writers of the Scriptures were inspired; but beyond this all is vague and obscure. The divinity and sanctity of the Sacred Scriptures do not consist in their having been given through *inspired men*, but because *they themselves*, as well as those through whose instrumentality they were *revealed*, were *inspired*.

Inspiration, as the term implies, is an *in-breathing:* the *inspiration* of the inspired writers consisting in this, that "holy men of old wrote" as the *in-breathed* Spirit of the Lord, or rather as the Lord by his Spirit, *dictated* to them. Thus the inspiration of the Word consists in its being inspired with God Himself, who is as much present in its truths as He was in the Israelitish Tabernacle. He as really speaks in the *Word* now as when He spake it of old by the prophets; and the precepts of the Gospel are as fully inspired with the vital Spirit of the LORD at this day—and will be to eternity—as they were when they fell fresh from the lips of the Saviour. He now speaks also to those who are without—*i.e.* to those whose ideas of the Bible are altogether natural—*in parables;* whilst to those who follow Him into the *sanctuary* of truth "it is given to know the mysteries of the kingdom of heaven." The evidences of the Lord's presence in his Word abound in almost every portion of the Sacred History. Whence had the *ark* of the *testimony* its miraculous power? Why was it that at its presence the waters of the Jordan receded? Why fell the walls of Jericho before it? And why was Dagon, the idol of the Philistines, cast down? It was because the LORD, by his Divine Commandments, was present there. But in what did his presence reside? Could it be exclusively inclosed in a space two cubits and a half in length and one cubit and a half in breadth and the same in height? By no means. God is Infinite; He was present in the *living truths* inscribed by his own direction on the two tables of stone, and on which, we are told, hang all the law and the prophets. It is the very sanctuary of God, in which He can be present with the minds of all his intelligent creatures,—with angels in heaven by its interior or spiritual truths, and with the members of his Church universal on earth by its *literal* expressions; through this He also leads man, so far as he is capable and willing to be led, into a perception of its *spirit* and *life;* and it is from this interior *spirit* and *life* that it is divinely inspired in every syllable. The letter of the Sacred Scriptures contains within it all the spiritual truths which had been *revealed* to men before the period of its commencement and present form; it is also the continent of other principles, of which it is the only exponent. The literal sense of the *Bible* is the ultimate form of all Revelation,—a form suited to the wants of the ultimate condition into which the fall has brought mankind. In this form of Divine *Revelation* all Divine, heavenly, and spiritual truth is, in its fullness, its sanctity, and its power. By this man has consociation with angels above, and by this he attains conjunction with his FATHER in the heavens; and every doctrine of the Church, to be truly instructive, must be drawn from the literal sense of the Word and confirmed by its testimony.

From what has been advanced, we trust it will be seen that the *Word of* GOD, like the heavenly *ladder* seen in vision by the patriarch, rests on the earth and reaches to heaven,—nay, even to the throne of God. Through the

Word, heaven and the future world are opened to us; by it angels are present with us, and heavenly influences are brought down to the sincere and devout worshiper in all our Sabbath assemblies, in our sacramental elements, and at our family altars; and our prayers and devotions, like incense, are borne up, as in angels' hands, to their heavenly abodes, where *their* aspirations mingle with ours, and thence ascend to the Only Wise God, our Saviour,—The *Word* that was God, The Creator, Redeemer, and Saviour of men. Amen.

DISCOURSE V.

ON CREATION.

Genesis i. 1.

The connection between science and religion has ever been a subject of deep interest to enlightened and reflecting minds. Yet, often has the theologian, on the one hand, looked with jealousy upon science, as if fearful that its influence might be hurtful to the cause of true religion; while, on the other hand, the man of science, in the pride of a skeptical spirit, has scorned the idea of an alliance between science and theology. Both these opinions are erroneous; and they have operated disastrously as well upon science as upon religion. The position we take as Bible-Christians is, *that scientific truth, rightly understood, is religious truth;* and *that religious or Bible truth, rightly interpreted, is ever in union and harmony with the* truths of science.

The subject of the *creation of the world* is one on which both theologians and philosophers have written largely; and in many cases their opinions are as different, as far from harmony, and as wide of the genuine testimony of either Creation or Revelation, as are the poles of the globe. They have erred, either on the one hand, "through not knowing the Scriptures," or on the other, through the delusive luminosity of their own imaginary and self-derived intelligence.

The theologian denies the scientific facts of Geology, because it refers the origin of the earth to a higher antiquity than, he says, is assigned to it by the Mosaic account of creation; and he considers that this theory undermines our faith in the inspiration of the Bible, and in all the animating prospects of the immortality which it unfolds. Here, however, the theologian is obviously wrong, because the writings of Moses do not fix the antiquity of the globe, nor make any such allusion to it.*

It is not, however, our purpose to enter into any controversy relative to the age of the earth, or the successive changes it may have undergone previous to the creation of mankind. Our purpose is rather to see the order and origin of Creation, and to demonstrate the operation of an Infinite Intelligence in the production of the world and all its parts; and to show that the Creator of the universe is at the same time the Creator, the Redeemer, and the Regenerator or re-creator of man. A careful study of the most ancient portions of Divine Revelation will evidently demonstrate that the Almighty from the beginning selected a peculiar and symbolic mode of communicating his will to mankind; doubtless because He saw it would convey most effectually the clearest spiritual ideas in relation to his own Essence and operations, and be most powerfully adapted to man's mental faculties. The Sacred Scripture, or Word of God, therefore, employs the terms by which physical objects are expressed, to communicate ideas respecting metaphysical or spiritual existences. The chief object of Scripture, however, in the employment of one class of natural things is not, as some have supposed, to

---

* The putting dates to the Bible, in regard to the era of creation, and thus making the present age of our globe about six thousand years, is altogether gratuitous, conjectural, and arbitrary.

signify another class of natural things; but objects existing in material creation are selected to symbolize objects of a spiritual nature. The spiritual, in the works of the Creator, can only be indicated by means of natural or material existences; and it is only as we view the Scriptures in this light that we are enabled to apprehend the first principles to which they point, and so to comprehend their real import or meaning. One of the first principles unfolded in the text recorded at the commencement of Divine Revelation, is, that "the heaven and the earth were created." This is an idea not found in any other ancient writings. Among the Egyptians, Greeks, and numerous other heathen nations, the earth was either represented as eternal, or it was said that matter was eternal, and that by some kind of fortuitous operation the particles of eternal matter were so brought together as to form the solid earth. The Bible, however, informs us, "the heaven and the earth were created," had a beginning, and that their creator was God. How sublime and important is this first truth of Revelation! The proper mode of viewing the subject of Creation is to regard it as an *outbirth* of the Divine mind,—as a production essentially distinct from the *producing cause*,—but yet, bearing, through all its parts, to that *Infinite Producer* and to the infinite essential attributes and properties existing in Him, a constant and an immutable relation. This shows the fallacy of the heathen notion that the world is eternal,—self-produced and self-formed, and the source of all things; and it manifestly evinces the absurdity of another notion, prevalent even among professors of religion, that God formed the universe out of nothing. But to create this world out of nothing is an absolute impossibility. Nothing is nothing; out of nothing, nothing can be produced. Nothing is not anything; and that which is not anything, cannot become anything, can have no possible existence. But some may be ready to say in support of this *nothing* hypothesis, God is Omnipotent, and He can do all things. He is Omnipotent, but He can do nothing inconsistent with his own Divine order and nature.

He cannot do anything that is really sinful;* and thus, also, in a number of instances, God cannot do this or that, although Omnipotent. He cannot act in opposition to his own Infinite Wisdom and Goodness.

The question then arises, Whence came matter? It could not be created from nothing; it is not eternal; what then can it be but an *outbirth*, a *creation*, or *formation*, from the Divine Creator? God created matter from Himself. It cannot be made from nothing. Behold the vastness, the boundlessness of Creation,—contemplate the immense number of stars, and suns, and worlds, scattered throughout the universe,—the wonderful works of the Omnipotent hand of the Lord; formed of different elements, and furnished with an indefinite variety of objects of various forms, natures, and uses,—look at the immensity and magnificence of the universe, and then say, if you can, that all these vast orbs, and suns, and worlds, and beings were once nothing—that out of nothing they were all produced! How inconsistent! Nothing always was nothing, and nothing will it always remain.

But, again, Whence came matter? Swedenborg, the celebrated philosopher and enlightened theologian, informs us, "There are two suns, by which all things were created from and by the Lord,—the sun of the Spiritual

---

* He doeth all things well: his perfections render wrong-doing impossible for Him.

world, and the sun of the natural world. The sun of the spiritual world, from which all things issue as from their fountain, is the first of all substance in intense activity, proceeding from the Lord God, who is in the midst of it. That sun itself is not God, but is from God, and is the proximate or primary sphere from Him. It is the first proceeding of the Divine Love and Wisdom. The sun of the natural world is pure (elementary) fire, and is created and produced (through intervening circles of atmospheres) from the spiritual sun. From this spiritual sun, as a great centre, proceed circles, or atmospheres, around it, one after another, even to the last, and where their end is, subsiding in rest: these circles are spiritual atmospheres, which the light and heat from that sun fill, and by which they propagate themselves to the very ultimate circle; and in that last, by means of the preceding atmospheres, and afterwards by means of the natural sun and its atmospheres which are emanated from it, the creation of the earth was effected.

"That substances or matters like those on the earth were produced from the sun by its atmospheres, is affirmed by all those who think that there are perpetual intermediations from the first to the last; and that nothing can exist, but from a prior self, and at length from the *First:* and the *First* is the sun of the spiritual world; and the *First* of that sun is the Lord.

"Now, as the atmospheres are the prior things by which the sun presents itself in ultimates, and these continually decrease in activity and expansion to ultimates (or last), it follows that when their activity and expansion cease in ultimates, they become substances inert, like those on the earth. In the substances of which the earth consists, there is, indeed, nothing of the DIVINE IN ITSELF, for they are deprived of all that, being the ends or terminations of the atmospheres, whose heat has ended in cold, whose light ends in darkness and their activity in inertness; but still, they have brought with them, by continuation from the *spiritual sun*, that which was there from the *Divine*, viz., a sphere from the Lord; from which, by continuation from the (natural) sun, proceeded, by means of the atmospheres, the substances of which the earth consists."

Thus, according to this philosophy, the proper mode of viewing the creation is to regard it as an *outbirth* from the Great Creator, yet as essentially *distinct* from the Great Producing Cause.

In the Gospel it is recorded, "The Word was with God, and the Word was God; all things were made by Him." Paul further says, "The things which *are seen* were not made of things which do appear." All things that exist, in heaven, in the universe, and on earth, exist from the infinite love and wisdom of the Lord: these are the only essence and source of all things. These form the Divine and ever-living sun of heaven, giving heat and light to all its glorious and happy inhabitants. This Divine sun is, as we have already stated, the proximate sphere of the Lord's glory, beaming forth its heat and light to the immense and boundless worlds above;—every beam of whose heat is Divine Love, and every ray of whose light is Divine Wisdom. From this sun of heaven spiritual atmospheres are produced, within which angels and the spirits of the just and good live; and from this sun, with its spiritual atmospheres,—which are no other than the divinely emanated sphere of the Lord, proceeding from his essential love and wisdom, surrounding, filling, and blessing all the heavens with their countless happy inhabitants,— from this sun and its spiritual atmospheres all things in the spiritual worlds are produced, formed, and have their existence; and from the same source or sphere, proceeding farther and farther, as it were, from the great spiritual and Divine centre, the natural sun is produced and formed as a body of pure elementary fire, the vitality of which is that spiritual sphere or creative principle by which it was produced, and from which it has its perpetual existence. From this natural sun, vivified by a spiritual power from the Lord, and thence made active, natural atmospheres are formed, which in their proceeding become more and more dense and inert, and ultimately form earths and material worlds such as exist in our solar system, derived from the sun, and mediately supported by it. In our natural sun, in the atmospheres, in the earth, and, indeed, in all nature, there is a certain spiritual principle of life and activity, from the Lord, which is their inmost life, and without which they could not exist one moment. Thus, the world was made by the Word of the Lord,—his wisdom proceeding from his Divine love, forming the sun of the spiritual world, the primary sphere of his unutterable glory; from this, spiritual atmospheres, as the living substance of all substances, "the wheels or circles within wheels" of the prophet; thence the sun, the universe, worlds and earths were created, exist, and will endure forever.

But although the things which constitute and form this natural world are *from* the Lord only, they are, nevertheless, *not* the Lord. This may, perhaps, be illustrated and made still plainer from the consideration of the fact that there is a certain *sphere* exhaling from and surrounding every human being, and likewise all animal and vegetable existences; this sphere, in many instances, is palpable to our bodily senses. Such a sphere emanates from every man, yet *it* is not the man; when passed from him, it is void of his life; and it no otherwise makes one with the man, than in that it accords with him, being produced from the peculiarities of his bodily organization, which are the forms of his life, or ruling affection. Thus, in the substances and materials of which the world consists, there is nothing of the Lord in them, although they are from the Lord; they are devoid of all that is Divine, being the ends or terminations of the spiritual atmospheres proceeding from the sun of heaven, in which is the Lord, and becoming ultimated through the natural sun and its atmospheres. And though the heat of those spheres has terminated in cold, their light in darkness, and their activity in inertness, there is nevertheless a certain degree of heat, light, and activity in and encompassing them from the Lord, according to his own Divine order in the creation of the universe.

Among the objects of the visible portions of creation, man, the acknowledged image of his Maker, stands in the highest degree of relationship to Him, and the inert substances of the mineral or inorganic kingdom in the lowest. This truth is not invalidated by the fact that this latter, according to Geology, came first into existence. It must be true that, in the creation of the world, the globe of earth and water, or the unorganized parts of its composition, though lowest in rank, must have been the first that were formed; for this reason, because their uses were indispensable to the higher order of existences, to afford them nutriment and a basis. Then, doubtless, the vegetable kingdom succeeded; because, without both these, animals could not exist. Thus, the higher orders of creatures must have appeared by degrees, and last of all man; as he could not begin to exist till everything necessary for his use was provided. Still, it was for the *sake of man* that all inferior things were produced: man was in the *Divine mind* throughout the whole process: thus everything produced was an image of something that was to exist in him, and the spiritual and moral essences of all inferior things were concentrated in him; as he himself was to be an image of the Creator, in whom alone exist, in their first principles and Divine essences, all the powers, faculties, and virtues which were to exist derivatively in mankind. The Great Creator, in the work of creation, cannot be considered as operating at random, producing things which have not in Himself their Divine prototypes or germs of being. To produce such things the Creator must step out of Himself, which is impossible. As the tabernacle, with everything in it which Moses was instructed to make, was to be made after the pattern or antitype shown to him in the mount, or was to be an outward type of such things as exist in heaven, so, no doubt, when the Lord created heaven and earth, with their respective inhabitants, He formed everything after the image of Divine prototypes existing in Himself,—after the pattern of the ineffable attributes and perfections which exist only in his own Divine essence. Thus the whole universe, instead of being, as it is sometimes inconsiderately regarded, a production of mere caprice, without order, and little better than the offspring of blind chance, was unquestionably what may most expressively be called an *Outbirth* of the Divine *mind;* and, as such, it must bear in all its parts an immutable relation to the attributes or essential properties which belong to the nature of the Omnipotent Creator.

And now, Christian friends, we trust you will see something of the order according to which worlds were created and formed, from and by the Lord, as the one only source and substance of all things; and this in the most impressive and beautiful light, more especially if you will elevate your minds to the Lord our God, whose essence is Divine Love and Wisdom; the inexpressible glory of which forms the sun of heaven,—the sun of righteousness,—with its pure heat and light,—the spheres and atmospheres of which heavenly sun the angels and good spirits inhabit; and whose spheres, proceeding farther, and becoming more dense, produce and form all the substances and materials of which suns and worlds are composed; the spiritual power and influence from the Lord giving them respectively their activity, life, and perpetual existence, and that, too, in the most perfect harmony and order, through all the varied revolutions of time.

Our observations have been concise, but, we hope, sufficiently full to satisfy you that the world is not eternal; that it was not created out of nothing;—an idea of the grossest kind, for out of nothing not anything can possibly come.

We have endeavored to show that the Lord Himself is the alone Creator of all worlds and all beings,—the only essence and substance from which all things are; and we may add that creation is perpetual. Our intelligent hearers will admit that there are, besides our world, suns and worlds innumerable scattered throughout the universe. The *Creator* is Infinite; the sun of heaven, or the proximate sphere of his love and wisdom, is forever the same, forever operating. His creative wisdom and power, therefore, are forever given forth in the same way, according to the order we have briefly described, creating and forming suns, and worlds, and beings in every variety, in agreement with his own infinite love and mercy; that by such means He may perpetually elevate and draw towards Himself rational, sentient, and immortal beings, to enjoy his love and favor, to be happy in his presence, and dwell everlastingly in his own immense and immeasurable heavens, which can never be filled through all the boundless ages of eternity.

Let this view of creation sink deep into your minds,

then, beloved, viz.; that in wisdom, love, and power, the Lord is the creator of all worlds,—that "In the beginning He created the heavens and the earth." Reflect, with the deepest humility, the sincerest gratitude, and the most ardent affection, that He has created our world, and worlds on worlds, and that He will unceasingly create, with this most benevolent design, that all we, and countless millions like ourselves, should be the recipients of his wisdom and rejoice in his love; and that, after a short existence of trial and tribulation in a material world, we may be prepared for an elevation into the fullness of heavenly love and light, of peace and joy, of felicity and glory in the heavenly mansions of the Lord our God,—in the bosom of his infinite goodness, and in that kingdom where we shall forever live as heavenly angels, perfect in blessedness. And while you are contemplating the wonders of the Lord's creative power, remember also the Bible testimony in regard to his redeeming love, his saving mercy, and his divinely benevolent design in all these operations to make you angels of his kingdom. Improve, therefore, your brief earthly existence; it will soon end,—we know not how soon: shun every known evil, and labor to insure the Divine approbation by a life of faith, of love, and of obedience to the principles of the Everlasting Gospel: elevate your thoughts and affections, your understandings and hearts, towards heaven, while mercy spares you time and opportunity so to do, and while truth points to you the way to a glorious immortality: then, that Great and only Creator, Redeemer, and Saviour of men, who created the heaven and the earth in the beginning, will raise your spiritual bodies from this primary state to his own eternal kingdom; will constitute you angels there, and make you perfectly happy in his love and in his glorious presence forever. Amen.

DISCOURSE VI.

ON THE ORIGINAL STATE OF MAN.

Genesis i.

In our last monthly discourse, we endeavored to aid our hearers in attaining an apprehension and understanding of the Bible testimony regarding Creation, and more particularly the creation of the world in which we are placed. We purpose this morning directing your attention to another department of the creative power, and operation of the Great Creator of all things in heaven and on earth, as the narrative is recorded in the chapter we have just read.

In order correctly to understand the written documents of antiquity, it is necessary to know something of the genius of the people among whom, or respecting whom, those documents were produced. Without such information, we should be liable to great mistakes. It is known that very different styles of writing have prevailed among the same nations, at different periods of their existence; and the deeper we penetrate into their mental history, the less of what is literal, and the more of parable, of analogy, or of poetry, shall we find to have been in their methods of expression. This fact is not to be disregarded in prosecuting our inquiry into the original state of man now before us. It bears forcibly on the subject. To us it seems evident that the Lord, in causing a Revelation to be made to mankind of spiritual wisdom and heavenly goodness, has at all times had respect to the peculiar genius, temperament, and leading disposition of the people to whom such revelation was vouchsafed. This is clear from what are called the Jewish Scriptures. The letter of the Revelation relating to that people, and of which they were made the depositaries, was constructed in the *historical style* in which we find it, in consequence of the remarkable *mental condition* of that singular people, who, as a nation, were most external and sensual. Of spiritual things, beyond their national rites and religious ceremonies, they had generally but little conception; and because of these characteristics, the Revelation, which, in its external form, is peculiarly theirs, partook of that *historical* and *worldly* appearance by which we see it is distinguished. If, then, it be true that the literal style of Revelation has always assumed a form in conformity with the genius of the people to whom it was first made,—if it be true that the most external style of Revelation to be found in the Bible was adopted in consequence of the external and sensual condition of the Jewish people, to whom it was first committed, —then it will follow that the Revelation granted to a *prior* and *mentally superior people* could not have been of so external a character. If the genius of the people among whom the early portions of the book of Genesis were produced was eminently heavenly, and if the narratives are constructed in conformity with such a character, then the literal sense of that Revelation ought to be differently understood from that given to the descendants of Abram. It would be contrary to all just criticism to suppose that the literal form of the Revelation granted to a people who were acquainted with heavenly subjects and were influenced by spiritual principles, was the same as that given to a community who, generally speaking, were utterly ignorant of such things. It is admitted there is a peculiarity in several of the first chapters of the book of Genesis, produced among a people who lived long before the time of Abram; and there is much reason to believe that they were revealed in those periods which poets and philosophers have spoken of as the *Golden Age*,—an age in which an Oriental people were intelligent on heavenly subjects, because they studied interior and spiritual truths, and were acquainted with those things among the outer existences in nature which were the symbols of such truths; an age in which mankind would speak of heavenly subjects by means of those objects they knew to be their symbols or emblems in the world of nature.

The minds of mankind, during the purity of the Adamic periods, were influenced by very interior, elevated, and heavenly sentiments: the affections of their *wills* were, doubtless, directed towards the Lord their Creator, and their *understandings* were enlightened by thoughts concerning Him and his kingdom. In such an intellectual condition, *nature*, to them, must have been a sort of mirror, reflecting internal and heavenly ideas. Such minds would regard the things of the world by which they were surrounded as the *symbols* of some mental state,—some spiritual experience, or heavenly truths, belonging to the Lord's kingdom in their souls. This mental state would, indeed, enable them to "look through nature up to nature's God," and to behold in all its objects the expressive types of heavenly realities. To such minds, Creation must have afforded a rich display,—a sort of photographic exhibition of objects mirroring forth interior and heavenly principles relating to the Creator and his kingdom.

With regard to the Creation and original state of man, Revelation informs us that, according to original creation, he was distinguished by an *internal* and an *external* nature; that he was endowed with immortality, and that he was placed in a state of responsibility. But what may we suppose were his *mental* and his *moral* possessions? We can scarcely think of his being created with the *experience* and *information* which mental exertions and moral qualities would seem to imply. His original condition, in these respects, could have differed but little, we imagine, from those states into which men have since been born. He must have been *ignorant,* but *innocent;* still, possessing all the capabilities for having developed the loftiest perceptions of *wisdom* and the holiest principles of *love.* The state which has attended the beginning of man in all ages may have been designed to inform us what his condition was when first originated. Of the process by which this was accomplished we have no specific Revelation; but we are told something of the mental characteristics that first belonged to man. "The earth" is said to have been "without form, and void," to denote that, as to his external nature, he was destitute of the *order* which arises from enlightened teaching, and *void* of that living excellency which springs out of active goodness. "Darkness" also is said to have been "upon the face of the deep," for the purpose of declaring to us the ignorance which then prevailed upon the perceptive capabilities of the human mind.

Thus it appears that mankind, by original creation, did not intuitively possess either the knowledge or the love of Divine things. This destitution did not, however, arise from the voluntary *rejection* of those excellencies, as has been the case with mankind in after-ages; but because, as yet, they had not been communicated. Man's original state, therefore, must have been one of passive innocence and mental docility. He was gifted with capacities that were afterwards to be developed, and by the cultivation of which it was intended that he should attain to the love of his God above all things, and of his neighbor as himself. He was created perfect in the degree of his primeval existence, but not with the actual possession of those high qualifications in which his mental faculties could result. The degree was a faculty to *become* great, but was not greatness itself. It is this peculiarity which distinguishes *man* from the *beast*. The beasts were at once endowed with all that they were capable of, and so at once were beasts; but man was created with capacities or faculties only, to the end that by their proper use and education he might knowingly progress in all that is wise and good, and so be a man. The perfection of the *beast*, therefore, is its imperfection; while the deficiencies of *man* become the groundwork of his eminence. How long mankind continued in this primeval state there is no historic information, nor is it necessary for us to know how long or how short was its duration.

We have stated that the spiritual creation of the human principles, or mental capabilities of religious life and actions, is treated of in this chapter under the symbolic language of a natural creation. The narrative teaches us not only the order by which, from being "void" and dark, man was successively filled with spiritual principles and gifted with intellectual light, but it records a fact which distinguished him as an early inhabitant of our world. He was actually raised into that spiritual and celestial eminence so beautifully and forcibly expressed by being made in the *image* and *likeness* of God. And now, in what sense are we to view this man? Is *Adam* to be considered merely as an individual, or is the term to be regarded as comprehending a community? We maintain that the latter, and not the former, is the true idea connected with this problem; and we believe this idea to be clearly recognized in the very expression *Adam* (mankind), as well as in general statements. Although this part of the Bible testimony is probably more allegorical than literal in its meaning, yet its language and intimations are constructed on the idea of the existence of society, and may fairly be referred to as affording evidence upon this question, which may be received as important, especially by those who insist upon the literal sense as expressing all that is meant. There are several circumstances so mentioned as to imply the existence of human society apart or distinct from that of *Adam* or his *posterity.* When, according to the common reading of these narratives, there were only *three* inhabitants of the earth, we find that Cain, after the fratricide he had committed on Abel, said, " My punishment is greater than I can bear ; and it shall come to pass, *that every one that findeth me shall slay me."* A mark also was set upon him, *" lest any one finding him should kill him."* These statements evidently imply the existence of society. Why should Cain fear every one that found him, if there had been none to find him but his parents? Of what use could have been the *mark* set upon him, if there had been but Adam and Eve, his father and mother, to see it, and be warned by it? They must have known him without such a sign. These circumstances show not only that society then existed, but also that such society was in a state of civilization so elevated as to be influenced by a moral sentiment that could reject and condemn a murderer's crime. But there is another fact, equally strong, bearing upon this point. When Cain went into the land of Nod, he is said to have taken a wife, and built a city, which he named after his first-born son, Enoch.

If there had not been society, where could Cain have obtained his wife? Where could he have procured the workmen necessary for such erections as are implied in the building of a city? Moreover, of what use could have been such a city if there had been no society to inhabit it? From these facts it is legitimately to be inferred that a people were at that time in existence for whom no relationship can be traced to Adam and Eve, and of whose origin we have no history. It clearly teaches that the doctrine, popular as it unquestionably now is, that the human family is all from that *one pair*, is not sustained,— nay, is absolutely without foundation in the Word of God; and we may be permitted to add that science demonstrates the utter fallacy of such an idea.

Now, if there were such a people in no way related to Adam,—and of this, after what has been said, we are persuaded there can be no well-founded doubt,—why may not the term Adam, which Gesenius and other learned Hebrew scholars do not consider as the proper name of the first man, but as an appellative referring to the race, and meaning mankind,—why may not this term *Adam* mean and indicate the existence of a *community*, an association or a Church that had been gradually separated and gathered from the general mass of human society, and had associated themselves under those virtues, graces, and excellencies of character which we have said distinguished the people of the Golden Age? That which is apparently predicable of an individual may with equal propriety be said of a number of persons; and therefore the narratives relating to Adam, instead of being the personal history of *one man*, may be the ecclesiastical or spiritual history of a highly cultivated people constituting a Church; and because it is the oldest of which we have any record, it may with propriety be called the *Most Ancient*, or the Adamic Church. There is surely nothing irrational in this view of the matter. But some of our hearers may perhaps feel disposed to say, Is there not some more distinct proof of such an idea? We think there is; and that, as we have already intimated, it is to be found in the Word itself. When the Lord said, "Let us make man," the proposition could not refer to the individual, but to the human race. Man, or the Hebrew word *Adam*, is put for *mankind*, and so it is to be taken as expressing that wider sense: this is evident, for it is immediately added, "and let *them* have dominion." But the original word, translated *man*, is *Adam*, and this is thus distinctly asserted to have a *collective* signification, for it is written that the Lord " called *their* name Adam in the day when *they* were created." Both male and female are here specifically meant; and there are many other instances in the Scriptures where the term Adam is used in the sense of *mankind*, or the *human race* in general. And that this is its true import, is evident from the circumstance of its never being found in the *plural* form, though there is no grammatical difficulty in the way of its being declined by the *dual* and *plural* terminations and the pronominal suffixes. The term *Adam* occurs in the second and third chapters of Genesis no less than nineteen times, and in every case it is put with the definite article. As then the word Adam is not the actual appellation of an *individual*, but a *nominal*, expressive of the *kind* or *race*, it will follow that the term *Adam* or *the man* in those Scriptures must be received as describing the *people*, the *community*, the *society*, the *Church*, or whatever other word may be thought more fitting to express the idea of a *human association* possessing the solid acquirements of a genuinely spiritual and heavenly religion.

From what has been said, our hearers will understand that while the first chapter of Genesis appears to describe the creation of the world, it also spiritually describes the creation and original state of man, and his successive progress through the varied conditions of being, until he attained to the *image* and *likeness* of his God; that is, until his *understanding* became so far receptive of the wisdom of his Creator, and his *will* the recipient of the *love* and purity of the Lord, as to be an image and likeness of the Divine Perfections. On account of this receptibility of the love and wisdom of the Lord, and of a spiritual and heavenly life in obedience to such an influence, he was called *Adam*, or *man*. We are not *men* from our mere external form. Shakspeare says, "All are not men who wear the human form." But we are men because we possess that which no other created beings possess. *Beasts* have no powers above what has been called *instinct* ; but *man* has mental faculties,—he has a *will* and an *understanding*, he has capabilities of affection and science,— reason, intelligence, and wisdom: these constitute his *manhood*. The successive developments of character, described in our chapter as *Adam*, were the progressive advancements or regenerations of the original human *community* of a *whole people*, who lived in some exceedingly remote period of the past, and who, from the superiority of their character, their highly cultivated and innocent minds, constituted what we prefer to call a *Church*,— the Adamic or most Ancient Church, because it is the earliest of which we have any revealed or authentic records. It will thus be understood that we are *men* because of our mental capabilities. Our moral and intellectual faculties are bestowed on us, not that we may eat and drink as mere animals do, but the grand prerogative of our *manhood*—of those noble capabilities and faculties which are spiritual and immortal powers—is that we can rise above the things of time and sense; we can direct our minds to the great Creator,—the GRAND MAN of the Universe, from whom we become men in the degree that we receive his love, his wisdom, and his life, and are thus transformed into images and likenesses of the Lord our God,—prepared by a process of regeneration to live eternally in his kingdom, as happy and glorious angels. Amen.

DISCOURSE VII.

ON THE POPULAR DOCTRINE OF ORIGINAL SIN.

Ezekiel xviii. 2.

"What mean ye that ye use this proverb, saying, that the fathers have eaten sour grapes, and the children's teeth are set on edge?"

If the maxim be true, that "The proper study of mankind is man," it is surely a matter of importance that we should endeavor to know the real situation of man on his becoming an inhabitant of the world, and what are the responsibilities resting upon him. It is well known that the doctrine of *original sin* is very generally taught as a leading principle in the system of Christianity, and that it is popularly admitted as a Bible truth; but it does not necessarily follow, because this doctrine has gained an almost universal popularity, that it is therefore "the pure milk of the Gospel;" for it is equally well known that many doctrines, both in religion and philosophy, have been propagated and for a time generally admitted as true, which, on a closer investigation and a more mature consideration, have been discarded as mere phantoms of imagination, and as the production of error. Hence a fair and rational inquiry into the doctrine of *Original Sin* is a duty of vast importance; for upon the truth or falsehood of this doctrine will depend most of our religious exertions, as well as much of the nature of our intercourse with the world around us.

In speaking to our hearers on this interesting subject, we will first state this doctrine as it is commonly taught and generally received, and then proceed to demonstrate its utter destitution of truth, and that it has no foundation in the religion of the Bible. The generally received doctrine of *original sin* maintains that Adam, as the first man, "was the moral principle of mankind. In the first treaty between God and man, Adam was considered, not as a single person, but as the representative of the future human family, and contracted for all his descendants by ordinary generation; his person was the fountain of theirs, and his will the representative of theirs. Hence his vast progeny became a party in the covenant, and had a title to the benefits contained in it, upon his obedience; and was liable to the curse, with all its fatal consequences, upon his violation of it." This is the foundation of the doctrine; and hence, as Adam was the confederal head of the whole human race, his disobedience and sin do not remain with him only, but are imputed to all mankind; all the families of the earth have suffered for the folly and transgression of one, and, consequently, the curse denounced on Adam, for his single act of folly, is effective on the whole of his posterity. By the single act of one, all mankind are declared to be sinners, and deserving of the wrath and damnation of God. The Augsburg Confession of Faith, from which all the leading doctrines of the Reformed Church are drawn, says, also, concerning *Original Sin*, "Since the fall of Adam, all men are *born in sin*, which brings damnation and eternal death upon those who are not regenerated, and that the merit of Christ is the only means whereby they are regenerated,—the only remedy by which they are restored. That original sin is such a total corruption of nature, that there is no spiritual soundness in the powers of man, either as to his soul or body: that in spiritual and Divine things which regard salvation, he is like the *pillar of salt* into which Lot's wife was turned, and like a *stock* or a *stone*, without life, which have neither the use of eyes, mouth, nor any of the senses." Such is the doctrine respecting *original sin*, as set forth in this orthodox and curious work we have referred to, and from which we have quoted; and who can read or hear its sentiments without being deeply impressed with horror at its bold and presumptuous clauses? If its teachings be true, the Sacred Scriptures, which were given—and mercifully given—after the fall of man, to be his rule of life, and for his guide to restoration and immortality, can be of no manner of use to him. The Scriptures contain the strongest and most powerful appeals to the hearts and understandings of men that can be imagined; but where is the wisdom of addressing such powerful appeals to "pillars of salt"? Of what avail can sympathy, clothed in the most impressive language, be, when directed to senseless "stocks and stones"? Why should the Lord speak to mankind, who are said to be so dreadfully depraved, so wretchedly polluted at the very core, as to be compared to things without life, having neither the use of "eyes, mouth, nor any of the senses"? No folly, in our estimation, can be compared to this infatuated supposition. If man, in regard to spiritual things, be really dead,—a mere "stock, stone, or pillar of salt,"—so senseless that he can neither move, speak, nor understand, to what purpose are all the beautiful and energetic exhortations of Divine Revelation made, and to whom are they addressed? Can it be supposed that the Lord, who is infinitely wise, would require the creatures of his hand, as we all are, to do such and such things, when He knows that we have no power to do them? And will this infinitely wise God punish us for disobedience, when He knows we have not the least power to obey? To teach this doctrine is not only dishonorable to GOD, and prejudicial to mankind, but, as Bible-Christians conceive, fatally and desperately wicked. And yet, in regard to *original sin*, the doctrine is deemed evangelical orthodoxy. When we are all earnestly called on in the Bible to do the work of Repentance, and "put away the evil of" our "doings," upon the theory of the doctrine of *original sin*, might we not say, We cannot "put away the evil of" our "doings," we cannot do the work of Repentance, we are "pillars of salt," devoid of all ability to repent? When the Lord says, "Come unto me, all ye that labor and are heavy laden, and I will give you rest," we might, with great propriety, say, We cannot *come*, for we have no power; we are "stocks and stones." "Comfort ye, comfort ye my people, saith your God. Speak ye comfortably to Jerusalem, and cry unto her that her warfare is accomplished." We cannot speak, for we have no mouth. "Come hither, and *hear* the words of the Lord your God." We cannot come, for we have no power; we cannot hear, for we have no ears. "Look unto me, and be ye saved, all the ends of the earth, for I am God, and there is none else." We cannot look, for we have no eyes. "Come, now, and let us reason together, saith the Lord." We cannot *reason*, for we have no understanding. Now, if the doctrine of *original sin* were true, might not such answers as these, with great propriety and reasonableness, be given to these and all other invitations of Scripture? How can we *do, come, look, hear, speak*, or *reason* without possessing the needful faculties, and the power of using them? It would be altogether impossible. But we do possess these faculties; by the possession of these and other mental powers, we, as human beings, are distinguished among the various existences which surround us, and we are endowed with the power of using them; our very existence and all our actions in life prove the fact, and it is in vain for the transgressor to attempt to plead a palliation for his life of iniquity, under the idea that the lamentable effects of *original sin* have deprived him of all power of doing good, and of co-operating with the Lord in the important work of the salvation of his soul.

But here it may not be inappropriate to ascertain and define what SIN is; for, unless we know what is to be understood by the term, we may come to very erroneous conclusions in regard to it. We may be permitted to say, then, that where there is no *reason* there is no liability to sin; nor can any one, compelled by an irresistible power or by a sort of fatal necessity to the performance of certain actions, thereby *commit sin;* for if the action be bad and sinful, the sin does not lie in the agent, but in that irresistible power which compelled, the agent having no control over the action.

It is generally admitted, by all professing Christians, that man, mentally considered, is composed of *Will* and *Understanding:* these two are so united as to make up the entire and perfect man. These constitute his manhood. The Will is the seat of all the affections, motives, propensities, and desires, and may be said to form his love and his life; the Understanding is the seat of all his thoughts, perceptions, and intellectual properties, and constitutes his rationality, judgment, and power of discrimination. No work or action of an individual can be *sinful* unless produced by the joint exertion of both *will* and *understanding;* the will prompting to the commission, and the understanding examining into the nature of the suggested action before it is executed. The evil desires and propensities of the *will* are constantly endeavoring to break forth into open acts of violence; but the understanding is a *restraining power*, given to guard and protect man from the dangers and snares into which the vitiated desires of his will would lead him; and while the understanding continues to exercise its power of judgment and discrimination, in its true and proper order, under the principles of conscientiousness, no *sin* can be committed. "Sin," says an apostle, "is the transgression of" (a known) "law." We must make a careful distinction between *evils* and *sins:* they are entirely different, and if they be carefully defined, distinguished, and acknowledged, we shall be convinced of the impossibility of "man being born in sin." The term *evil*, as used in the Bible, refers to the vitiated desires and propensities of the *will;* but *sin* relates to a corrupt state of the understanding, in permitting the evil propensities of the *will* to break forth into actions contrary to the dictates of truth and to conscientiousness or justice. Since the fall, man is born into the world with evil desires, propensities to evil, and with impure inclinations, and these are hereditary, that is, are communicated from parents to children; but these are not *sins*, neither do they condemn before the Lord. They have not yet passed the understanding, received its sanction, nor been made the individual's *own*, by the actual commission of crimes contrary to *truth* and *conscientiousness* marked out by the understanding.

Bible-Christians, therefore, maintain that *no man is born in sin.* He is born with hereditary propensities to evil, derived from a more or less corrupt ancestry; but these do not become *sins* until his rationality or understanding is formed, and he then brings those hereditary evils into actual life and practice; then they are *his own*, then he is a *sinner*, and then he is *accountable*. If it be still contended that man *is born in sin*, and if it be also true that without repentance *sin* cannot be forgiven, and if it be likewise true, what our Lord says, "If ye die in your sins, whither I go ye cannot come," what, then, becomes of that vast portion of the human family which dies in a state of infancy? It is of no use to evade this question by saying we cannot tell, because we can tell, and the inference is certain: for if *man is born in sin,* and he *dies* before he is in a state capable of doing the work of repentance, which is the case with all infants, then we are forced into the conclusion, however shocking, that all who die in infancy are consigned to the dark regions of misery and woe. Such a doctrine would surely be one of the blackest that ever emanated from the dark and direful regions of the bottomless pit. What said our Lord on this subject, when He took the dear children in his arms and blessed them, saying, "Of such is the kingdom of God"? The great doctrine of Bible-Christians in regard to this is, that of all the families of the earth those who die in a state of infancy, of whatever religion or country, whether the offspring of pious or of impious parents, are initiated immediately, through the instrumentality of angels, into all the delights of heavenly joy and angelic wisdom.

But we will now turn to the testimony of Scripture. Perhaps there is no passage in the whole Bible which appears to be more favorable to the doctrine of *Original Sin* than this, "Behold, I was shapen in iniquity, and in sin did my mother conceive me." This passage is brought in on all occasions to prove the doctrine, and upon this it is thought to rest. Bible-Christians want no stronger testimony than this passage in proof that *man is not born in sin.* Who can discover from it, that man *is born in sin?* It is not even remotely declared: the terms *iniquity and sin* are not applied to the child which is here said to be *shapen* and *conceived,* but to the mother. Thus the passage says, "Behold, I was shapen"—In what? "in iniquity," "and in sin did my mother"—What did she do in sin?

"conceive me." Thus the literal and obvious meaning of this passage is, that the mother was *iniquitous* when the child *was shapen*, and *sinful* when the child *was conceived*. The terms *iniquity* and *sin* do not apply to the *child at all*, but only to the spiritual condition of the mother.

It is a little remarkable that the doctrine of *Original Sin* should be so strenuously insisted on, when there is not one single text in the Bible which says or teaches that the sin of *Adam* is communicated to his posterity. It is true the Apostle Paul says, "By one man *sin* entered into the world, and death by sin," but here is no mention of an actual *transferring* of the identical sin of Adam to his offspring. All that *is said* we readily admit, viz., that by the *disobedience* of one man *sin* entered into the world; for *disobedience* is the cause of sin, and those who follow in the path of *disobedience* become *sinners* equally with their forefathers, and are, consequently, subject to like penalties. Those who maintain the doctrine of *Original Sin*, and suppose that the sin of *Adam* is *transferred* to his posterity, agree readily with the *old proverb* we have selected for our text, "The fathers have eaten sour grapes, and the children's teeth are set on edge." But if we turn to this chapter, Ezekiel xviii., and examine it carefully, we shall find that the LORD, instead of approving, condemns the proverb, and, in language that cannot well be mistaken, points out the erroneousness of *Original Sin*. Upon this doctrine the prophet writes thus: "The word of the Lord came unto me, saying, *What mean* ye that ye use this proverb concerning the land of Israel, saying, The fathers have eaten sour grapes, and the children's teeth are set on edge? As I live, saith the Lord God, behold all souls are mine; as the soul of the father, so also the soul of the son is mine: *the soul that sinneth, it shall die*." Here we find no mention of the imputation of the *sin* of one man to another, but it is plainly declared that "the soul that sinneth shall die." The very reverse of the doctrine of Original Sin is inculcated; for the prophet, in describing the wicked man, says, "Now, lo! if he beget a son that seeth all his father's sins which he hath done, and considereth and doeth not such like, *he shall* NOT *die for the iniquity of his father, he shall surely live.*" Again the Lord saith, "The soul that sinneth, it shall die. The son shall NOT bear the iniquity of the father, neither shall the father bear the iniquity of the son." How plain is this language of the Bible! How clearly is it affirmed that no actual sin or transgression of one man can be imputed or transferred to another! Every man's condemnation depends upon his *own actual* sin,—upon his own voluntary and internal state and life.

That man is not born in sin is further obvious from the Gospel. We there read, "As Jesus passed by, he saw a man who was blind from his birth, and the disciples asked him, saying, Master, who did sin, this man or his parents, that he was born blind?" Our Lord answered their question in a way that totally overthrows the notion of original sin. He says, "Neither hath this man sinned, nor his parents; but that the works of God should be made manifest in him." And the works of God were literally manifested in him, by the miraculous bestowing of sight. But an appeal is made to the decalogue in support of *Original Sin*. It is there said that the Lord "will visit the iniquities of the fathers upon the children unto the third and fourth generation." But this in reality gives no sanction nor support to the doctrine: it is one thing *to visit* the iniquities of the fathers upon the children, but another *to punish* the children for the sins of the fathers. The visitation implies the power by which the sinful father communicates to his children those evil propensities and impure inclinations which reside in the will,—the will of the flesh,—but which never do become sins until the understandings of the offspring are formed and they bring them into life and practice, in opposition to their better judgment and to the known dictates of truth and conscience: then they become the sins of the offspring, and condemnation follows as the necessary effect of such actual transgression. But this visitation of the fathers upon the children is not said to be made upon all mankind, but only upon a particular class of persons, that is, upon those that *hate* the Lord: "Visiting the iniquity of the fathers upon the children unto the third and fourth generation of *them that hate me;*" but mercy is to be shown to the thousands of those who *love the Lord* and keep his commandments.

And now, beloved, may we not conclude that the popular doctrine of Original Sin, as commonly taught and believed, is a vile error, dishonorable to the goodness and love of the Lord our God, whose "tender mercies are over all his works"? Have we not good reason to conclude it has no foundation in the Bible? Let us turn from the dark picture, and listen to the voice of the Lord Himself, by his prophet: "Wash you, make you clean: put away the evil of your doings from before mine eyes; cease to do evil; learn to do well: then, though your sins be as scarlet, they shall be as white as snow; though they be red like crimson, they shall be as wool." These invitations are not made to "*pillars of salt,*" nor to *stocks and stones,* but to men,—to all mankind,—to rational and intelligent beings, capable of understanding the invitations, and of co-operating with the Lord in the great work of their salvation.

The Bible teaches that if we turn our souls to the Lord, and remember that "The soul that sinneth, it shall die,"—if we strive to do his Holy Will, and rely upon his power and goodness, which will accompany us through all our days,—if we cease to do evil, and learn to do well, then will the Sun of Righteousness gild our declining days with mental peace and heavenly tranquillity; and when time shall remove us, the voice of our Heavenly Father shall gladden each of our joyous souls with, "Well done, thou good and faithful servant; enter thou into the joy of thy Lord." Amen.

DISCOURSE VIII.

ON THE GARDEN OF EDEN AND ITS TREES.

GENESIS ii. 8, 9.

IN our lecture on the Original State of Man, we endeavored to convince our hearers that the idea so prevalent among religious professors respecting the unity of the race, or the whole human family being descendants from Adam and Eve, was not sustained by science, nor even by the Bible itself when correctly interpreted. We showed that the term *Adam* was not the name of an individual, the first created man, but a generic term denoting mankind; and that as used in the book of Genesis it is expressive of a religious community, or the first true Church among men on earth. The language of our text to all appearance describes the first natural garden,—a garden that was the result of the Creator's planting; there are also some intimations of its geographical situation, and the adjacent features; but instead of this being the instruction that the text is intended to convey to us, if we examine it and other portions of the early chapters of Genesis we shall have strong evidence for believing they treat of the most Ancient Church, or that our text in particular treats of the state of religion among living men, and is not to be considered as descriptive of the mere vegetable productions of the insensible earth. All that is revealed with regard to this first or Adamic Church is presented to us in the language of poetry rather than of history: still, it is a Divine poetry in an historical form. There are many acknowledged instances in which Jesus Christ has presented spiritual principles to the consideration of his disciples under the appearance and character of fictitious history. His parables are remarkable instances of this fact. Many, notwithstanding, have believed that the beginning of Genesis was real, literal history; that the earth and all the vegetable and animal existences were produced in the order and time mentioned; that there was a real earthly garden or paradise, created and formed purposely for two individuals to occupy, and in which they dwelt till the time when they partook of the forbidden fruit; that this garden was a spot of peculiar beauty and of delightful productions, and in every respect was a locality superior to every other part of the then known world. Many have devoted much time in seeking to discover such traces of its existence as would enable them to say precisely where, or in what particular part of the globe, this garden was placed; but all their study and researches have amounted to no more than uncertain conjecture, and where the locality of the Garden of Eden was is, literally speaking, wholly unknown to the learned. But had those persons considered the word of God in its primary and true light,—as a book revealing to mankind religious, spiritual, and Divine principles,—they would have thought less about an earthly garden, embellished with shrubs and flowers and fruit-bearing trees, and have given themselves less trouble about ascertaining the particular place of its existence. The earth was formed for the habitation of men, and they who first dwelt on it no doubt occupied certain parts of it; and those of whom we have spoken as a religious community, under the appellation of *Adam* or the most Ancient Church, whilst they remained in their primitive integrity, were distinguished for their wisdom, their love of God and of goodness, and then, with such mental virtues, an Eden bloomed around them. All nature, even in its external form and appearance, was in agreement with the internal condition of their minds, and administered external delight and pleasure both to their minds and bodily senses, so that it may be justly said the whole earth was then a paradise.

Let us for a moment look at the external world. Is it not beautiful in all seasons and in all hours?—from the rising of the sun to the time of its going down; even in the solemn midnight hour, when the moon and the stars assert their peaceful reign. This wonderful world, so pleasing to the natural sight, in all the plenitude of its beauty and magnificence, when religiously considered, is but a type, a symbol or shadow of another, a spiritual and interior world, —a spiritual universe. In this outer world we perceive there is a sun which forms, as it were, its heart and centre, and from which, as from a vast fountain, every manifestation of beauty and of order proceeds. So also in that other inner world there is likewise a sun. But the sun of that world is a living sun. It is the proximate sphere of the love and wisdom of the Almighty. And the Lord Jesus Christ in his glorified manhood, as "God over all, blessed forever," is in the midst of that sun,—the Sun of Righteousness. And He is our Creator, Preserver, and Redeemer,—the Alpha and the Omega, the Beginning and the End, the First and the Last,—who is, and who was, and who is to come, the Almighty. His government in our hearts ever gives the spiritual Garden of Eden, the garden of delights to our souls. That this Garden of Eden and its trees described in our Bibles were allegorically understood, their very names evidently imply. What is a tree of life? Solomon in his book of Proverbs answers,

"Wisdom is a tree of life." And may we not ask, Did you ever find life growing on any material or earthly tree? Has life more than one source? and is not the glorified Jesus the Way, the Truth, and the Life, itself? Again, do we not find this same Tree of Life, here represented as in the midst of the garden, declared in the book of Revelation to be in the midst of heaven? "To him that overcometh," it is said, "I will give to eat of the Tree of Life, that is in the midst of the paradise of God." Once more we find the "Tree of Life" in the midst of the New Jerusalem, and on both sides of the river. "In the midst of the street of it, and on either side of the river, was there the Tree of Life, which bare twelve manner of fruits, and yielded her fruit every month; and the leaves of the tree were for the healing of the nations." The holy influence of the Lord, in its twofold character of *love* and *light* within our minds, is the Tree of Life. This, if we are in the way of regeneration, is in the midst of the garden in our souls. This is the source of the joys of the heavenly inhabitants. This is the centre, and this pervades all the principles of the true Christian Church on earth. The *Tree of Knowledge* of good and evil is equally indicative of a spiritual existence; for on what other tree does knowledge grow, save on that of the human mind? And knowledge grows only as we desire to know. The knowledge of external things may well be called the knowledge of good and evil, for it is the knowledge of the effects of religion and of irreligion, of order and of disorder, of truths and of appearances. This knowledge is a tree that has its uses in the garden of the soul, but its fruit is not to be eaten. Our own knowledge is good to know and to use, but not to eat or confirm, and as it were to make part of ourselves. The popular but idle fancy that this tree was an apple-tree, cannot be called even a thought: it is a mere fancy, and wholly devoid of any scriptural or rational foundation. The other trees of the garden, that are "pleasant to the sight and good for food,".are our perceptions of heavenly wisdom and love; and of these we may freely eat,—they are in unison with Him who is the Truth itself. When we speak of our perceptions, we mean a certain interior sensation which the spiritually-minded man has from the Lord, enabling him to know as it were at once whether a thing be good and true, or the contrary. It is what he calls conscience. A man dead in trespasses and sins is devoid of such conscience, and without this intellectual perception. The Sacred Scripture is exceedingly particular in keeping up the distinction between these three kinds of trees,—the tree of life, the tree of knowledge, and the trees pleasant to the sight and producing fruit for food. Of the fruits of the last-mentioned trees, mankind were originally directed freely to eat. "Behold, I have given to you every herb bearing seed, and every tree in which is the fruit of a tree yielding seed, which is upon the face of all the earth ; to you it shall be for food." The trees pleasant to the sight and good for food, as well as the herb and grain, are said to have been on the *face* or *surface* of the *earth:* it is not so said of the trees of life and of knowledge. The originally prescribed food for mankind was herbs, grains, and fruits; for a period of more than sixteen hundred years, or to the time of the flood, this was the only, the universal food of mankind. The Creator and Lawgiver appears to have deemed these productions all-sufficient for the nourishment, the health and strength, of the human family. An illustrious and learned expounder of the Scriptures, alluding to the original food of man, says, "Eating the flesh of animals, considered in itself, is something *profane;* for the people of the most ancient time never ate the flesh of any beast or fowl, but only seeds, especially bread made of wheat, also the fruits of trees and esculent plants ; to these they added milk and what is produced from milk, as butter, etc. To kill animals and to eat their flesh was to them *unlawful*, and seemed as something bestial ; they only sought from them *services* and *uses;* but in succeeding times, when man began to grow fierce like a wild beast, yea, fiercer, then first they began to kill animals, and to eat their flesh." They were permitted so to do, as they are permitted to do every other kind of evil, such, for example, as drunkenness and all other carnal indulgences. The diet God prescribed for man in Eden, He pronounced to be "very good ;" a diet which, from experience and observation, we can honestly say is fully adapted to our nature, preservative of our health, calculated to prolong our days upon earth, to give vigor and energy both to our physical and our mental faculties, and, as such, is a diet worthy of universal acceptation.

But we must speak more fully of this Garden of Eden. It is evidently regarded in the Sacred Scriptures as a symbol of a regenerated, cultivated, and sanctified state of the human soul ; it is the emblem of the kingdom or Church of the Lord on earth ; it denotes the intelligence and wisdom by which this first religious community, or the members of the Adamic Church, were favored from the Lord,—the *love* and *goodness* in which their minds were principled. For as a well-planted and properly-cultivated garden is not only stored with fruits of every variety, with vegetables, grain, and flowers for the *use* of man, but is, in its beautiful aspect, also both pleasing to the eye and delightful to the mind, so when an individual is truly receptive of intelligence and truth, of love and faith, and of other religious and heavenly virtues from the Lord, that individual is then spiritually a *garden* and an *Eden;* his life and conduct are orderly, beautiful, and useful ; he brings forth and bears to perfection the pure graces, virtues, and fruits of the kingdom of heaven; he is amiable and pleasing in the sight of God, of angels, and of men; and as the prophet Isaiah saith (xli. 3), "He is then made like Eden, and the garden of the Lord; joy and gladness are found in him; thanksgiving and the voice of melody." Thus, beloved, have we laid before you what is truly and spiritually meant by the Garden of Eden and its trees; and this fruitful, useful, beautiful, and happy state was the real, religious, and spiritual condition of the religious community called Adam, or the most ancient people or Church of whom we have any account in the pages of Divine Revelation.

From what has been submitted to your calm and Christian consideration, we trust that when you think of the Garden of Eden you will not only think of the beauties of a natural garden, but of the magnificence of what is spiritual; that is, of the state of the human mind when truly fruitful and useful in all the doctrines, virtues, and graces of the Christian life and its heavenly nature. We hope, in the *tree of life*, you will see a symbol of those Divine principles of love to the Lord, and faith in his name and Word and Gospel. Such a believer is the blessed one whom Jesus Christ calls "a good tree, bringing forth good fruit;" he is planted in the Church, in the house of his God, by the river of living waters; and in the course of Divine Providence he will subsequently be transplanted to mansions in the eternal heavens, to flourish there as a tree of Paradise, an angel of light, a son of the Lord's love, and a happy citizen of his kingdom forever. Our fervent prayer is, that your souls may all become Gardens of Eden,—gardens of delight; that the Tree of Life, the Divine love and faith from the Lord, may dwell in your inmost hearts, and transform you into Edens,—gardens of delight, each producing spiritual virtues, heavenly graces, and celestial qualities, and that you may be so devoted, useful, and amiable in the garden of the Lord as to be duly prepared, whenever He sees fit, for being transplanted to the Paradise above,—the kingdom of our adorable Lord and Saviour,—there everlastingly to enjoy the unutterable perfections of that heavenly world as glorified spirits and angels throughout the boundless ages of eternity. Amen.

DISCOURSE IX.

ON THE FORBIDDEN FRUIT, AND THE TEMPTER.

Genesis ii. 7, iii. 1.

The subjects we are about to present to the consideration of our hearers this morning are confessedly somewhat mysterious, though of the most interesting importance to our understanding of the sacred pages. Commentators have conceived and published opinions and conjectures on the subject of our text, so vague and inconsistent, that reasoning and judicious minds have been led to disbelief, rather than to a conviction of the truth of the narrative. The whole account given in the first chapters of Genesis is either a simple narration of facts, or it is an allegory. If it be an historical relation, its literal meaning should be sought out; if it be an allegory, then is it equally necessary that we should be acquainted with the facts presented in that form of Revelation. The literal interpretation of this part of the Bible, as we have shown in our last two lectures, has been involved in doubts and difficulties from the earliest periods, and the recent developments of physical science have tended rather to strengthen these doubts and increase these difficulties. The peculiar language applied to the tree bearing the forbidden fruit, and called the tree of the knowledge of good and evil, shows evidently that the record should be looked on as an allegory or figurative representation. The learned Jewish Rabbi,

Simon bar Abraham, says, "Know that in the trees, fountains, and other things of the Garden of Eden, were the figures of the most curious things by which Adam (or the most Ancient Church) saw and understood spiritual principles." Rabbi Maimonides says that the serpent has relation to the mind of man; and that in the account that is given of creation, the ancient Rabbis, from the time of Moses, held that these things, reduced to an historical form in the first chapters of Genesis, were not to be literally understood, but that this was the method by which, in ancient times, they instructed the people. The teachers of primitive Christianity maintained that the whole account was purely allegorical; and whoever examines the Scriptures with care will find that similar instructive allegories were used by the sacred penmen throughout the Scriptures of the Old and New Testaments. The confessed difficulties in comprehending what is meant by the trees of the Garden, though different in kind, are the same in principle. Concerning the fruit of the forbidden tree, a physical notion has been conceived by many professors of religion as well as by modern commentators; whereas a *mental* condition of the *soul* is really meant. "Life" and "the knowledge of good and evil" are not vegetable productions; they are spiritual and intellectual existences. Yet professing teachers of the Bible have very generally believed that this forbidden tree was a real vegetable production in Eden, having its branches, leaves, and fruit like other trees. What particular kind of tree it was, has been a matter of considerable controversy among the learned literalists: some say it was a *vine*, others the *fig-tree*, and others again are persuaded that it was an apple-tree. Now, does it not seem something very extraordinary — something quite out of the order and the nature of things—that any mere tree, or the fruit of any tree, whether *fig, apple,* or *grape,* should have in its nature the power to make man *wise,* or to give him knowledge and understanding superior to what he had before eating any such fruits? Wisdom and intellectual knowledge are not material things;—they grow not on any trees of the vegetable kingdom: they are things of a spiritual character, and can only be communicated to mankind in a spiritual way. The very idea of supposing that to eat an *apple,* a *fig,* or a *bunch of grapes,* or indeed any other fruit from a tree of the ground, will give wisdom and intelligence to man's mind, is a notion so extravagant, so out of the order and nature of things, and so contrary to the Divine economy, that it is difficult to conceive how men of learning and intellectual attainments could possibly give way to such a sentiment; more especially when, by a little attention to the testimony of the sacred pages, they must perceive that though trees are therein frequently mentioned, this is always in such a connection as to show demonstrably that *not* material trees, but things of an intellectual and spiritual kind, of which trees are the outward emblems, are signified by the trees of the Bible. Thus, the prophet Isaiah, treating of the Lord's people, says, "They shall be called trees of righteousness;" and in the Gospel it is said, in speaking of the men of the Church, "The tree is known by its fruits;" and "Ye shall know them by their fruits." Again, "The axe must be laid to the root of the trees; every tree which bringeth not forth good fruit is hewn down, and cast into the fire." How plainly is it to be seen, then, that earthly trees are not what is here intended to be understood, but that the language has reference to men, and what immediately relates to men! What, then, are we to understand by this tree of the knowledge of good and evil, bearing the forbidden fruit, the partaking of which was attended with such serious and lamentable consequences to the human race?

In a former lecture it was shown that the Hebrew term *Adam* was not the name of an individual, the first created man of the human race, but that it was a generic term literally meaning mankind, or the Lord's first Church on earth; that by the Garden of Eden was denoted or described the religious and spiritual condition of that Church and its members, as it regarded their love and faith in the Lord, with all the varied and heavenly graces, virtues, and other religious and spiritual qualities they then possessed. By the tree of life, or lives, it was also shown that by it was denoted the Lord in man, and man in the Lord, by man's reception of the *Divine life* and eternal principles from the Lord, the Fountain of all life, and of all goodness. And so long as the men of this most Ancient Church remained faithful, and were steadfast and immovable in the love and fear of the Lord, they tasted not of the forbidden fruit; all their thoughts and affections were directed to the Lord as the Supreme object of their adoration; to Him, and to Him only, they looked for love and life, for wisdom and every good; on Him they affectionately depended, and in Him they were happy.

> "Ah! who their virtues can declare! Who pierce,
> With vision pure, into their secret stores
> Of health, and life, and joy? The food of man,
> While yet he lived in innocence, and told
> A length of golden years; unfleshed in blood,
> A stranger to the savage arts of modern life."

How long mankind continued to live in this primeval state of innocence and bliss in the Garden of Eden, we are not informed: it may have been and doubtless was for a long series of years. But in process of time mankind began to look to themselves and not wholly to the Lord; to look outwardly instead of inwardly; to judge by appearances instead of realities; to lean on their own understandings and intellectual attainments, their senses and their own wills, as they had the capacity to do, being created free agents: thus seceding from the Lord, they began to conceive their own intelligence and knowledge were wholly self-derived, instead of acquiescing in the Divine prohibition, as a *caution* of merciful love and wisdom, warning them that if they preferred the appearances of their own knowledge and intelligence to the lessons of heavenly intelligence symbolized by the other trees of the mental garden, they would descend or fall into a carnal state of mind, and thus realize what the apostle has said, "To be carnally minded is death, but to be spiritually minded is life and peace." The forbidding mankind "to eat of the tree of knowledge of good and evil" is in reality a Fatherly and merciful spirit of caution; pointing out unto them and to us likewise the inevitable consequences of slighting the Lord's will and wisdom and leaning on their own intelligence, their own wills and understandings. It is from this source, even in the present age of the Church, that so many now reject the love and wisdom of the Lord, and follow the dictates of their own carnal hearts, and perish in ignorance and vice. If we turn from the light of heaven, we become mentally *dark;* if we turn from the warmth of heavenly love, we become spiritually *cold;* and if our thoughts and affections remain with the lower principles of our nature, and will not advance to the higher, we become *selfish* and *carnal;* and spiritual *darkness, coldness,* and *selfishness* constitute spiritual *death.* In the day, in the very hour, that we adopt these principles and act from them,—that we thus eat or appropriate the products of the tree of the knowledge of good and evil,—we spiritually die. It was thus the most Ancient or Adamic Church died, by eating this forbidden fruit.

But this subject will appear still plainer by considering what is meant by the *serpent*, that creature being said to be the medium by which the woman, or, as we have said, the most Ancient Church, was *tempted* to eat of the forbidden fruit. Who or what this *serpent* was, the religious world, with their learned commentators, have ever been at a loss satisfactorily to determine. Great difficulties have always been experienced in the way of a satisfactory understanding of the narrative. We cannot believe in the existence of a talking serpent; we do not think that the Creator ever endowed a reptile with the capability of reasoning; nor can we conceive that mankind were seduced from their integrity by the utterances of a snake.

There is such a phenomenon as feeling a thing to be true, even although there may be difficulties in the way of its clear utterance and demonstration. This we call *perception:* and the honest and good heart which loves truth for its own sake will often *perceive* the truth of a subject more clearly in its proposition than in the argument for its support. Under such perceptions we proceed to the examination of the question *who* or *what* the serpent was by which the fall of man was accomplished.

Serpent, in our language, comes from the Latin word *serpens*, signifying *creeper;* but the Hebrew term is *Nachash*, and has no relation to the form or motion or any external attribute of the serpent: it is a term descriptive solely of mental properties, being derived from a verb signifying *to search, to scrutinize closely, to divine* or *use enchantments, to find out by experiment,* and *to practice augury* or *divination.* The name, therefore, is obviously more appropriate in its original application to the *propen-*

sities, the *passions*, and the *principles* of the human mind, than to a brute or an unintelligent reptile. But it is very generally agreed by religious professors that, whatever might have been the instrument or agent, the real tempter was the *devil;* and that for this purpose he crept into, or assumed the form and appearance of, a *serpent.* But no devil is even alluded to in the account of the transaction: "The serpent beguiled me, and I did eat." Now, considering the subject literally, and remembering the term used in the original is expressive of mental properties, we cannot admit the idea of a talking and reasoning serpent.

Dr. Adam Clarke, like other commentators on the passage, considers the whole affair as a narrative of facts, and, after the use of much Hebrew and Arabic learning, arrives at the conclusion that the serpent was not the creature meant, but that an *orang-outang* was the tempter, and that the chattering and babbling of which it is now capable are the remains of the speech with which it was once endowed, and, of course, the evidences of its curse. If we considered the record as a narrative of literal facts only, we would reject both the *serpent* and the *orang-outang,* and at once assert the *tempter* to have been a *man.* The term implies *mental properties* which are not possessed by either of these creatures, but are peculiar to mankind. Man alone is endowed with rationality, and consequently with speech. In our former lectures we traced mankind from their primeval state, declared in the Sacred Scriptures to have been of the earth, dark and void; we stated that thus their original condition was the lowest degree of human life, and that thence they were gradually and successively elevated to the highest degree of human excellence by the teaching which they received through the voice or Word of the Lord in Eden. That low degree of life in which mankind originally stood was doubtless of a sensual nature, though not then of an evil quality; for evil had not yet come into existence. This sensual nature is the kind of life into which mankind now first comes, though its quality, in consequence of *the fall*, is now more or less tainted with hereditary propensities to evil. As an infant, man is the mere creature of *sensation;* and the life of the *senses*, or sensual principle, is first developed, and must be so before the higher degrees of intellectual and moral life can be unfolded. To this sensual principle the people of the most Ancient or Adamic Church gave the name of serpent. This was the allegorical tempter; and by giving heed to the suggestions of this principle in themselves they fell: this was the *fall of man*. After the men of the Adamic Church had lived in a state of innocence, rectitude, and happiness for a series of ages,— how many we are not informed,—they began gradually and imperceptibly to recede from their innocence and purity. They leaned or reposed on their own wills and understandings, instead of looking only to the Lord; they seceded from the Divine centre of love, of life, of wisdom, by indulging and trusting in the gratification of their sensual principle in a forbidden or unconstitutional manner. Thus, self-love and the love of worldly things having gained the ascendency over their previous innocency and integrity, they ultimately sank into a state of actual evil.

" The tree of the knowledge of good and evil," therefore, implied that they were free agents; they had liberty to do good, or to do evil, but they were required for their own happiness not to secede from the Lord. They were to acknowledge receiving all love, and life, and wisdom from Him; they were to depend upon Him and regard his will as their surest guide; but if they seceded and relied on their own wills and understandings, they would assuredly *know*—*i.e.* experience—*evil* as well as good. They would not only think they were wise and good in themselves, but they would descend into self-love, the love of earthly things; thus their intellects would be darkened and their wills perverted, and they would sink lower and lower into what is sinful, till the evils of a perverted sensual principle would hold dominion in their souls. This sensual principle, then, is what is meant by the Serpent or Tempter. And are we not all aware that there are many persons who suffer themselves to be so absorbed in sensual indulgences as to lose all enjoyment and taste for everything nobler? These become altogether sensually-minded persons. They prefer earth to heaven, and the things of time and sense to those that are eternal. These, like Dan in the tribes of Israel, are "serpents in the way." Man, however, is formed not by one mental principle only, but by many; and he has not lost any of them by *the fall:* that calamity deteriorated their quality and perverted the order of their existence, but it obliterated none.

The Serpent or Tempter which seduced the inhabitants of Eden from their innocence and wisdom is the same tempter as that by which transgression and guilt have since been perpetuated. Man is its exclusive author, and not anything or any creature extrinsic to him. To charge it on some other being, whether serpent or orang-outang, is only another act of self-delusion.

The "tree of life" is the heavenly life of love and faith prevailing in the human soul; the forbidden fruit is all the evil and sin that is opposed to the life of heaven within; the Serpent or Tempter is the sensual and the now depraved principle of our nature: if, therefore, beloved, you desire to regain your true Eden,—the Divine favor, and a place of unspeakable felicity in the kingdom of heaven,— look unto the Lord alone; give up your will to his will, cease from appropriating to life all forbidden fruit, eat of the "*tree of life,*" cultivate a pure and heavenly love towards the LORD JESUS CHRIST, obey his most holy laws, and the Eden, the garden of delights above, even the "Paradise of God," the heavens of boundless peace and joy, will be your blessed portion and inheritance for ever and ever. Amen.

DISCOURSE X.

BIBLE TESTIMONY ON ABSTINENCE FROM THE FLESH OF ANIMALS AS FOOD.

CHRISTIAN FRIENDS:

It is with feelings of peculiar pleasure that I meet with you on each returning Sabbath in this place,—a house which we have consecrated to the worship of Almighty God, and in which we have periodically assembled each returning Sabbath, for a series of years, to worship and honor and magnify his Holy Name. But it is with the utmost gratification that I have the pleasure of meeting you here to-day, to celebrate once more the anniversary of our Church in this the land of our voluntary adoption. Twenty-three years ago, a few of us landed at this city, strangers, in a strange country, far from those scenes and associations that had been dear to us from childhood, and widely separated from our relatives and former friends. Poor and unknown were we to all whom we beheld around us, and there were none from whom we had any especial reason to anticipate the sympathies and consolations of friendship. We were not, however, discouraged by what we beheld, nor cast down by our seemingly disconsolate condition. Our motto was, "The Lord will provide." Like Abraham of old, we had left the land of our nativity to accomplish an important work. Our purpose was nothing less than to introduce principles of religion and knowledge among a free people, which we believed to be essential to the happiness of all men here, and indispensable to their peace and everlasting salvation hereafter. With such ends and purposes in view we crossed the waters of the mighty deep; with such views we disembarked on the shores of this fertile land; and the blessing of the Father of all Spirits has been on our every religious effort. Our labors, though not attended with that display which some Christian professors have experienced, have yet been crowned with signal success, and with the Psalmist we can truly say, in relation to our progress, "It is the Lord's doing, and it is marvelous in our eyes."

It has been customary with us, in commemorating these Anniversaries of our Church, to address you on some one or more of those peculiar doctrines which we entertain as Bible-Christians, and by which we are distinguished from other denominations; and it is my intention, this morning, to pursue the same course, and to present to your serious and Christian consideration the Scripture Testimony, so far as I may be enabled of the Divine Mercy to do so, on one of those subjects wherein we deviate, both in theory and in practice, from the great body of our Christian Brethren.

You are all aware that the propagation of tenets of a peculiar nature, or the adoption of habits that are singular or unique, has a tendency to attract the attention of inquisitive minds, and will often lead them to inquire into the origin and foundation of such deviations from the prevailing opinions and practices of men. In these cases it is a duty incumbent on the adopters of such peculiarities, whether in faith or practice, or in both, to be "always ready to give an answer to every man that asketh the reason of the hope that is in them." These are precisely the circumstances, then, in which we are placed: we differ from others, and should be ready to point out the cause;

hence the duty of searching after truth devolves upon us imperiously, not only that we may be able to display our views with clearness and perspicuity, to the edification of our brethren, but also that we ourselves, by our efforts to benefit others, may progressively approximate to the perfection of that wisdom which is in CHRIST JESUS OUR LORD.

As a religious community we have adopted a mode of life, in regulating the appetites and fulfilling the physical and organic laws of the body, altogether different from the practices of other Christian professors. We have long discontinued the habit of feeding on the flesh of butchered animals, and have confined ourselves wholly to vegetable productions. We have long resisted the allurements of the intoxicating bowl, and have been contented to satisfy our thirst from the limpid stream. The system of temperance which we thus religiously practice, furnishes us with strength and activity sufficient to support the most laborious occupations, secures one of the all-important blessings of life,—the possession of health,—and qualifies us for the enjoyment of a more perfect mode of being and intellectual delights than ever falls to the participation of the "winebibber or the glutton."

Deeply impressed with the importance of the doctrine that "It is good neither to eat flesh nor to drink wine," and knowing it to be the duty of a minister of the Word of GOD faithfully to communicate to his congregation whatever information he may deem requisite "to build them up in the faith," to assist them to understand the Divine Record, and to remove every probable objection to the truth, the credibility, or the practicability and usefulness of his doctrines, I purpose on this occasion, the annual assembly of our Church, with Divine assistance, to present you with such a development of the doctrine of the Bible, in relation to abstinence from the flesh of animals, as, it is to be hoped, will go far to satisfy you of the correctness of a vegetable diet, and of its consistency with enlightened reason and harmony with the laws of our nature, and the plain testimony of the Word of God.

It is not, however, the intention of your speaker to enter into any illustration of the subject from anatomical or physiological facts, though this might be done very effectually, if here requisite or proper. Looking on the subject, however, in a religious light, we propose to treat it as such, and to be guided in our labors by the Sacred Scriptures. They are confessedly the foundation of all moral and of all religious principle. It is in them we have presented to our contemplation an unlimited source of knowledge. In them is recorded, for our edification, a Revelation of the will of the Almighty. Here we find those Sacred Precepts according to which we are commanded to regulate our lives, so that we may become the children of GOD. Here we have unfolded to us the astonishing work of Creation, and the still more wonderful operation of Redemption and Salvation for all that believe. Here also we are taught to know aright the nature and Divine attributes of the Creator, and the Immortality of our own souls. Here is presented to us a display of the end of our existence, the proper means by which to preserve that existence, and how to perpetuate our health, prolong our days, and participate in the happiness intended for us by our Maker. To the evidence of the sacred pages, therefore, on the proper food for sustaining life, in accordance with the will of God,—on preserving health and enjoying "a sound mind in a sound body,"—and at the same time on progressively gaining more and more of heavenly wisdom, our inquiries will this morning be particularly directed.

At the very commencement of the book of Genesis we find this plain and important commandment prominently set forth, as one of those laws of direction essential to the health and happiness of new-created man :—"*Behold, I have given to you even every herb bearing seed which is upon the face of the earth, and every tree in which is the fruit of a tree yielding seed; to you it shall be for food.*" This primeval law of Divine Revelation was undoubtedly given to direct the families of mankind in the selection of their appropriate food. That food, according to the precept, was to be wholly vegetable. The productions of the earth alone were to be to them for meat. These the Creator of all things deemed fully sufficient to sustain his new-formed creature, man. And who will presume to be wiser than the Omniscient? Were not the regulations of this original Law such as were calculated to preserve the health, support the vigor, sustain the power, and secure the physical happiness of the human race? Have after-ages ever disputed the reality of the enjoyments of the primitive race of men, especially whilst they continued in their integrity? Encompassed, as they were, by the lovely scenes of Paradise, and guided and influenced by the mild principles of this Divine law, whether they contemplated the glorious vault of heaven, or their eyes reposed on the beautiful verdure of the earth, whether they listened to the sweet music of the murmuring brook, or wandered in pleasing reflections amid the umbrageous solitude of the forest, their enjoyments would doubtless be more intellectual, more spiritual, and every way superior to anything experienced in our day by degenerated human nature. So entirely have men, in all subsequent times, been persuaded of the truth of this view of the subject, that the period has been emphatically denominated the *Golden Age.*

> "Men of the Golden Age, who fed on fruit,
> Nor durst with bloody meats their mouths pollute;
> Then birds in airy space might safely move,
> And tim'rous hares on heaths securely rove;
> Nor needed fish the guileful hook to fear,—
> For all was peaceful, and that peace sincere."

What, then, Christian friends, shall we say more concerning this original Law,—this first Revelation of the will of the Creator of all things, relative to the diet of his creature man? Shall we be justified in concluding that it was intended by its all-wise Author to be applicable only to Adam, and that merely during his continuance in Paradise? In so judging we should undoubtedly err; we should be putting a partial construction on the Divine Record, when we are most unequivocally assured that the "Scriptures are of no private interpretation," but that "all Scripture is given for our edification and to make us wise." Hence the law we are considering is for us, as well as for those to whom it was first given; its principles, whether dietetic or spiritual, or both, concern us all, and it is for us to apply those principles, according to their fair and reasonable interpretation, to the regulation of our lives, the government of our appetites, and the subjugation of all our unhallowed propensities. It appears, indeed, to be an incontrovertible fact, that till after the deluge, or for a period of over sixteen hundred years, mankind were sustained wholly by vegetable food; it is also clear from the nature of the Law, as recorded in the text before us, that man was originally *intended to live upon vegetables only;* and, as no change appears to have been made in the organic structure of men's bodies, after the flood, nor any extraordinary alteration in the vegetable world, to render its productions less nutritive than they were before, it is not probable that any change was made, or intended to be made, in the nature of their food. An illustrious expounder of the Sacred Scriptures has justly remarked, "Eating the flesh of animals, considered in itself, is something *profane;* for the people of the most ancient time never ate the flesh of any beast or fowl, but only seeds, especially bread made of wheat, also the fruits of trees, esculent plants, milk, and what is produced from milk, as butter, etc. To kill animals and to eat their flesh was *unlawful*, and seemed as something BESTIAL; they only sought from them *services and uses;* but in succeeding times, when man began to grow fierce like a wild beast, yea, fiercer, then first they began to kill animals and to eat their flesh." The diet at first prescribed was declared by Infinite Wisdom "to be very good," and it would be derogatory to his character to suppose He had erred. We cannot otherwise believe, therefore, but we are justified in concluding that the dietetic principles presented to our consideration, in this first law of God to man, are adapted to our nature, preservative of our health, calculated to prolong our days upon earth, to give vigor and energy both to our physical and mental faculties, and are worthy of all acceptation.

Were we to judge of the opinions of some of our fellow-Christians, however, by the manner in which they speak and write on this subject, we could come to no other conclusion than that our heavenly Father had found it necessary to abrogate one of his first laws to mankind as *imperfect*, and had seen good to substitute another in its place, of a nature wholly different from the former. Strange as it may appear, there are, nevertheless, those to be found among professors of Christianity who have seemingly thus judged of the ways of the Almighty. Professing to believe in Revelation and in the immutability of its Author, they yet contend, particularly when reasoning in support of the carnivorous habit of feeding on the mangled bodies of butchered animals, that an error of a most serious nature must have been committed when man was directed to sustain his physical existence by mere vegetable food! "Morbid debility," say they, "induced by an often unfriendly state of the atmosphere, together with the labor of cultivating the ground, would necessarily require a higher and more stimulating nutriment than the vegetable kingdom could supply." This imaginary error is supposed to have been "found out" about the time of the deluge, and as soon as God had made the momentous discovery, He is represented by them as having promulgated a new law, as if in order to counteract the effects of the unfortunate error attributed to Him. "*Every moving thing that liveth shall be meat for you.*" "Here," say such reasoners, "we have indubitable proof that it is now lawful to eat flesh! Oh, how very gracious is our God! How comforting the information contained in this indulgent law! Is it not as plain as language can express it that we are here allowed to eat of *every moving thing that liveth*, without any restraining self-denial, or any needless mortification of our bodily appetites?"

We shall not stop to dwell on the inconsistency nor to enlarge on the blasphemy of representing the Omniscient as capable of erring, or of finding out a mistake in his legislation, which had continued undetected by his Infinite Wisdom for sixteen hundred years! But we shall bespeak your serious and unbiased attention whilst we inquire a little more minutely into the correctness of the generally received acceptance of this new law,—this supposed indulgent grant to feed on "*every moving thing that liveth.*"

In the first place, then, it appears to us evident from the history and experience of all ages and of all nations, that "every moving thing that liveth" has never been considered as fit for meat, by any one class of people on the face of the whole earth; even the ferocious cannibal of the forest, who would feel no compunction at feeding on the flesh of a fellow-mortal, would shrink from the odious practice of eating *"every moving thing that liveth."* True it is, mankind, in the aggregate, have treated the animal part of creation much after the manner that the poet has represented the Mohammedans as treating their Prophet's mysterious charge, in relation to a certain portion of the swine, that no good Mussulman may taste:

> "With sophistry their sauce they sweeten,
> Till quite from tail to snout 'tis eaten."

So, one man will eat beef, but not pork, another will eat mutton, another fish, another bear's-meat, and perhaps another may be found that would not object to a dish of frogs or snails; but nowhere can the man be found that will eat "every moving thing that liveth." Can we, then, reasonably believe that the Maker of all things ever gave forth such a precept?

In the second place, the commonly accepted interpretation of this law is not in agreement with the declarations of the context: *"Flesh with the life thereof, which is the blood thereof, shall ye not eat: for surely your blood of your lives will I require; at the hands of every* BEAST *will I require it, as at the hands of* MAN." The most inveterate devotee to the habit of flesh-eating will not surely contend that God, in this text, commanded men to eat flesh, and yet accompanied that precept with a clause in which He declares He will require the *"blood of your lives"* for every beast slain. If He had intended us to feed on flesh, would He have accompanied the grant with such a clause? Would He, as our Creator, have implanted in our bosoms a feeling of commiseration so hostile to his purpose?—sympathies so potent for the suffering victim?

Could He intend that we should eat our food with perpetual compunction and unceasing disquietude?—that every morsel should be purchased with a pang, and every meal empoisoned with remorse? And to increase our consternation to the utmost, would He have imperatively declared He would require the *blood of every slain beast at our hands*, and have inspired his Prophet to announce unto us most solemnly that "*he that killeth an ox is as if he slew a man*"? Yet all these interrogatories must be admitted affirmatively, if God has commanded us to eat "*every moving thing that liveth.*"

To justify the common interpretation of this law, however, and to avoid the force of what we have already advanced, it is contended, by some who have undertaken to comment on the Scriptures, that the term in the Hebrew Bible translated *beast* implies not only an animal, but that it is also applied to an *uncivilized* or *ignorant* person, or to such as were in a state of Gentilism; in support of which they refer us to the Prophet Jonah (chap. iii.), where not only the citizens of Nineveh were commanded to repent, but even the *beasts* also were directed, by the proclamation of the King, to *spread out their hands and cry mightily to the Lord!* Admitting the propriety of this appeal to the Hebrew text; not disputing, for the present, the correctness of the interpretation for which they contend; grant it all,—and does it prove that God has here allowed man the privilege of feeding on flesh with impunity? We think not. We will appeal in our turn to the import of the original, in connection with such facts as will not fail, if we are not too sanguine in our conclusions, to convince all minds, untrammeled by the traditions of men, or unenslaved by the chains of appetite, that the law under consideration, as given to Noah, has no reference whatever to eating reptiles, snakes, snails, or any other creeping thing of an animal nature, all of which are expressly prohibited or forbidden in the Levitical code (chap. xi. 41), but that it relates wholly to the productions of the vegetable kingdom,—that it is only an extension, a fuller illustration, a more particular specification of the principles comprehended in God's first law to man. If we were called on to give a translation of what is rendered *every moving thing*, we would say, rather, "*every creeper.*" But there is a great variety in the kinds of creepers. There are vegetable creepers, as well as animal ones. "The Vine," says the intelligent author of the "Wonders of Nature and Art," "is a noble plant of the *reptile* or *creeping* kind." Animal creepers, we have already seen, were expressly forbidden as articles of food. The creeper of which Noah was by this law *allowed* to eat, was, in our apprehension, the vine, or grapes, *of every kind*, IN COMMON, or for food, *even as they did the green herb*, which fruits the antediluvians had probably used only for sacred or religious purposes. In corroboration of this view of the subject, and as if designed to prevent any misapprehension as to the nature of the *creeper* meant in this text, it is expressly written in the very same chapter that "Noah planted a vineyard, that he drank of the wine, and that he was satisfied." There is, moreover, a further provision in the context of the law, that deserves our notice: by this they were mercifully prohibited from using the fruit of these creepers when *the* FLESH *with the* BLOOD — that is, the *pulp* with the *juice*—had acquired a *life* or *spirit* by standing together in a crushed state till they had spontaneously fermented, and, in consequence of this process, had actually become inebriating wine,—alike injurious to the physical and the moral life of man.

Such, my Christian friends, is the plain, unvarnished sense of our understanding of the law before us; a sense which neither militates against the wisdom nor the immutability of God; a sense in perfect harmony with the first dietetic law given to mankind.

Our views, then, on the subject of a vegetable diet as being that regimen designed for man by his Creator, so far, at least, as relates to the antediluvian world, or for a period of more than sixteen hundred years, are acceded to, without disputation, as being correct, and as borne out both by the natural and revealed laws of God; and though the supposition has been exceedingly prevalent, particularly among modern professors of religion, that the Noachic dispensation commenced with a grant, or precept, directing men to "kill and eat," we trust the exposition of the testimony we have here given will go far to impress your minds, if not fully to convince your understandings, that they have "foolishly imagined a vain thing,"—that they have suffered their judgments to be biased rather by the influence of appetite and the power of habit, than their minds to be convinced by the testimony deducible from the works and the Word of God. In brief, Christian friends, we think it must be no difficult matter to see that the superstructure erected in defense of gratifying an unnatural, inhuman, and carnivorous appetite is built on a "sandy foundation" and cannot stand; already, in fact, it is shaken to its very basis, and in a few more revolving years, as the light of moral, physiological, and religious truth becomes more general on the subject, it must inevitably sink into its merited oblivion, and become a mere matter of history, at which to wonder.

We come next to the examination of that part of the Sacred Oracles which primarily related to the people of Israel. It is a portion of Scripture of deep, and often of thrilling, interest to the Christian mind, evincing the Providence of God, as exercised over that peculiar people for good; and we are persuaded, with the Divine Blessing, you will be led to agree with us, that on the subject of our present inquiry there is much also recorded that tends to corroborate our principles in relation to diet.

Among those important commandments promulgated by JEHOVAH from Mount Sinai, for the edification not only of the children of Israel, but of generations yet to come, there is one with which we shall commence our remarks on this part of the Scripture Testimony: "*Thou shalt not kill*" is the precept to which we allude. If we can succeed in satisfying you that this has any bearing upon the subject under investigation, or that the Great and Merciful Author designed it to be understood as extending to "the cattle upon a thousand hills," we shall not fear, in such case, to persuade you that eating animal food constituted no part of the Divine Economy with the House of Israel.

But, it will be said, this law is not commonly looked upon by the orthodox portion of the community as having any reference whatever to the subject of our inquiry; that its obvious design was only to prevent the murder of human beings, or to deter man from imbruing his hands in the blood of his brother; and that any interpretation beyond this must be foreign to the intentions of the Author. We will attempt to meet this conclusion by-and-by; in the mean time we cannot overlook the fact that the history of all nations, in all ages that are gone by, abundantly evinces that this precept has had a very inefficacious effect in regulating and directing the conduct of mankind. Wars have existed between man and man, and between nations of men. Individuals have been and still are trained up, educated, and supported by the public, for the very purpose of murdering their fellow-beings, and wars and desolation, blood and carnage, have covered the earth. If we ask of History, where is her Babylon, if we inquire, where is Persepolis, where is Phœnicia, Tyre, Sidon, Jerusalem, Thebes, or Athens, we shall be answered, they are desolated by the sword. Where the remnants of their glory? Wasted by the ravages of an invading army. The sword has devoured them. Even the very weeds that wantonly spring up around their ruins, owe their luxuriance to the blood of their murdered citizens. In a state of war, this precept, and indeed every similar institution of GOD, are entirely superseded by the murderous declarations of man. Theft is no longer stealing. Killing, in such case, is not murder. In national warfare it is declared to be *just* and *honorable* to plunder and to kill, and he who proves to be the most barbarous and successful acquires the greatest share of renown. What, then, is the influence which the commandment before us has had in staying man from murder? The poet has given us a powerful, eloquent, and just picture of man's reckless disregard of this Divine Law:

> . . . . "'Twas man himself
> Brought Death into the world; and man himself
> Gave keenness to his darts, quickened his pace,
> And multiplied destruction on mankind.
> With joy Ambition saw, and soon improved
> The execrable deed. 'Twas not enough
> By subtle fraud to snatch a single life:—
> Puny impiety! Whole kingdoms fell
> To sate the lust of power: more horrid still,
> The foulest stain and scandal of our nature
> Became its boast. *One* murder made a villain;
> *Millions* a hero. *Warriors* were privileged
> To kill, and numbers *sanctified the crime!*"

But, to come again to the import of this commandment. What certainty have we, Christian friends, that not to kill men is the only true and proper sense, morally speaking, in which it ought to be understood? It is certain they could not eat flesh without killing. You will observe that the language of the precept, however, is altogether indefinite. "Thou shalt not kill"—what? Who has authority or presumption to limit this precept to killing men? Is it not recollected by my hearers that we are peremptorily enjoined "not to add to the law, nor yet diminish aught from it"? May we not reasonably believe that its application was benevolently intended to reach the animal creation? "The cattle upon a thousand hills are mine," saith JEHOVAH, "and not even a single sparrow falleth to the ground without the knowledge of your heavenly Father." Would not the principles of mercy and the sympathies of the human heart lead our judgments to such a conclusion? For our own part, we believe most sincerely that this law was engraven not only on the table of stone on Mount Sinai, but that the finger of GOD *has written it also on our hearts;* hence that there exists within us, whilst uncorrupted by the world, a repugnancy to killing animals, and also an aversion to feeding on their flesh! Had GOD intended us so to live, He would not have imparted the milk of kindness to our bosoms. He always adapts his *means* to his *ends*. He would rather have filled us with unfeeling ferocity,—given us hearts incapable of humanity, of sympathy or mercy, and armed us, as He has done the hyena or the tiger, with fangs and claws, to lacerate and tear, *without remorse or compunction*, the palpitating limbs of agonizing life.

> "Ah! then refrain the blood of beasts to spill,
> And, till you can create, forbear *to kill!*
> Unthinking man! renounce that horrid knife,
> Nor dare to take for food *a creature's life.*"

But we rest not here alone. We pass on to the consideration of other facts, recorded in the history of this remarkable people,—facts which, in our apprehension, evince in the most unequivocal manner that it has been the will of the Author of our nature at all times that his creatures should derive their subsistence from the productions of the vegetable kingdom, and that they should not imbrue their hands in the blood of innocent creatures for food. It is recorded in the Bible that while this people were sojourning in the Wilderness they were daily fed, by the bounty of their heavenly Father, with *manna*, and that this display of his providential and paternal care was exercised over them for forty years in succession; nor did the manna cease to fall till the people began to eat of the fruits of the Promised Land. It will not be denied that the same Omnipotence, exercised in the continuous production of the manna, had it pleased the Divine Being so to employ his power, could have furnished, with equal facility, *flesh* for his people in the Wilderness. But it was obviously the will of the Great Furnisher that his people should be sustained by bread. "Behold," says He, "I will rain *bread* from heaven for you; and the people shall go out and gather a certain rate every day, that I may prove them, whether they will walk according to my law or no." In what way could JEHOVAH have given a plainer indication of his intentions respecting the food of this his peculiar people?

The Land of Promise was presented to the Israelites as a land flowing with milk and honey,—a land of wheat, barley, figs, pomegranates, and other rich vegetable productions, without even once mentioning any kind of animal food, or depicting the country as adapted to the purposes of grazing, with the view of fattening cattle. The promises made to them as the blessings of obedience were "the dew of heaven and the fatness of the earth;" and it is, my Christian friends, an important and remarkable fact, though neither generally known nor acknowledged, that whenever JEHOVAH *prescribes* or *appoints* a diet for mankind He never mentions the flesh of animals as constituting any part of that which "is good for food." We would wish you, Christian friends, to particularly note,—we say, *prescribes* or *appoints*. We are not here speaking of what He *permits* a sinful nation to do. He appointeth one thing, and yet, under certain circumstances, He permitteth another that is opposed to his appointment. We will illustrate our meaning. He appointed, from the beginning, "that man should leave his father and his mother, and should cleave unto his wife, so that they twain should become intimately one;" but, "because of the hardness of their hearts," a law was given by Moses *permitting* the Israelites to put away their wives, by giving them a writ of divorcement. He *appointed* from the beginning that mankind should live on vegetable food alone; but when the people of Israel, in their disobedience to GOD'S will, and in the wickedness of their hearts, *lusted* for FLESH, and longed to return to the fleshpots of Egypt, He *permitted* them to eat flesh; and this permission, the Bible tells us, was extended not merely for one day, or two days, but for a whole month. And now mark the dreadful consequences resulting from the permission of this disobedient people to gratify their sinful desires: "While the flesh was yet between their teeth, ere it was chewed, the judgment of the LORD was against the people, and they were afflicted with a great plague." So great, indeed, was the fatal effect of this transgression, that the place was subsequently denominated "the sepulchre of the lusters." These instances of Scripture Testimony will enable you to understand our meaning in relation to the *appointments* of JEHOVAH in contradistinction to the *permissions* of his Providence. We repeat the observation, then, hoping we are now understood, that whenever JEHOVAH *prescribes* or *appoints* a diet for his people, that diet is always vegetable, without any admixture of the flesh of animals. "He maketh the grass to grow for the cattle, and the *green herb for the use of man.*" The writer of the book of Ecclesiasticus (xxxix. 26), in describing those few things that are requisite for man's welfare, says, "The principal things for the whole use of man's life are water, fire, iron, and salt, flour of wheat, honey, milk, and the blood of the grape, and oil and clothing." There can be no reasonable doubt but that such was the light in which the subject was viewed by the faithful among the ancient Israelites. The refreshments David received at different times, for the support of himself and his six hundred faithful followers, from Abigail, from Ziba and Barzillai, and likewise what was brought to him at Hebron, indicate very decidedly that such was the case. The provisions furnished on the various occasions I have named consisted of *bread and wine, wheat and barley*, and *flour of each kind, beans, lentils, parched corn, raisins, summer fruits, dried figs, honey, butter of kine* and *cheese of sheep*, and *oil*. These were furnished in quantities sufficient to supply David and his army. The testimony of Judith (chap xi.), though not considered canonical, is yet admitted to have such claims to authenticity as to give importance to whatever is found in that ancient record. Judith, then, declares most unequivocally that the flesh of animals was expressly forbidden to the Israelitish nation. In her interview with Holofernes she says, "Our nation shall not be punished, neither can the sword prevail against them, except they sin against their GOD. But they have determined to lay hands upon their CATTLE, and purposed to consume all those things that GOD *hath forbidden them to eat by his laws!*" Such were the declarations of one of the most eminent and pious females of the Jewish nation in her day.

And can any one presume to doubt her apprehension of the nature and extent of the Divine prohibitions?

The noble example of Daniel and his companions, who refused to eat the meat from the king's table and to drink the wine, and who solicited *pulse* to eat and *water* to drink, is also strongly corroborative of our views. It appears, indeed, from the narrative of the facts as recorded in the first chapter of his Prophecy, that vegetable food is not only the most nutritive,—"for their countenances were fairer and fatter in flesh than all those that ate the portion of the king's meat,"—but that it contributes exceedingly to strengthening the intellectual faculties of man; for "in all matters of wisdom and understanding they were found by the king ten times better than all the magicians and astrologers that were in his realm." In a work published by Paxton, entitled "Illustrations of Scripture," the author declares that the ancient Jews, like the modern Hindoos, abstained entirely from the use of flesh; and the justly celebrated Dr. Lightfoot informs us that even in the days of JESUS CHRIST, the Pharisees taught that it was unlawful to *eat flesh* or to *drink wine*.

Before proceeding to the evidence of the Gospel on the subject of our inquiry, we propose briefly to meet one or two of the many and various objections that will probably be brought forward in opposition to this system of abstinence from the flesh of animals, which we are feebly attempting to advocate. The first we shall notice is one that has the appearance of much plausibility: it is founded on the distinction between *clean* and *unclean* animals as described in the Levitical Law. We apprehend the nature of the distinction in that law has been generally misunderstood. The prohibitions there given are respecting the animals that give milk not fit for the use of man. In consequence of such animals not ruminating, their milk is crude and unwholesome: hence they were not to be *touched* in the operation of milking, nor should they be domesticated for such a purpose. Strange as it may appear to men of our times, it is nevertheless an important truth, in relation to the people of Israel, that the *milk* and the *fleece* were the principal objects for which herds and flocks were kept by them and the Patriarchs who preceded them. Hence it is that we find a charge delivered by Solomon to this end: "Take heed that thou have goat's milk enough for thy food, for the food of thy household, and for the maintenance of thy maidens." Paul also reiterated the like sentiment: "Who," says he, "planteth a vineyard, and eateth not of the fruit thereof? Or who feedeth a flock, and eateth not of the *milk* of the flock?"

My hearers will doubtless remember that we read in the Bible of a law having been given to man, almost immediately after his creation, prohibiting him from "eating of the tree of knowledge of good and evil;" from which we at once infer, without any difficulty of apprehension, that he was not to eat of the *fruit* of that interdicted tree. Now, we understand and interpret this law rightly, and that for this very simple reason,—we have not been accustomed either to eat *wood* or the *branches* of *trees*, or to see our fellow-beings doing so. But when we read of certain animals being allowed and others interdicted, we do not so clearly see, nor with such facility understand, that we are thereby prohibited from eating, or are allowed to eat, their *fruit* or produce,—that is to say, their MILK. The cause of this "slowness of heart to believe," and unwillingness to admit the force of this important truth, is obvious. In the present depraved state of human appetite and human feeling, we behold mankind everywhere around us, like so many *beasts of prey*, tearing and devouring with the greatest avidity the mangled limbs of butchered animals;

but had we been placed in community with the Brahmins of Hindostan, and imbibed from infancy their mild and humane principles, we should never have believed ourselves tolerated, by the recorded distinction between the clean and unclean in the Levitical Law, to feed on the *bodies* of a portion of animated existence. For it is unquestionably true that as in the case of "the tree of knowledge" the *fruit* of the tree was meant, so in that of the allowed and forbidden animals the *milk* of the clean was allowed, but that of the unclean interdicted.

Were it here requisite, or if time permitted, we might reason in a similar manner in relation to those animated existences comprehended in the law that do not come within the limits of the preceding remarks; but our time will not allow us to go into all the details of the matter. Reasons, however, equally potent, and consistent with our views of the vegetable character of the aliment of the human species, can readily be assigned for all the distinctions enumerated.

Another objection will probably be raised on the misapprehended testimony of the Bible respecting the sacrificial worship of the Jews. It will perhaps be contended that the Jews, by the command of JEHOVAH, offered animals in sacrifice, and ate of their religious offerings. We are ready to admit that they offered sacrifices, and ate of that which was thus consecrated. But we have a few remarks which forcibly tend, if we are not much mistaken, to show that flesh-eating can derive no sanction from the Bible account of sacrifices, especially when we are willing to listen to a rational and consistent interpretation of these Jewish ceremonies. Every one will be apt, on the first thought, to wonder how so horrible a rite—an ordinance so repugnant to some of the finest and strongest feelings of human nature—as that of sacrificing innocent animals, could ever have been tolerated among mankind, and especially by the then most civilized portion of them, for a single moment; much more, how it could have been so extensively and constantly practiced among the various nations of antiquity, as history seems to indicate was the fact. We are of the number of those who do not believe that the Israelites, in their integrity, ever offered living animals in sacrifice, or that JEHOVAH commanded any such rituals; and we think our principles are borne out by Scripture testimony. A satisfactory theory of the origin and nature of sacrificial worship is among the great *desiderata* of modern religious science; and surely it must be agreeable to every intelligent and candid mind to contemplate so curious a subject in a light which invites and gratifies the understanding rather than excites feelings of horror. To enter fully, however, into inquiries necessary to such an investigation would require a volume of itself; a mere sketch, chiefly for the purpose of supporting our statements, is all that we can here offer.

We will first see what the Scriptures say in relation to animal sacrifices being *commanded* by JEHOVAH. I need scarcely say the prevailing opinion upon this subject is that they were instituted by Divine Appointment. But David says, " Thou desirest *not* sacrifice, else would I give it; thou delightest *not* in burnt-offerings; *the sacrifices of* GOD *are a broken spirit : a broken and a contrite heart*, O GOD, *thou wilt not despise.*" The Prophet Hosea represents JEHOVAH as saying, " I desired *mercy*, and not *sacrifice*, and the *knowledge of* GOD, rather than *burnt-offerings.*" So also in Jeremiah, " I spake *not* unto your fathers, nor *commanded* them, in that day I brought them out of the land of Egypt, concerning *burnt-offerings* and *sacrifices;* but this thing I commanded them, saying, Obey my voice, and I will be your God, and ye shall be my people;

and walk ye in the ways that I have commanded you, that it may be well with you." Here we infer that animal sacrifices were not of Divine appointment; on the contrary, as a portion of the fruits of their wickedness and hostility to the Divine Will, it is emphatically declared, "I gave them also *statutes that were not good*, and judgments *by which they ought not to live.*" In other words, he *permitted* these statutes and rituals because of the hardness of their hearts.

Authority equally perspicuous is susceptible of being produced in proof that the Jews, during their faithfulness to the commandments of their GOD, did not sacrifice living animals in their worship,—did not imbrue their hands, nor stain their altars, with the blood of innocent beasts. Let us simply consider the Bible account of the dedication of the Temple; let us view the narrative, not according to our prejudices, but in the light of impartial reason, and, after maturely reflecting on all the circumstances, let us solemnly ask ourselves whether popular opinion on this subject can possibly be right. Who can tell us how *one hundred and twenty thousand sheep* and *twenty-two thousand oxen* could possibly be *butchered* and *burned* in one day in the Temple then just built by Solomon? Who can tell us how such a number of animals could all be consumed on an altar of small dimensions, made of wood and overlaid with thin plates of metal? Whence came all these sheep and oxen, and the fuel necessary for the consumption of their bodies? The very act of numbering the animals mentioned here as given by King Solomon at this consecration, at the rate of one hundred and twenty each minute, would occupy full *nineteen hours and three-quarters!* How, then, we inquire, could they all be sacrificed and consumed in a single day? Again, what kind of conceptions must those persons have respecting the

Great JEHOVAH, who seem seriously to believe that He was delighted with the sacrificing of sheep and oxen, and fancy that the stench of burnt flesh was a sweet-smelling savor in his nostrils? Who can conceive that the magnificent structure raised by Solomon, and consecrated to the worship of JEHOVAH, could not be deemed an appropriate place for the manifestation of the DIVINE PURITY, until it became filled with the fumes of burning victims and defiled with the filth and blood and garbage which must obviously be the concomitants of such *butchery?* Would such a scene as the Temple must have presented, if living sacrifices were really made, be calculated to inspire a congregation with devotional feelings? Would it not rather produce abhorrence and disgust? The sacrifices of the early Jews were no doubt widely different from that view which has been palmed on the world through the darkness of human tradition, and which they doubtless offered in their perverted state. In the Scriptures the names of *animals* are applied to vessels made of their respective skins, and used in sacrifices ; to *moneys*, stamped with their appropriate figures, and brought to the Temple as offerings; to *pastry images* of animals, made of fine flour and other ingredients as specified in the Levitical Law ; to *human beings*, and to individual spirits or *societies*, as seen above by Prophets, Apostles, and other holy men of old, enveloped in bestial spheres. We merely add, that the sheep and the oxen offered by Solomon at this consecration were doubtless pieces of money of the value of the animal with whose image they were impressed and by whose name they were designated.

We come now to the testimony as it is recorded in the Gospel Dispensation in relation to the subject of our investigation. And here, my Christian friends, let us not deceive ourselves by imagining, as some have done, that

JESUS CHRIST, *the Author and Finisher of our Salvation,* came into the world to abrogate or destroy the law or the Prophets, as given under a previous dispensation. "I came not to destroy, but to fulfill." Neither let us erroneously conclude that the Gospel develops a system of legislation differing in any of its essential principles from that order instituted by Infinite Wisdom from the very creation of the world. "With him there is no variableness, nor even a shadow of changing." He never departs from the laws of Divine order which He immutably established at the beginning. The Gospel, in our apprehension, is simply the manifestation of those means, always provided of the Divine mercy of the LORD, by which the children of men, degenerate as they had even then become, might be restored to that felicity which, through transgression, they had unhappily lost; that they might be re-exalted to that estate from which, through sin, they had lamentably fallen. The effect of those means, in the renewal and restoration of Human Nature, is fully exemplified in the history of the Redemption and Glorification of *that nature* by JESUS CHRIST. "He came that He might save, and that He might save unto the uttermost." But you will call to mind that in the renovation of our nature, which He assumed, He observed the law, He fulfilled even that primitive law first given to man. "He was a Nazarite from the womb." "Butter and honey shall He eat," says the Prophet, "that He may know to choose the good and to reject the evil." If such is the kind of testimony presented in the Gospel, is it not the duty of his followers to walk in his footsteps, and imitate with all their ability his bright and glorious example? His forerunner, John the Baptist, the messenger to prepare his way before him, lived on locusts (the fruit of the locust-tree) and wild honey; and yet it is emphatically said of him that "of those born of woman there has not arisen a greater than John." "Be ye wise as serpents," says our Redeemer, when instructing his disciples, "and harmless as doves." The serpent is described by naturalists as one of the most watchful of all animated existences; and the dove as an innocent and inoffensive creature, that feeds only on the productions of the vegetable world. Such, then, it appears to us, should the followers of the meek and humble JESUS be; such the *circumspection* of character, and such the *dietetic conduct*, of all his faithful followers.

Soon after the commencement of the Christian Church the Apostles held a council, whence was subsequently promulgated a decree to the churches, composed principally at that period of Gentile converts. In that important document, the members of the first Christian Council declare, "It seemeth good to the Holy Spirit, and to us, to lay upon you no greater burthen than these necessary things: that ye abstain from meats offered to idols, and from blood [that is, the blood of the grape, in your religious feasts, when rendered intoxicating by fermentation], and from things strangled," or, in other words, "which have suffered a violent death." But do not all animals which fall a sacrifice to the butcher's knife suffer a *violent death?* Are we not, then, as Christians, enjoined to abstain from eating such things, as a necessary part of our "obedience unto the faith"? The light in which the Apostle Paul apprehended this decree is easily perceived. He was a member of the Council, and subsequently one of those deputed by its authority to deliver the decree to the churches. He voluntarily took upon him the fulfillment of the delegated duty, and his declarations to the churches are remarkable. "*It is good*," says he, "*neither to eat flesh nor to drink wine.*" Did the Apostle to the Gentiles not understand the will of the

Council? It will scarcely be contended that, in announcing it to be good neither to eat flesh nor to drink wine, he transcended his powers or that he misrepresented the sentiments of this primitive Christian Council. Such an inference will not readily find a place in any mind wishful to see the truth as it is in JESUS.

It is said that Peter, James, and John were fishermen, with Zebedee their father; and yet, says the justly celebrated *Calmet*, "they never ate either fish or flesh or fowl." In brief, Christian friends, there are many testimonies tending to induce the belief that the doctrine for which we are contending was that maintained by the whole Christian Church for upwards of two hundred years. Philo, accordingly, in writing of the Christians of his own time, says, "They not only abstain from eating flesh, but none can be found among them that voluntarily engage in manufacturing darts, arrows, swords, helmets, breastplates, nor even such weapons as might be converted to bad purposes in time of peace; much less do any of them engage in war or its arts."

In opposition to our views, the language of our Redeemer, as delivered to the Pharisees, will probably be cited: "Not that which goeth into the mouth defileth the man." But does any one seriously imagine, and really believe, that our SAVIOUR, by this declaration, meant to give full license to gluttony and intemperance, or that his followers might eat or drink anything with impunity which the law of GOD had forbidden to be used? The sense in which these words were intended to be understood must be attained by a consideration of the reason and the occasion of their being spoken. The context informs us that the Pharisees, being offended, murmured at the disciples of JESUS for sitting down to meat with unwashed hands. In answer to their murmuring, JESUS said, "Not that which goeth into the mouth defileth," etc. In other words, not any little soil taken into the mouth by eating with unwashed hands can be said to defile the man. This, we apprehend, is the plain and obvious meaning of the passage. It is further worthy of remark that these words were spoken about twenty years prior to the apostolic decree to which we have already directed your attention; and it is not probable the apostles would make a decree directly in contradiction to the declaration of HIM whose cause they advocated, and by whose authority they had stood forth as the champions of the Gospel dispensation.

The vision of Peter, as recorded in the Acts of the Apostles, is often adduced by those who would sustain the flesh-eating system, as proof indubitable that man is sanctioned by the Christian Scriptures in eating flesh. The language recorded as addressed to Peter on that occasion is, "Rise, Peter, kill and eat." But, before we acquiesce in such an interpretation, let us first inquire, if Peter was directed by this vision and this language to kill and eat animals and other reptile existences, did he do as he was commanded? He certainly did not; for, after being exhibited before him three times in succession, he expressly says, they " were *all* drawn up again into heaven." Let us again inquire whether there is anything like reasonableness in concluding that living animals, of flesh and blood, were actually let down from heaven in a sheet, when we are assured that flesh and blood cannot enter the kingdom of heaven. Again let us ask, What instruction *did* Peter derive from this vision? "Of a truth," says he, " I perceive that GOD is no respecter of persons; but that in every nation, he that feareth Him and worketh righteousness is accepted with Him." Thus, as the testimony appears to us, Peter learned not to call any *man* common or unclean. He was taught to look upon the *animal appearances* exhibited to his view as representatives of the Gentile nations; but we have no reason to believe he learned anything by this vision respecting killing cattle or eating flesh, or that he was intended to derive any such instruction from the vision. Peter, in common with the rest of the Jews, was prejudiced against the Gentiles; by this vision his prejudice was corrected, for after it he went in *to eat sacramentally* WITH men that were uncircumcised, on their becoming Christians,—God having in this way taught him so to do. The rendering of the language to Peter is, "*Rise, Peter, consecrate and eat.*"

> "O mortals! from the flesh of beasts abstain,
> Nor taint your bodies with a food profane;
> While corn and pulse by nature are bestowed,
> And planted orchards bend their willing load;
> While labored gardens wholesome herbs produce,
> And teeming vines afford their gen'rous juice:
> Nor tardier fruits of cruder kind are lost,
> But tamed by heat or mellowed by the frost;
> While kine to pails distended udders bring,
> And bees their honey redolent of Spring;
> While earth not only can your needs supply,
> But, lavish of her store, provides for luxury;
> A *guiltless* feast administers with ease,
> And *without blood*, is prodigal to please."

It will also be objected, especially in regard to *fish*, that our SAVIOUR fed the multitude with loaves and fishes, that He ate of a broiled fish and a honey-comb, and that several of his disciples were fishermen. To this we reply with all possible brevity,—first, that there are various sorts of fishermen, as pearl-fishers, coral-fishers, fishers of submarine and water-plants of various kinds, as well as of the living or animal fish; and secondly, that the term used for fish in the Gospel does not mean fish in its common acceptation. PARKHURST, in his Greek Lexicon, says, and his authority will be duly respected, "It seems not very natural to understand the Greek word *opsarion* (John xxi. 9) as signifying fish. It signifies some other kind of provision, of the *delicious sort*, that may be eaten with bread." In short, we believe there is reasonable ground for our argument that the Scriptures, rightly interpreted, do not sanction the eating of either fish or flesh or fowl. There is, we believe, testimony sufficient in them as they are, to raise doubts in inquiring minds; and the apostle says, "He that doubteth is condemned if he eat; for whatsoever is not of faith is sin."

Lastly, Christianity inculcates *self-denial* as one of the duties of her votaries; a term that denotes a relinquishment of everything that stands in opposition to the Divine commands, or that would be detrimental to their spiritual welfare. She calls upon her followers to deny themselves and take up their cross daily. She entreats them to mortify the body with its deeds; to shun fleshly lusts, to avoid luxury, intemperance, and gluttony, and whatever is done, that it be done in the fullness of faith, without doubting, and in the fear of the LORD. She represents the blessings of Eternal Life as attainable only by keeping the commandments. She exhorts her believers to be humane and merciful, as their Father in the heavens is merciful; to mortify the fleshly mind, which is ever contrary to the mind of CHRIST; to keep the body under subjection to the precepts of the Gospel; not to live to the flesh, but in all things, whether they eat or drink, or whatsoever they do, that it be done to the glory of their heavenly Father. She calls upon her followers peremptorily to renounce all those pleasures of sense, worldly examples, and unhallowed practices that are prejudicial to their physical well-being, or injurious to the spiritual interests of immortal souls.

And shall Christianity hold out to us these blessed truths of our holy religion in vain? Shall we continue rebellious to her purifying and heavenly doctrine of self-denial? Shall we be unwilling to take up our cross, to die daily to an indulgence in the pleasures of an over-excited sensation, whether arising from *eating flesh* or *drinking wine*? Shall we not be ready "to present our bodies, a living sacrifice, holy, acceptable unto GOD, which is indeed but our reasonable service"? Shall we not labor with all diligence, by living according to the order of our nature and the commandments of our GOD, to attain unto that holiness of spirit without which no man can see GOD; and even strive to prepare our very bodies, that they may become appropriate "temples of the Holy Spirit"? Shall the voice of Humanity, Reason, and Christianity plead with us to no purpose? Shall we continue to make a god of our appetites, and not turn from following the corrupting example of "riotous eaters of flesh"?

Christian friends, let us endeavor to impress the importance of this subject upon our minds. Let us ever remember that all religion which does not produce its appropriate effect upon the life is futile and useless,—mere vanity and vexation of spirit, instead of life and peace in the Holy Spirit. Let us never forget that one of the most exalted attributes of the Christian is that of consistency in practical life with the theoretic principles he professes. It is this which pre-eminently distinguishes the devout and sincere professor from the common mass of mankind. Let us bear in mind that to us most especially, my Christian friends, the world turns for such an example; that to us pure and undefiled religion calls for such a conduct; to the consistency of our practice with the clemency and humanity of our profession, as believers in the Bible-Testimony, that it is good neither to eat flesh nor to drink wine, bleeding Christianity looks as her only refuge. Let her not look in vain. Stand for the cause of Truth against all the efforts of those "who live to the flesh." Stand as the soldiers of your Redeemer, in the blessed armor of the Gospel, with the shield of faith and the breastplate of righteousness, having for a helmet the hope of salvation, and girded with the sword of the Spirit, which is the WORD OF GOD. Yet contend not, my Christian friends, in the temper of angry controversy, for the battle is the LORD's, and He demands of us the spirit of meekness and holiness, the spirit of supplication and prayer, the spirit of a diligent co-operation with Him, the spirit of benevolence and an affectionate solicitude for the souls of all men. Fear not, then, that the rays of this heavenly doctrine, if faithfully mirrored in the lives of our little community, will be wholly lost in the darkness that surrounds us on this subject. In such case we shall know and feel that we have strength and power from on High; and we cannot doubt that the sober wishes of the moral, the intellectual, and the virtuous, of every creed, will always be with us. We are not, indeed, to expect that immediate and complete success is to crown our infantile exertions in this self-sacrificing cause. *The storm and the whirlwind* of human prejudices and erroneous sentiments *must* first *pass by* before the *still, small voice* of Christian clemency, meek-eyed mercy, and childlike humanity can be beneficially heard. Our aim is not *violently* to snatch the fatal knife from the bloody hands of the butcher, nor ruthlessly to tear the *feast of death* from the teeth of the *riotous eaters of flesh*. Our high object is to instruct, to correct general sentiment, and to determine the principles of public habits so as to cherish universal humanity; believing that in proportion as the minds of the moral and intellectual among our fellow-mortals are sufficiently awakened to the importance of the *dietetics* of the Bible, they will withdraw themselves from a system of cruel habits, which involves a portion of the animal creation in needless suffering and untimely death, and which has unquestionably a baneful effect upon the physical existence and the intellectual, moral, and religious powers of man.

In conclusion, my Christian friends, if we would seek to invigorate and expand the principles of our own faith, or be instrumental in effecting the conversion of others, let us not confide in our own strength, but rather look unto HIM who is the author and finisher of our salvation, and who alone knoweth the unruly wills and darkened understandings of sinful men, for his blessing on our feeble labors. Let us remember that the most convincing argument is the spectacle of a pure and consistent example; that while controversy, uninfluenced by prayer, has a natural tendency to irritate and inflame, to increase the obstinacy of prejudice, and rivet the stubbornness of self-will, devotion will frequently soften, kindness will conciliate, and affection will reclaim.

And now, may HIS blessing for the future so guide our course and prosper our efforts that we may find cause to rejoice in the extension of pure and undefiled religion, and not only experience its increasing influence within our own souls, but behold its present growth among our fellow-mortals, until every domestic hearth shall have its altar; until the WORD and Spirit of the MOST HIGH shall govern our country and the world; until carnal-mindedness, inhumanity, vice, and profanity, intemperance, wretchedness, and immorality, shall vanish, the whole earth be filled with the knowledge of the LORD, and the period come when, according to JEHOVAH, by his Prophet, "They shall neither HURT NOR DESTROY in all my Holy Mountain"!

DISCOURSE XI.

ON THE SACRIFICES OF THE JEWS.

I. Kings viii. 62 to the end.

Under the Jewish dispensation it was customary for the people of that Church to make use of various rituals and ceremonials in their religious worship; rituals which appear to us to be a strange and an incongruous method of worshiping a Being of Infinite Mercy, Benevolence, and Love. The prominence of animal sacrifices in their religious and devotional exercises is so evidently set forth in the sacred pages as to have impressed many with the idea that such worship was commanded by Jehovah; and yet the varied sacrifices of innocent animals, as is generally supposed, are of a character so repugnant to his Divine Attributes, and so contrary to the purest and strongest feelings of our nature, that we are astonished to think how such a practice could ever have been tolerated by any people having the smallest claims to civilization and humanity; and we are prompted to inquire, Why were sacrifices instituted? And what do they mean? The word sacrifice literally means what is devoted to God,—made holy, or consecrated to his service.

The first observation which impresses our minds when we read of worship by sacrifice, is that such worship, like all the other customs of the Jewish services, was symbolical of the nature of that spiritual devotion which is required to be offered in the Lord's spiritual Church. As Christians, we are to do what was typified or represented by the Jews, and by Solomon, when he and they brought their gifts and offerings to their altars. These were their dedications of good things to the Lord, according to their sacred rites of worship. Their rites and ceremonies were all emblems of things spiritual; of things that are to be done by us in the Lord's Christian Church. They had an altar which was an emblem of the Lord Himself; and to this altar they anciently brought offerings of fruit, bread, wine, and other things; and these dedicated objects they called *offerings* or *gifts*. The act of offering them was typical of the spiritual worship we should offer to the Lord our God. They were called gifts or presents, because they were tokens of love to the Lord, good will and friendship to man: they testified a desire to establish certain relations between the parties, or rather to maintain the relations which should exist between those who offered and those who received the gifts,—relations which should exist between men and their God,—a desire to acknowledge Him as the Author and Giver of life, and the Source of every good; an acknowledgment that *He* should rule and reign in the minds and lives of men, and that men should dedicate themselves to *Him* as his people and servants. All this is Divine worship; and we perform such worship when, as Christians, we engage in pious exercises,—when we pray and praise the Lord, reverence and worship Him at various times, and in various ways. Our Sabbath days are more especially times when we come together with offerings to the altar of the Lord. We come, or should come, with offerings of penitence, and sacrifices of broken and contrite hearts. Our offerings, gifts, or sacrifices are either accepted or they are not. Our Sabbath worship in the Lord's Temple, like every act of piety, is always accepted, if it be true and genuine; without these qualifications it is non-accepted. Before the ritual law was given to the children of Israel, it is evident that they were in the habit of offering sacrifices in the wilderness; for immediately after coming up out of Egypt, while Moses was gone up on Mount Sinai, to receive the Law, and before its annunciation to the people, they had made a molten calf, erected an altar, and had offered burnt-offerings upon it. That the custom of offering sacrifices was at that time prevalent also among the Gentile nations is obvious, for it is recorded that when the idolatrous priest, BALAAM, of the city of Pethor, was consulted by BALAK, king of Moab, he commanded the king three times to build him seven altars, and to offer a bullock and a ram upon each altar. From profane history it is also an undisputed fact, that the custom of offering sacrifices was of general prevalence among all the ancient heathen nations. We are authorized, therefore, in concluding that the custom of offering sacrifices did not originate at the time when the laws relating to sacrificial worship were given to the Jewish Church from Mount Sinai, but that it had an origin earlier even than the existence of that nation; and also that the practice of offering sacrifices was by no means confined to the Jews, but that it was a practice which prevailed generally throughout the various nations of the Gentile world.

On various occasions we have stated that we did not believe the ancients, in the performance of their religious ceremonies and during their integrity, ever butchered and offered animals that had lived and breathed, and tasted of the sweets of life; or that JEHOVAH ever commanded or approved any such cruelties in coming before Him. It is universally allowed that in the earliest ages of the world the religious sacrificial ceremonies of most other nations consisted principally in their offerings of fruits, bread, and wine before GOD. Such was the offering of MELCHIZEDEC, of which Abraham partook. Ancient history also informs us that offerings of bread, wine, oil, and even milk, were in use at an early period among the Romans, and that at their sacrificial festivals they presented their libations in cups or vessels beautifully modeled and finished, and bearing the name of the ram or other animal whose head was embossed thereon. It is well known also to persons acquainted with ancient history, that the Athenians had a *coin* called *ox*, from the figure of that animal enstamped upon it. The Romans had a coin on which the impress of a *sheep* was marked, thence it is called *pecunia*. This ingenious substitute of coin for living animals the Romans might have derived, says Dr. GREGORY, from the Hebrews, to whom the pastoral life was more eminently peculiar, and who applied the names of certain animals to the vessels used in their sacrificial ceremonies, in their tabernacles, and in the Temple, and likewise to moneys or coins stamped with their appropriate figures. The offerings made by *Solomon* of *one hundred and twenty thousand sheep* and *twenty-two thousand oxen* on the day of the dedication of his beautiful Temple, we are persuaded, were not living animals, presented to be butchered and burned in a place constructed and solemnly consecrated to purity and holiness, but *pieces of money*, of the value of the animal with whose image they were respectively impressed, and by whose name they were also designated. Let us briefly consider the Bible account of this dedication of the Temple. Let us view the narrative not according to our prejudices, but in the light of science, history, and religion, and after maturely reflecting on all the evidence, let us solemnly ask ourselves whether the popular notion on the subject of animal sacrifices can possibly be right. Who can tell us how one hundred and twenty thousand sheep and twenty-two thousand oxen could possibly be sacrificed, and their bodies consumed, or, as others say, *cooked*, in one day in the Temple then just built by Solomon?

If animals were intended for the food of mankind, why such a useless waste? If not, why so great a destruction of animal life and enjoyment? Who can tell us how such a number of animals could all be consumed on one altar made of wood and only overlaid with thin plates of metal? Whence came all these sheep and oxen, and the fuel necessary for the consumption of their bodies?

Other believers in Divine Revelation, we are aware, have a different opinion respecting the Scripture sacrifices. They conceive these sacrifices were living animals, and that the Temple was little other than a splendid slaughter-house. A correct view of the origin and nature of sacrificial worship that should present a symbolical and spiritual development of the subject, would doubtless be exceedingly gratifying and instructive to minds inquiring after the truth. In the language of Job, then, on a different occasion, we venture to say to our hearers this morning, "Hearken unto me, I also will show you my opinion." These sacrifices of the Bible have long been considered in the religious world as all pointing to the crucifixion and bodily death of the LORD JESUS CHRIST, as typical of what is called the *great sacrifice* which He offered of Himself for the sins of the world, in suffering Himself to die, in order, as they say, to appease the wrath of his Father and to satisfy the claims of his Divine justice, and by this means to open a way of pardon from God for guilty man, through faith in his atoning blood. But from the testimony of the Bible it appears that sacrifice was *never required*, but that obedience to the truth was and is: "Sacrifice and offering thou didst not desire; mine ears hast thou opened: burnt-offering and sin-offering hast thou not required. Then said I, Lo, I come: in the volume of the book it is written of me, I delight to do thy will, O my God: yea, thy law is within my heart." (Psalm xl. 6–8.) This is said even of the great sacrifice of Christ itself; it was not *desired, it was not required.* But all that was required or desired in the Divine law was devotion in his heart. Now, this *was required,* and to devote himself to the will of God was his delight. That we are not mistaken in our application of this passage to the Lord Himself, may be seen by its quotation and application to Him in the Apostle Paul's Epistle to the Hebrews: "Wherefore when He cometh into the world, He saith, Sacrifice and offering thou wouldst not, but a body hast thou prepared me: in burnt-offerings and sacrifices for sin thou hast had no pleasure. Then said I, Lo, I come (in the volume of the book it is written of me) to do thy will, O God." In the next verse it is said, "Sacrifice and offering and burnt-offerings and offering for sin thou wouldst not." In the verse after it is repeated: "Then said He, Lo, I come to do thy will, O God." (Hebrews x. 5–9.) So plainly are we assured that doing the Divine will, not sacrifice for sin, even in the case of our Lord Jesus Christ, is that which is required. And, lest the matter should be overlooked, it is several times repeated. It doubtless behooved Christ to suffer as a thing *permitted,* but not as a matter of *requisition.* So also the Jewish sacrifices, whatever may have been their nature, were *permitted,* not *commanded,* not required. That people's obedience was *required,* but sacrifice was not. For says the Psalmist, "Thou desirest not sacrifice; else would I give it: thou delightest not in burnt-offerings. The sacrifices of God are a broken spirit." (Psalm li. 16, 17.) Solomon in the Proverbs (xxi. 3) says, "To do justice and judgment is more acceptable to the Lord than sacrifice." This matter is also expressly decided in Hosea (vi. 6): "For I desired mercy and not sacrifice; and the knowledge of GOD more than burnt-offerings." In the Gospel it is recorded that one of the scribes put this question to our LORD, "Which is the first commandment of all? And Jesus answered him, The first of all the commandments is, Hear, O Israel; the Lord our God is one Lord: and thou shalt love the Lord thy God with all thy heart, and with all thy soul, and with all thy mind, and with all thy strength: this is the first commandment. And the second is like unto it, namely, this, Thou shalt love thy neighbor as thyself. There is none other commandment greater than these. And the scribe said unto Him, Well, Master, thou hast said the truth: for there is one GOD; and there is none other but He: and to love Him with all the heart, and with all the understanding, and with all the soul, and with all the strength, and to love his neighbor as Himself, is more than all whole *burnt-offerings* and *sacrifices*. And when Jesus saw that he answered *discreetly*, He said unto him, Thou art not far from the kingdom of God." (Mark xii. 28–31.) The scribe was *discreet* in placing the love of God and our neighbor above all whole burnt-offerings and sacrifices. He was, consequently, no advocate of a vicarious atonement, and yet our Lord sanctioned his *discreet* answer. The Sacred Scriptures are, indeed, remarkably uniform in their representation of the *permissive* nature of the Jewish sacrifices. It is said in the Prophet JEREMIAH, "Thus says the Lord of hosts, the God of Israel: I spake not unto your fathers, nor commanded them in the day that I brought them up out of the land of Egypt, concerning burnt-offerings and sacrifices: but this thing I commanded them, saying, *Obey* my voice, and I will be your God, and ye shall be my people." (vii. 21-23.)

In the fiftieth Psalm (8-15): "I will not reprove thee for thy sacrifices, or thy burnt-offerings, to have been continually before me. I will take no bullock out of thy house, nor he-goats out of thy folds. For every beast of the forest is mine, and the cattle upon a thousand hills. I know all the fowls of the mountains: and the wild beasts of the forests are mine. If I were hungry, I would not tell thee: for the world is mine, and the fullness thereof. Will I eat the flesh of bulls, or drink the blood of goats? Offer unto God *thanksgiving;* and pay thy vows to the Most High." In this passage sacrifices and burnt-offerings are *disclaimed;* but the offering of *thanksgiving* is *required*. In Isaiah (i. 11-14) we read: "To what purpose is the multitude of your sacrifices unto me? saith the Lord: I am full of the burnt-offerings of rams, and the fat of fed beasts; and I delight not in the blood of bullocks, or of lambs, or of he-goats. When ye come to appear before me, who hath *required* this at your hands, to tread my courts? Bring no more vain oblations; incense is an abomination unto me; your new moons and your appointed feasts my soul hateth; they are a trouble unto me; I am weary to bear them."

The numerous passages we have now repeated to you, Christian friends, are abundantly sufficient to show that the Jewish sacrifices were not *required* or *appointed*, but that, like the law of divorce, they were "*permitted*, because of the hardness of their hearts." Neither are they typical of a vicarious sacrifice for sin, in order to render God propitious, and willing to bless his people.

We maintain that living animals were not originally sacrificed. But whether the Jews offered in sacrifices the slain bodies of animals, which had lived, breathed, and enjoyed life, or whether their sacrifices were of a different character, they did what was not *required*, and in the case of animal sacrifices they did what was absolutely wrong. They had no authority from the Almighty to inflict pain or take away the life of any of his sentient creatures.

"When man his sacrifice of beasts began,
He also forged the sword to murder man."

The names of the animals mentioned in the Bible as having been used in sacrifices are lambs, sheep, oxen, goats or kids, turtle-doves, and pigeons. A consideration of the typical character of each will assist us in the understanding of the subject. The *Lamb* is named in the Word of God as the symbol of *innocence*, and it is so expressive of this virtue that it is almost a household word. *Sheep* are the types of the gentle principles of *Charity*, or sympathizing brotherly love. *Oxen* are the types of the *dispositions to duty* and *obedience*. The ox was the animal anciently used for plowing, an operation spiritually typical of the preparation of the soul to receive the knowledge of heavenly truths. The *goat*, whose delight is in leaping from rock to rock, is the symbol of a *disposition* in the man of the Church to regard the truths of Faith with great pleasure. *Birds*, from their soaring power, are the symbols of *intellectual thoughts*. *Turtle-doves* and *pigeons* are the types of those *tender thoughts*, and that yearning after the heavenly life, which the soul experiences in the early part of its regeneration.

All these types, then, of good affections and heavenly thoughts, abundantly confirm the view we have drawn from the Sacred Scriptures that the sacrifices, bearing the *names of birds and animals*, represented the good things and principles dedicated to the Lord by true believers, in their worship of his glorious Being. The nature and quality of the worship, which men render to the LORD in all ages, are always according to the state of their *thoughts* and *affections*, and to the idea which they form of the *Divine Character*. When mankind became natural and carnal, they also became external in the quality of their worship. And it was then, and not till then, that they began actually to kill, and to offer in sacrifice, those animals the NAMES of which, in a state of *higher intelligence* and *purity*, had been used simply as types or emblems of those spiritual thoughts and affections in which all true worship ever consists. Such, we believe, is the Scripture view of the nature and origin of offering burnt-offerings and sacrifices.

But it may be asked why the Jews, a people selected by the Divine Being to be the medium of a Divine Revelation, were apparently commanded, but in reality only *permitted*, to offer sacrifices and burnt-offerings to God.

We have shown that the practice of sacrificing had an existence among them before the giving of the Law. The command, therefore, for them to offer sacrifices was given in consideration of their mental condition or spiritual degradation, and it is to be regarded as merely a *permission*. Being themselves so carnal as to be incapable of understanding the nature of *spiritual worship*, they were mere performers of external rites and ceremonies, which were so regulated by the laws in the Levitical book as to represent correctly true spiritual worship by symbols or *analogies*. They were selected that they might be the medium of giving to the world the external representative form of spiritual principles and a spiritual religion. In this sense only were they a chosen people,— chosen as the agents by whom there might be given to the world a representative form of true spiritual worship,— that the Word might be given by analogy or correspondences for the use of the future Church. When thus set apart or chosen, their custom of sacrificing was not *prohibited*, but *restricted* and regulated by a code of ceremonial laws and ritual observances as recorded in the Mosaic institutions. They were strictly forbidden to offer any animal in sacrifice which was not a true type or emblem of the pure and spiritual affection required to be exercised by the spiritual worshiper in the circumstances of the offering. They were *permitted* to offer only those *beasts* and *birds* from the animal kingdom, and those offerings from the vegetable world, which were the true types of *good affections* and intellectual thoughts. On one occasion they were required to offer an *ox;* on another, a *ram*, or a *goat;* on another, *oil, flour*, or *incense;* yet the occasion and the circumstances of the offering were always such as according to the law of analogy called for the specific offering, or the exercise towards God of that peculiar affection of the mind which was thus typically represented by the object sacrificed.

Such, Christian friends, was the principle in accordance with which the custom of offering sacrifices originated and was restricted and regulated in the Jewish Church.

For the sake of the Church in after-ages, these sacrifices which *they* were *permitted* to offer were restricted by the Mosaic law, and so regulated as to represent truly, by analogy or symbol, the spiritual affection which was at first, and ought ever to have been, the real offering presented, and the offering which would in the future be presented, when mankind under a new dispensation would form a true idea of the character and attributes of God, and thus be able to understand the nature of that sincere spiritual worship which alone is truly acceptable unto Him.

As we, then, beloved, endeavor to follow the Lord in

the renewal of our lives, and as we advance from natural to spiritual mindedness, the ceremonial law of the Jews will receive its fulfillment individually in our own minds. We shall learn to offer in our worship those thoughts and affections which were outwardly represented in the rites and ceremonies of the external sacrificial worship of the Jewish Church, and at the dedication of Solomon's Temple. We learn by experience, also, that in order to follow the LORD we are every one of us required, as Bible-Christians, to consecrate unto Him all our *natural affections* and *desires ;* and even to offer our very bodies as living sacrifices, holy and acceptable unto GOD, which is (as it should be translated) our spiritual worship.

Looking in this manner at Solomon's sacrifices, and at the ritual laws of the Mosaic institutions, we can see as in an image what the burnt-offerings and sacrifices of the Jews represented, as applied to the Redemption and glorification of the Lord and Saviour, JESUS CHRIST. They represented not a vicarious sacrifice, but the consecration of all the affections and desires of the *assumed human nature* to the *Divine nature*, from and by which it was assumed, for God was *in* Christ; the offering up and hallowing to the Essential Divinity of every affection and desire of the assumed humanity; and, finally, the offering up of the assumed humanity itself, as a *living* sacrifice, to the Essential Divinity within Him, so that it, *i.e.* the assumed human or manhood of Jesus Christ, not his material, murdered body, became the *brightness of God's glory* and the *express image of his person,*—the *Way*, the *Truth*, the *Life*,—for in *the face* of the glorified LORD and SAVIOUR, JESUS CHRIST, *shines forth, to the comprehension of his people, all the fullness of the* GODHEAD *bodily.*

In this sense our Lord offered Himself as a sacrifice for

the sins of the world. Instead of performing outwardly the ritual, sacrificial worship of the Jewish Church, He performed inwardly and spiritually, until He had offered up *every affection, every desire* and thought of the human assumed, and in this spiritual way had consecrated the entire human nature, as a temple; as a Lamb that was slain without spot or blemish, by whose blood we are redeemed to GOD; *blood* meaning not that which was wickedly shed on Mount Calvary from his material body, but *blood*, the emblem of the *Divine Truth*, which He continuously imparts for the sanctification and salvation of his people. Hence, again, the symbolic language, *"Except ye eat the flesh of the Son of Man, and drink of his blood* [that is, appropriate of his Divine Love and Truth to the nourishment of your souls], *ye have no life in you."*

Beloved, the Christian emblematical sacrifice or sacrament here prepared is the token of the marriage covenant between the Bridegroom and his Church. You are invited in the language of our Redeemer Himself: "As often as you come together, *do this in remembrance of me."* From the nature of our remarks in this discourse, you will readily see that by the Lord's *body* or *flesh* is represented and meant *the bread of life*,—all the *good* that gives spiritual life to our souls; *coming down from heaven*, transmitted from the Lord to all who *come unto Him* in the spirit of love and obedience. You will also perceive that by the Lord's *blood* is meant *the blood of the new covenant*, the *Divine Truth* proceeding from his all-glorious person, *shed for the many*, revealed in his Holy Word to all who *believe on Him*,—who acknowledge and obey Him as the Only Wise God, our Saviour, the *Way*, the *Truth*, the *Life*. "Blessed are they that come to the marriage supper of the Lamb." Amen.

DISCOURSE XII.

ON THE TEN COMMANDMENTS.

Exodus xix. 16, etc.

We purpose directing the attention of our hearers to a few remarks intended to illustrate those sacred laws delivered to Moses on Mount Sinai, by the voice of Jehovah, amidst the most solemn and extraordinary scenes ever presented to the world. When we read of the tremendous preludes to the announcement of those Ten Commandments, which were given to direct innumerable millions of beings, and intended to govern the whole brotherhood of man, the circumstances should impress our minds, and lead us to desire to know their inexpressible importance.

It is very generally imagined that the thunder and lightning, the smoke, the clouds, and the fiery appearances, were indications of the Divine displeasure against the people of Israel; these accompanying experiences are also thought to demonstrate clearly that the revealed laws were laws of condemnation and spiritual death, manifesting to mankind their guilt and their duty, without giving them the ability to shun the one, or the power to fulfill the other; and therefore these laws are frequently deemed fiery laws, denouncing a curse upon every one who did not obey them; and as all mankind had sinned, it is supposed no one *could* obey them; hence they were deemed to them laws of condemnation and spiritual death, and on that account were introduced by clouds and smoke, thunder and lightning, fear and trembling, even the mountain shaking, and the presence of Jehovah appearing as in fire. Such are the ideas that have obtained in the religious communities of Christendom; hence it is common for religious professors to maintain that these laws are not binding on believers in Christ; that they as Christians are not under them, but that they are under grace; Jesus Christ fulfilled these laws *for them*, and *bore* and *removed* their curse *in their stead*, and all that is required of them is *faith* in these views of his redeeming operations. Such notions have originated from mistaken ideas of God, and are maintained in the continuance of ignorance regarding his true character, his love, justice, wisdom, and unbounded benevolence. Can any of our hearers imagine that anger, or anything like *wrath*, condemnation, and spiritual death, can come from the Lord? He is infinite in love, and his tender mercies are over all his works. Can any suppose that *fiery wrath* is embodied in those laws revealed to his often-erring children, to guide their feet into the paths of righteousness? All the scenes, all the appearances which took place at the time of the promulgation of the Decalogue, were such as arose from the peculiar state of mind which then existed in the Israelitish Church; they were such as were emblematical of the spiritual states of that people, and of the effect of the truths of Revelation on their minds. We will not enlarge on these appearances at present, and we shall only briefly observe that in the symbolic language of the Bible, thunder and lightning are typical of the manifestations of Divine truths given forth to the Church on earth; the cloud was an emblem of the mental state of the people of Israel, who were in the shade and in the darkness of ignorance with regard to all spiritual knowledge; the *trumpet sounding,* denoted the announcement of Divine and heavenly truths to the people; the congregated multitude trembling, implied a holy fear and reverential feeling; the smoke was indicative of the obscurity in which the truths were seen by the Church, and the fire in which Jehovah descended on that important occasion was a symbol of his Divine Love towards the human race; and to those who were living in evil among them, this Love appeared as a consuming fire, whilst to those who are living in the love of goodness from the Lord, and in obedience to the Ten Commandments, the Lord's Love is the heat and life, the comfort and happiness, of their souls; and by the voice of Jehovah heard on the mount are denoted his influx and dictation in revealing his laws to the Israelitish Church and people. These are some of the prominent circumstances typified by the appearances on Mount Sinai when the law was given, the mountain itself being a symbol of the *love* and *goodness* of the Lord. These ten laws were thus given by Jehovah because they are not merely *moral* laws, but because they are *spiritual* and *Divine;* they were revealed in all these sublime appearances to convince mankind, in every age of the Church, that they are indeed not only laws of natural, civil, and moral obligation, but likewise of the truly spiritual and heavenly life, and that always according to the degree in which they are disclosed to man's perception and applied to the regeneration of his heart and life. Hence these ten laws contain our duty towards God, as well as our duty towards each other; they contain all that is required of man in time, and of angel in eternity; for, like every other part of the revealed will of the Lord, there is in them a threefold sense or meaning,—a celestial sense, adapted to the perception and edification of celestial angels; a spiritual sense, adapted to the angelic inhabitants of the Lord's spiritual kingdom; and a natural sense, from which a religious meaning or doctrine is to be drawn for the use and instruction of men on earth, and for the formation and nourishment of the Church. This will be obvious from the consideration that these laws are preceded by the words, "God spake all these words;" for what God speaks is, like Himself, truth Divine; and his truth is designed for the instruction of all his rational offspring on earth and in heaven; it is so revealed as to be accommodated to the mental states and uses of all. In the highest, or what the Apostle Paul calls "the third heaven," its celestial or inmost sense is known; in the other heavens, its spiritual sense; and in the Church on earth, its natural sense. In heaven the word of the Lord assumes a form of development suited to the requirements of the angels there; on earth it is presented to us in a natural or literal form. These laws, or Ten Commandments, therefore, being a kind of *first-fruits* of the Word of God, and containing a *compendium* of all things relating to religion, or to love towards God and love towards our neighbor, are to be regarded as *most holy*,—are presented for our reception as a transcript of the Divine mind and perfections. They contain the religious and spiritual duties devolving on every one of us, as well as our civil and moral duties; in them are concentrated the sum and substance of all genuine religion; for they were written on two tables of stone, one of which contained all our duties to God, the other, all those we owe to the brotherhood of man. These comprehend the sum total of our religious duties; and they are all comprised in the laws of the Decalogue. From the character of these laws, as thus defined, we may easily see why these Commandments were delivered on Mount Sinai in so solemn and extraordinary a manner by the very voice of Jehovah; it was because all these precepts are holy, spiritual, and Divine,—infinite in truth and love, and unfolding the whole duty of both man and angel,—they were thus delivered to convince us of their *Divine sanctity*, and of their infinite importance as eternal, ever-binding rules of life; they are not to be looked on as laws emanating from God's *fiery wrath* and *hot displeasure*,—as laws of condemnation and death, or rigor and severity,—as laws showing us what we ought to do, condemning us for not doing it, while the power to obey their requirements is wholly kept from us; but, on the contrary, they are laws of pure mercy and love,—laws of Divine order,—our rule of action, and intended to be inscribed on our hearts and lives. Never, indeed, can we be perfectly happy until these laws are written on the tablets of our hearts, and inscribed on the pages of our every-day lives; and that, too, from the pure principle of love to the Lord and charity to man. We have said these laws of the Decalogue relate not only to our civil and moral conduct, but also to our spiritual and everlasting well-being.

Again, we frequently meet with persons who tell us the laws of the Decalogue *are abrogated* by the introduction of the *Gospel*, and that as followers of CHRIST we have nothing to do with these laws as rules of life. Such notions are dangerous errors: they would lead men to form false and unjust ideas respecting Divine laws in general, and even of the Divine Being Himself; they would supersede that line of conduct and duty which the law of God declares to be always binding,—that is, *obedience to the Commandments*. These laws *are* what those of the Medes and Persians *professed to be*, unalterable,—forever binding on the human mind. JESUS CHRIST declares, "He came not to *destroy* but to fulfill *the law*."

To one who asked Him what he must do to be saved, He said, "If thou wouldst enter into life, keep the commandments." In teaching his Christian converts, Paul said, "Do we make void the law through faith? God forbid; yea, we establish the law." And again says he, "The law is holy, and the commandment is holy, and just, and good." And every page of the Sacred Word calls upon us, as immortal beings, to regulate our lives and order our conduct according to these blessed and everlasting laws. The Commandments of the Lord are laws of mercy and love, and contain a *compendium* of every moral, religious, and spiritual duty. The very giving of the laws implies the existence of a *power* bestowed on mankind to keep those laws. Is it not a reflection on the wisdom of the Almighty to represent Him as enacting laws for the government of his creatures which He has not conferred on them the power or ability to fulfill? Would it not be solemn mockery in JESUS CHRIST to tell us we cannot enter into life unless we keep the Commandments, if we had not had ability conferred on us so to do?

We have already stated that the essence and substance of the Ten Commandments, and, we may add, of all the Divine laws of the Bible, rightly understood, is to love the Lord with all the heart, and to love our neighbor as ourselves; and the end and purpose of all Divine Revelation is to elevate mankind intellectually, morally, and spiritually into this blessed and happy state,—this mountain of heavenly love. To effect this desirable end, the order of the Divine mercy and goodness appears to be, that as man is now a fallen creature, and confessedly prone to evil, *redemption* is effected for him,—the system of Christianity is revealed in the Gospel, the glorified JESUS CHRIST is represented to us as "God manifest in the flesh," as the Redeemer and Saviour of men, as the all-wise and merciful Creator of heaven and earth.

Therefore, however low we have sunk through our

fallen propensities, which the Decalogue informs us "*are visited* unto the third and fourth generation," however much we are degraded by our actual iniquities, *in* HIM— that is, in his glorified HUMAN NATURE—is the power of full restoration.

What, then, does the Lord require of us? Does He say to us, "If you do not, by your own independent power, without my aid, fully obey my Ten Commandments, from your first existence to your last breath, you shall die in your sins, and be miserable forever"? Such is not the teaching of the Bible. From it we learn that the Lord graciously calls upon us all to *repent* of our transgressions and sins, to *turn away* from every known evil, and, assisted by his power, his Word and Grace, to *forsake* the errors of our ways, to *believe* in his Holy Laws, to have *faith* in Him, as "*God over all*," and to be *obedient* unto his *Commandments.* From the Bible we are taught that if we thus return to Him, in the way of his Divine appointment, we prepare our hearts for the reception of his love, and truth, and life, this *genuine Repentance* will open our minds for the reception of the principles of a sanctifying *faith*, of *love* to his holy name, and of *charity* to all mankind, and will establish these heavenly affections and other Christian graces in our minds. These are the Lord's principles and spirit in the human soul. By these our purification from evil is effected, our regeneration into the heavenly state is accomplished, and the salvation of our immortal spirits is secured. When, therefore, as true penitents, as spiritually-reformed Christians, living under the influence and guidance of these heavenly precepts, we follow the Lord in obedience to his revealed *will*, we may be truly said "*to keep the Commandments;*" and though in our obedience we may still be imperfect,—for no one becomes *instantaneously perfect*,—yet our chief desire, our ruling love, being, as we have said, *the love of the Lord* and *of mankind,*—a love derived from the glorified JESUS CHRIST, "in whom dwelleth all the fullness of the Godhead,"—we then obey these ten Divine precepts; for "*love* is the fulfilling of the law."

Such are the persons who have *the law* written on their hearts, manifested in their sanctified thoughts and heavenly affections, and who walk according to the Commandments of their God. In the Church, under the teaching of genuine Bible-Christianity, there will be continually rising up, in the good Providence of the Lord, persons of this character, advancing in purity, and in the knowledge and love of goodness, and becoming *images* and *likenesses* of the Lord. These and such as these, when they come to pass from the Church militant on earth to the Church triumphant in heaven, become angels of order, felicity, and honor in the kingdom of the Lord forever.

And now, beloved, let us seriously reflect upon these things, let us meditate on these Bible doctrines, and we shall then find these Commandments are every way suited to our state, our spiritual interests, and our real and permanent happiness. We shall then thankfully experience, and humbly acknowledge, that there is not a Commandment given in this whole Decalogue but what has emanated from infinite love and mercy, from a wise and affectionate Father, in order to promote our highest and true interests. We shall learn, further, that a faithful obedience to these laws will not only be every way congenial to our hearts, but it will be calculated, moreover, in infinite wisdom, to qualify us for the sublime, perfect, and eternal realities of the heavenly world. Every Divine law is a law of love, and tends to exalt and dignify us as immortal beings; every commandment leads to a glory that is unfading and passeth not away.

Let us, then, beloved, as humble followers of the Commandments, seek these heavenly qualifications from the glorified *Redeemer* and *Saviour*, the LORD JESUS CHRIST, and strive to live under the influence and guidance of these holy truths; then shall we with delight obey *the law of the* LORD, and be faithfully going forward, *day by day*, towards the realms of endless bliss, where we shall experience and realize the truth of the gracious declaration of the Lord of glory: "Blessed are all they that do his commandments, for they shall have right to the tree of life, in the city of the New Jerusalem, and shall enter in through the gates into the city." Amen.

18*

DISCOURSE XIII.

ON THE RESURRECTION OF JESUS CHRIST, AND THE DIVINE NATURE OF HIS RESURRECTION-BODY.

LUKE xxiv. 34.—"The Lord is risen indeed, and hath appeared to Simon."

THE great event of the Resurrection of the LORD JESUS CHRIST has been generally regarded as the main fact on which depends the Christian's hope. If CHRIST be not risen from the dead, as the apostle very justly observes, then is our preaching vain, and your faith also is vain. His remaining in the tomb would have proved Him to have been a mere man; holy and gifted He might have been, but, as such, wholly incapable of imparting any help to mankind, to lead them heavenward, except what might be gathered from his example and instruction; and these would not have differed from the example and instruction of other pious and intellectual men, except in their superior excellence. The power of imparting ability to the sinner " to put away the evil of his doings," to walk according to the principles of Divine Revelation, and to become saved with an everlasting salvation, could not possibly have been given had JESUS been merely a finite mortal, and had He shared the common lot of mortal men without a manifest Resurrection from the silent tomb; but, having risen to full and perfect union with the Essential Divine Spirit, or the Father, and through that *unition* or *oneness* attained, even as to his glorified Human Spirit or Manhood, the power of being perpetually and spiritually with his genuine disciples, He could truly say, "Lo, I am with you always, even unto the end of the world;" He was in possession of the ability of communicating to them the inward endowments necessary to empower them to obey his precepts, to follow his example, and to become in their degree like-minded with Himself.

That JESUS CHRIST did rise from the tomb is most certain. Not only did the female disciples receive an assurance from angels that He was not in the sepulchre, but was risen; not only did all the disciples see from without that the stone was rolled away from the door of the sepulchre, and nothing of a human person left within, but some of them entered it, and viewed the place where He had lain; and Peter and John, we are informed, beheld the linen cloths in which his body had been swathed, according to the custom of the Jewish people of that age, lying where they had been deposited, and lying, as it would appear, and as the original word implies, as if that which they had enveloped had emerged without disturbing or unfolding them, and as is expressly said of the napkin, which had been bound round the head, that it lay *wrapped together* in a place by itself.

And as it was thus so certain, on the one hand, that the body was gone, it is no less certain, on the other, that Jesus was alive; for He was repeatedly seen, both on the day of his Resurrection, and on various occasions for forty days afterwards. One peculiar circumstance which shows the Divine nature of this transaction is, that there were no human witnesses of the Resurrection itself,—of the act or manner of coming forth from the tomb,—and no description of it is given by any of the evangelists. What became of that *material* body which was taken down from the cross, wrapped in "grave-clothes," and deposited in the sepulchre, none of them positively inform us. When Jesus had, on a previous occasion, raised or resuscitated the widow's son of Nain, "He stopped the bier, and said, Young man, I say unto thee, Arise." And it is added, "He that was dead sat up, and began to speak; and He delivered him to his mother." So, again, when He had commanded the stone to be removed from the mouth of the grave of Lazarus, "He cried with a loud voice, Lazarus, come forth! And he that was dead," the record proceeds to state, "came forth, bound hand and foot with grave-clothes, and his face bound about with a napkin;" therefore Jesus said to those who were present, "Loose him, and let him go." All this is perfectly natural, and with respect to the resurrection from the grave of any finite being, in a body of flesh and blood, the circumstances could not well be otherwise. But such a person could not be *evolved* from the grave-clothes without discomposing them, nor be extricated from them when swathed up in many folds, as was the custom at that time, without assistance from others; and most certainly he could not come out of the sepulchre without, like Lazarus, walking forth. Yet nothing of this nature is recorded respecting the resurrection of Jesus. His grave-clothes were left, as we have seen, undisturbed in the place where his body had lain; and none of the evangelists give any account, except by remote and symbolical images, of the manner in which Jesus emerged from the sepulchre. An angel came and rolled away the stone from the entrance to the sepulchre, yet it is not said that the body of Jesus thereupon walked forth. According to the Gospels of Matthew, Mark, and Luke, the female disciples were invited by the angel to view the place where the body of the Lord had lain; and according to the Gospel by John, Mary Magdalene beheld two angels, one sitting at the head, and the other at the feet, where the body of Jesus had been placed; and the disciples all afterwards saw Him in various places *without* or outside of the sepulchre; yet neither they, nor the guards who had watched the sepulchre through the night, and who also were present when the angel came and rolled away the stone, saw *Him* come forth. Nor is anything regarding a coming forth ever stated respecting Him. The angels inside the place say to the women, "He is not here; He is risen," but they do not in any wise define the manner of his rising. The whole is left in the mystery and apparent obscurity so essential to the sublimity of such a subject. *Jesus* did not rise and go forth as a resuscitated mortal must have done; and the mode of his Resurrection could not have been described in other terms without departing from the Divine style of writing, in which alone the Word of God could be written; nor could any terms of human language more *plainly* describe the facts, without limiting and in a manner finiting a subject which, being of a nature purely Divine, can never be adequately apprehended by any mere finite intelligence. The Gospel, therefore, only speaks of it under figurative images, in which the whole Divine fullness of it is included, though to many, who limit their ideas to the literal expression of the Bible testimony, they seem to have no relation to the subject. Thus, the angel, it is said in Matthew's Gospel, rolled back the stone from the door of the sepulchre; but it is not said that Jesus thereupon walked out, as was the case with Lazarus, who at his call came forth. The reason is, because, to his coming forth, the rolling away of the stone was by no means necessary. That took place to typify an important circumstance connected with the subject; but the Resurrection of Jesus could have taken place as surely had the sepulchre continued closed with the stone from that hour to this. He who, the same evening, and subsequently on other occasions, suddenly appeared in the midst of the room where the disciples were assembled, though the doors were shut and fastened, for fear of the Jews, could not have been confined to the tomb had the stone never been removed from its entrance. Everything of the material body which was laid in the sepulchre must have been there *dissipated* by his own Omnipotent power. And, although it is said the angel rolled away the stone, it is not said in any of the Gospels that the Lord availed Himself of that circumstance to walk out at the aperture. But his Resurrection-body was a Divine, or, as the apostle says, "a *Glorious Body,* in which are hid all the treasures of wisdom and knowledge." (Col. ii. 3.) This Glorious Body, as well as the earthly body of Jesus, disappeared from the sepulchre without *discomposing* the grave-clothes, or requiring the removal of the stone from the door. His Glorious Body, being now in full participation of all the attributes of Divinity, possessed Omnipotence, and could no longer be localized or confined even to the boundaries of the material universe. Thus much with regard to the Resurrection of Jesus; and connected with this, the manner of his appearing to his disciples after that event requires to be noticed.

When it is understood that the Lord in his Resurrection-body is *Omnipresent,* many circumstances in the Gospel history become easily intelligible, which otherwise would be involved in inextricable mystery. The circumstances we have mentioned, of his Resurrection from the sepulchre while it was closed and watched by the guard, and his appearing in the midst of the room, the doors being shut, are at once made clear and easily accounted for: either by supposing his Divine *Omnipresence* in the midst of the disciples, and their spiritual eyes open to behold his presence in spiritual light, or by the exercise of his Divine

Omnipotence assuming a material investment from the elements of matter in the room, and thus becoming visible and tangible to the bodily senses of his assembled followers. "Destroy this body," says He, "and in three days I will raise it again." "I have power to lay it down, and I have power to take it again." In either case we have a view that is in all respects agreeable to the testimony of the Gospels, and which does no violence to any of our perceptions.

Another circumstance which becomes easy of comprehension when it is understood that the Lord's Resurrection or Glorious Body was Divine, and endued with *Omnipresence*, is that of his apparent journey with the two disciples to Emmaus; and this again proves that the risen Lord must have possessed these Divine attributes. For He was visible, it appears, to these disciples on their journey, and yet appeared to the Apostle Peter at Jerusalem at *the same time!* The Evangelist Luke informs us that two disciples, who were acquainted with all that had taken place at the sepulchre, and at Jerusalem in the morning of his Resurrection, went the *same* day to Emmaus, and that as they went Jesus Himself drew nigh, and went with them; and when they had arrived at the village whither they were going, He discovered Himself to them, and immediately afterwards vanished out of their sight, becoming invisible to them, as the original expressly says, no doubt by the closing of their spiritual sight, which had been previously opened. They instantly returned, with all speed, to Jerusalem, to relate what they had witnessed; "where they found the eleven gathered together, and them that were with them," who said, "The Lord is risen indeed, and hath appeared unto Simon." Thus, this appearance to Simon then took place *after* the two disciples had left Jerusalem, and *before* their return. Thus it seems Jesus was seen by Simon at Jerusalem at the very time that He was in company with the travelers to Emmaus, a circumstance which evidently shows that his body was no longer material, but Divine, and possessed of the attributes of Omnipresence and Omnipotence. How sublime, how magnificent is this view, which accounts for all these manifestations, by attributing to the Lord's Risen Person, or Glorious Body, the attribute of Omnipotence and the other attributes of Divinity! The whole transactions are thus seen to include nothing low, trifling, or derogatory to the now Divine Character of the Risen Lord; but, on the contrary, all inspire conceptions of perfect holiness, dignity, and majesty, and fill the mind with the profound and reverential feelings which properly belong to a subject so heavenly and Divine.

While our thoughts are filled with such grand conceptions of the Omnipresence and other exclusively Divine attributes of the Risen Jesus, we must never lose sight of the momentous fact on which the salvation of the human family then, and our individual salvation at the present time, was, and is, entirely dependent,—that is to say, the *glorification* of the *human nature*, or manhood, assumed. Jesus Christ did not *lay down*, or *divest* Himself of, the assumed Human nature or manhood, but only of the frailties and propensities peculiar to its fallen condition. These imperfections were all through trials and temptations overcome and removed by the process of redemption He effected while in the world. Though He rose again in all respects a GOD, yea, the ONLY GOD, besides whom there is no Saviour, his glorified *Human* having thus become the proper *Personal Form* of the *Father*, or Essential Divinity, and in full union or *oneness* therewith, yet He rose again also a *Man*, but a *Divine Man* complete. He put away all the infirmities and propensities which He had by his birth of a human mother, and gradually put forth into the assumed human nature as it became redeemed a Divine Human, from the Father who dwelt in Him, which is properly the Son of God, in the ultimate principles of human nature. All the residue of the infirmities of the assumed Human of Jesus Christ was, indeed, *rejected* by his *life, death, and burial*, and dissipated in the sepulchre; but all the fullness of the *Divine Human* was put forth into the very ultimates of the human assumed at his Resurrection. We must never lose the conviction, therefore, that in the glorified and Risen Jesus is the full and perfect union of the Divine and Human natures; that in Him, as the apostle says, "dwelleth all the fullness of the Godhead bodily;" that in Him GOD is MAN, and MAN is GOD. It is better, in our estimation, even to worship an idol, than to lose the idea of the *One only true* GOD in the "Glorious Body" of the Risen Lord and Saviour Jesus Christ.

But we must hasten to a conclusion. Instructed by the testimony of Divine Revelation, let us learn to adore the Risen and glorified Jesus as the "True God and Eternal Life." Let us learn to rise from earthly, low, and carnal ideas concerning Him to a sense of his infinite greatness. We must rise in our sentiments if we would obtain any just conceptions of his Divine character. Let us remember, too, what it is that is risen. It is not his Essential Divine Nature, for this could never cease to be the Supreme, the Most High. What is risen is the *Human Nature*, or Manhood exalted by the process of Redemption to perfect Oneness with the Inmost Divinity. Let us ever think of the Lord Jesus Christ, as to his Glorified Human Nature, as "God over all, blessed for evermore." Let us love and obey Him as such, and then, as He declares, "because He liveth, we shall live also."

In the language of the apostle, " He will change our vile body, that it may be fashioned *like unto* his Glorious Body, in which are hid the treasures of wisdom and knowledge." This He will accomplish according to the mighty working whereby He is able to subdue all things unto Himself. This is only another mode of stating the great truth, that by the Omnipotence which belongs to Him in his glorified Manhood, as the possessor of "all power in heaven and on earth," if we are faithful and obedient, He will re-create us into his own image and likeness. The Lord grant that this may be the experience of us all. Amen.

DISCOURSE XIV.

ON THE PASSION OF THE CROSS, OR SALVATION BY THE BLOOD OF CHRIST.

Colossians i. 19, 20.

In our remarks on the popular doctrines of orthodoxy, we are not actuated by any want of Christian charity towards the advocates of the religious opinions of the day, nor by a blind bigotry in support of our own peculiar doctrines: our leading purpose is to be instrumental in rescuing the Bible from "all false doctrines," irrespective of their popularity; and to the utmost of our ability to make manifest the purity of its truths, the practical, enlightening, and sanctifying tendency of its morals, and the necessity of conforming to its precepts in order to our attaining to a participation of its gracious promises. We trust, therefore, that none of our hearers will take offense at the freedom of our exposure of traditionary opinions, nor at the fervency and zeal with which we plead the cause of truth,—the cause of what we believe to be Bible-Christianity.

Salvation by the Passion of the Cross, or by the Blood of Christ, stands out in bold relief, as the most prominent and deeply interesting doctrine in the whole circle of what is called Evangelical Theology. Modern preachers have exhausted their utmost oratorical skill in describing the doctrine in the most fascinating and intensely exciting terms. The imaginations of their auditors have been wrought upon and inflated, and their feelings excited to the very highest pitch; and yet what has been the solid, the moral, and abiding result? Where are we now to look for such a view of the effects of this popular doctrine as at once to satisfy the demands of the intellect and the heart? The time has come when imaginative descriptions must give way to calm investigation and cogent reasons. In times past it used to appear as a most satisfying statement to present in strong contrast the dreadful suffering and the exalted character of the sufferer. A suffering and a dying God was regarded as an object of the deepest interest, and the contemplation of the event appeared to awaken the most delightful feelings and the noblest sentiments of devotion. The imagination was filled, the feelings were powerfully excited, and the mind, under this popular notion of Salvation by the Passion of the Cross and Blood of Christ, was soothed and satisfied. But minds of another cast are now succeeding to these. The human intellect has awakened as from a long and a deep sleep on religious doctrines, and men now feel themselves called upon to exercise their understandings, "to try all things and hold fast only to that which is good." No doctrine is more strenuously insisted on by modern professors of nearly all religious denominations than this, "Salvation by the Passion of the Cross, or the Blood of Christ." They unanimously contend that it is solely by virtue of the blood, or of the sufferings and death, of Jesus Christ, that salvation is at all attainable. They maintain that by no other means could the wrath of God the Father be appeased, seeing that He had condemned all mankind to eternal misery. They thus represent one God as having died to appease the wrath of another God,—a doctrine which is an obvious violation of the Divine Unity; a doctrine which represents the Father as a God of wrath and vengeance, and which assigns to Him passions and attributes the very opposite of love and goodness. When preachers and writers speak of the Passion and Blood of Jesus Christ, they always mean by the expression his physical sufferings and death. We admit that the sufferings and death of Jesus Christ were indispensably necessary to man's salvation; but they were so necessary not to appease the wrath of the Father as a separate *Divine Person*, but to complete the glorification of the Lord's assumed human nature, that is, to accomplish its entire assimilation to the Essential Divine Spirit, without which the influences of the Holy Spirit requisite to convey the gifts of salvation to us could not have been imparted to mankind. For the true doctrine of Salvation by the Blood of Christ is in perfect harmony with that of the *Indivisible Unity* of the Divine Being, and of the complete Oneness of the Lord Jesus Christ in his glorified manhood with the Eternal Jehovah, and with the attributes of Infinite Love and Wisdom, as constituting the Essential character of the object of our Christian worship and adoration. The passages of Scripture in which the whole of man's salvation is ascribed to the *blood* of the Lord Jesus Christ are far from being so numerous as a person would suppose from the manner in which the subject is so often treated in our modern pulpits. Many religious persons and preachers have the phrases, "The Passion of the Cross," "The Blood of Christ, or "The Blood of the Lamb," perpetually on their lips, and a stranger to the Bible would suppose from such a use of it that one or other of these phrases must occur in every verse, or at least in every chapter, of the New Testament. This, however, is far from being the case, and all the doctrines of the Christian religion, truly understood, might be fully expressed were it not used at all. When the Lord Himself in the Gospels spoke of his *blood*, it was always in connection with his *flesh*. Thus, when He declared to the Jews, "Except ye eat the *flesh* of the Son of Man, and drink his *blood*, ye have no life in you." So in the institution of the Holy Supper, "Take, eat; this is my *body:* drink ye all of it; this is my *blood*." In fact, He never speaks of the one without the other; but, then, when He does speak of his blood, his language is properly to be understood in a purely spiritual manner and light. We may here be allowed to remark that the genuine meaning of the "Passion of the Cross," or the "Blood of Christ," is the temptation-sufferings of our SAVIOUR; sufferings which his true disciples must also experience by crucifying the lusts and life of evil when assaulted by temptation, in order that in their degree they may become like Him, and by which spiritual crucifixion their minds and all therein will be purified, and so they will be made pure, "even as He is pure." Such, briefly, is the rational, practical, and edifying construction of these Scripture phrases, as resulting from the great first principle that the sufferings of Jesus Christ were pacificatory, or peaceful, not *penal* and *vicarious;* because many of the popular errors of doctrine originate in the erroneous principle assumed by the commonly styled Evangelical churches, that the Lord's sufferings and passion of the cross were *penal*, and were suffered for the human race in his person as their voluntary substitute. The question now, then, is, Were these sufferings of our Lord *penal*, or not? Were they of the character or nature of a punishment? or were they in their object like those human sufferings concerning which it is said that "God chasteneth us that we might be partakers of his holiness; because chastening yieldeth afterwards the peaceful fruit of righteousness unto them who are exercised thereby"?

Modern teachers *affirm* that the sufferings of the Redeemer were *penal*, and their public instruction, founded on this assumption, is generally so ingeniously contrived as to withhold from us the information contained in the Epistle to the Hebrews, that Jesus Christ "learned obedience by the things which He suffered," and that He was "*made perfect* through suffering."

So far, indeed, from drawing any doctrine from these plain and important declarations, the principles usually set forth assert quite the contrary: they assert that Jesus had no moral virtue to attain, and nothing of good to learn, because, as they say, He possessed from birth all fullness; that He had no perfection to acquire, for He was perfect and immaculate, and free from every imperfect propensity, even from his birth; and that it was on account of his possessing this exalted character on the mother's as well as on the *father's* side, that his vicarious sufferings and punishment were of such an infinite worth as to outweigh all that imperfect man, in the persons of the whole human family, could possibly suffer. It is in vain that JESUS Himself has declared that his assumed human nature required sanctification; He plainly says, "For their sakes I *sanctify myself.*" But the preachers of the Passion of the Cross and Sanctification by the Blood of Christ affirm, in contradiction to Him, that Jesus was already holy, and free from all evil tendencies, and that, being already sanctified, He could not require to be sanctified; and then they proceed, on *their own* authority, to declare that the word sanctified, when applied to the Lord, does not mean the same as when it is immediately after applied to his followers; that as applied to Him, it means, merely, "set apart;" but what *set apart* means they do not pretend to show. It is a mystery!

The view of the doctrine we repudiate does away or

nullifies the apostolic testimony as to the *immediate* effect of our Lord's sufferings—that is to say, the effect on his own assumed *human nature*, or manhood; and it *misstates* the ultimate effect and bearing of those sufferings upon mankind. Now, these two perfectly distinct effects are carefully distinguished in the writings of the apostles, and also by Jesus Himself. The *first* effect Jesus sets forth in his saying, "For their sakes [or benefit] I sanctify myself;" and the *second* or ultimate effect He refers to in what follows, where He adds, "that they also may be sanctified through the truth." So, also, the apostle testifies that JESUS entered by his sufferings into the holy place or state, as the immediate effect of those temptation-sufferings; and that, having thus obtained eternal redemption for us from the captivity of sin and hell, He had made provision for the cleansing of our consciences from dead works by his Spirit as the ultimate effect of those sufferings. Again, he shows that Jesus having *consecrated* his assumed human by his passion on the cross, as a new and living way of access for us into the holy place or state, into which He had previously entered, we may, with the assurance of faith, enter into that state by his blood, suffering, or Divine Truth as the procuring cause, since all Gospel blessings come to us by his Spirit, which flows to mankind from his glorified and sanctified human since his resurrection and ascension. It was thus that He suffered being tempted, in order to perfect the human assumed through the virgin, *to the end that afterwards* He might help us when we are tempted, and so perfect and sanctify us in his own image, renewing us in righteousness and true holiness by his Spirit.

But there is a more exalted sense belonging to the blood of Christ. Whenever spoken of by the Lord Himself in the Gospels, it means not the blood shed on the

Cross, but the communications of his Holy Spirit proceeding from his Glorified Human or Manhood, to convey spiritual life and salvation by this new and living way to mankind.

It is commonly supposed that the Lord's *flesh* and *blood* in the Holy Supper, which He gives to be representatively eaten and drunk under the types of bread and wine, are given merely to express his *death*, and as memorials of the *Passion of the Cross;* but if our hearers will, at their leisure, read over Christ's long discourse with the Jews upon the subject, as recorded in the sixth chapter of John's Gospel, they will be satisfied, we are persuaded, that *flesh* and *blood*, as there used, have reference to what is *spiritual*, communicated by Him, and received by those of mankind who believe in Him and obey his truth. *Flesh* and *blood* will be seen by every devout reader to be the symbols of his Infinite Love and Divine Wisdom. Every difficulty will vanish when we are once aware that Jesus Christ was continually in the practice of couching his Divine and spiritual meaning in terms borrowed from the objects of outward nature; not, however, in an arbitrary manner, but agreeably to a certain fixed law of analogy, established from the beginning, between the objects of the world of matter and those of the world of mind, or between the existences of the natural and those of the spiritual world: these are so formed that there is no spiritual existence which has not its proper emblem in the world of nature. Whenever, therefore, the Lord speaks of his *flesh* and *blood*, He refers to the two essential principles which constitute his Divine Frame,—as flesh and blood constitute the frame of man; and these, as we have already said, are his Infinite Love and his Divine Wisdom,—they are his Goodness and his Truth. Nothing else enters into the pure Essential Deity. Nothing else can constitute the interior essence of the human soul, particularly if it be renewed, and prepared to receive and enjoy God, or to *eat* and *drink* worthily of his Holy Supper. Hence it is, when the Lord speaks of his *flesh* and *blood*, that He speaks of them as being the proper food of human souls: "Except ye eat my flesh and drink my blood, ye have no life in you,"—that is, ye have no spiritual, no heavenly life,—nothing that can qualify your souls to live in heaven. That the Lord did not mean the flesh and blood of his natural body is evident from his answer to the murmuring and carnal Jews and his short-sighted disciples. The former said, "Can this man give us his flesh to eat?" And the latter, "This is a hard saying: who can bear it?" But He immediately explained Himself, by adding, "It is the *spirit* that quickeneth [or giveth life]; the flesh profiteth nothing: the words that I speak unto you, they are *spirit*, and they are *life*." When Jesus said that the natural *flesh* profiteth nothing, He, as a matter of course, meant the same in regard to natural *blood*. He therefore directs us to look for the spiritual signification of his words.

This, then, is also the most proper signification of "the blood of the Lamb." "Thou art worthy to take the book, and to open the seals thereof: for thou wast slain, and hast redeemed [or purchased] us to God *by thy blood*, out of every kindred, and tongue, and people, and nation." By the blood of the Lamb, by which man is redeemed or purchased and saved, is meant the Divine Truth, flowing from the Lord's Glorified Spirit, and offered for the quickening of man and the renewal of his heart to spiritual life. When this Spirit is received by us, we believe his Word, —we attain to a right understanding of it,—we allow it to purify our hearts, and we make it the director of our lives. It is a pure gift of the Lord's Divine bounty, and, when accepted by us, we are bound, we are *purchased* by it, to his service. Had He not assumed our nature and laid down his life for us, this reception of the *truth* and *life* of his Word must forever have remained beyond our reach; but these being presented to us through the glorification of his Human or Manhood and unition with the Essential Divine, to which the Passion on the Cross was an indispensable preliminary, presented in a form and manner which we can apprehend, we may now "put forth our hand unto the tree of life, and eat, and live forever." The *tree of life* is the Lord Himself, and its fruits are the spiritual graces of charity and faith of which He is the Author; and these, in the accommodated form of the flesh and blood of Jesus Christ, of bread and wine, or the Divine Goodness and Truth proceeding from Him, are offered to the acceptance of the whole human family. Whatever the variety of man's state, character, color, or attainments, the graces of salvation are made free to all.

And now, beloved friends in the Lord, permit us, by way of improvement, to inquire whether the view of salvation by the Blood of Christ which has been presented to you this morning is not a rational, and, what is of yet more importance, a Scriptural disclosure of the subject. We are persuaded you will hereafter lay aside preconceived notions and search the Scriptures with candor, prayerfulness, and sincerity of heart. Where, we would ask the professing world, do you find one word in the Bible respecting one Divine Person dying, in the most inexpressible tortures, to appease the wrath of another Divine Person, that would consent to be reconciled on no other conditions? We are, indeed, quite astonished how such a persuasion ever entered the human imagination. Dark and gloomy, and destitute of all light of intelligence, of all benevolence, veneration, sympathy, and love, must that mind have been which first conceived so monstrous a supposition,—a supposition which sets up not only two Divine Persons of such contradictory natures, but which assigns to the first of these Persons a nature totally opposite to that which must peculiarly and essentially belong to the great and gracious Father of the Universe. And what is most strange is that the originator of this notion should have fancied that he found it in the Bible, in which, nevertheless, not a trace of it is to be found. The doctrine of salvation by the blood of Christ, rightly understood, is, as we have shown, a doctrine of the Bible; but will any one, for the sake of maintaining this popular doctrine, adhere to this preposterous notion, when the real Scriptural doctrine of salvation by the blood of Jesus Christ requires no such melancholy inconsistencies to explain and uphold it? Jesus Christ did indeed suffer for us,—for our good, because otherwise we must have perished eternally; and He did thereby effect salvation for all who are willing to do his will; but He did not undergo this suffering as a punishment inflicted upon Him by another Divine Person as a commutation for our eternal punishment, but, as we have seen, because his assumed Human, or Manhood, could not otherwise be glorified; and without this glorification He could not have given us his *flesh* to eat, or his *blood* to drink; nor could He have imparted by his Holy Spirit, for the nourishment of our souls, the blessed communications of his eternal love and wisdom,—his infinite mercy and grace,—His Living Bread and New Wine. And since He is our Redeemer and Saviour, "The true God and eternal life," and has become the Author of "eternal salvation to all that obey Him," let us henceforward love and worship Him as "God over all, blessed forever." Amen.

DISCOURSE XV.

ON FAITH.

Habakkuk ii. 4.

The term *faith* comprehends a most essential and important branch of Christian Theology. It includes whatever is a matter of belief on the part of a convert to the doctrines of the Gospel. The principles' of the Word of God are the only proper constituents of a Christian's *faith;* for all that which may, for a time, be produced by mere appearances, representations, and false reasonings, can only be accounted as a *counterfeit faith*,—a vain *persuasion*, or an *illusion*, that will most undoubtedly fail to be effective of any saving good when the truths of Divine Revelation are brought to light. These truths plainly teach that genuine and saving *faith* is that which leads the believer's mind to look to the glorified *Jesus Christ* as the Lord *God,*—the world's *Redeemer* and *Saviour*. We scarcely need attempt to prove to this congregation that *Jesus Christ* is the only proper object of a true and saving *faith*, after what has been advanced by us on various occasions in regard to this interesting subject. As there is, and can be, but *One God,* and as *Jesus Christ* is declared to be "*God over all, blessed forever*," therefore Bible-Christians maintain He is that *One only God.* To say that *Jesus Christ* is *God*, and not exclusively the *Only God*, would evidently be to admit that there are more *Gods* than

One; and this would not only be contrary to the Bible testimony, but it would require a divided *faith,—a faith* in several *Gods.* Such a *faith,* instead of blessing, would distract the mind. The principles of *faith* in regard to *Jesus Christ* are that in Him *Divinity* and *Humanity* are united,—that He is *God* and *Man* in one and the same *Being,* consequently in one and the same Divine *Person;* for we cannot conceive that any one *Being* can be divided into two or three real and distinct persons. It ought further to be observed that, although *Divinity* and *Humanity* in *Jesus Christ* are distinctly the objects of our regard and faith, they possess not *two* opposite, nor even different, *natures.* Divinity itself is really *human,* and Humanity in its primary *essence* is really *Divine.* Whenever we speak of the *Divinity* of the Lord's *Humanity,* it is essentially important that we entertain clear ideas of what constitutes *humanity,—human nature* or *manhood.* In speaking of the *glorified Humanity, human nature,* or *manhood* of *Jesus Christ,* we never have any reference whatever to the material body,—the body that was crucified on the cross, and pierced by the spear of a Roman soldier. That quality or characteristic by which *we* are distinguished as finite *human beings,* is the fact of *our* being by creation in possession of a *Will* and an *Understanding;* and the perfection of these mental *qualities* consists in our *willing* what is *good,* and *understanding* what is *true,* so that the more good we *will* and *love,* and the more truth we *understand* and *obey,* the more *truly* are we *human,* and the more completely are we distinguished as human beings from the rest of the animal creation. If, therefore, it be *good* and *truth, willed* and *understood,* which make us *human,* then are these two the essential human principles; and in this point of view, to speak of a Divine or Glorified *Humanity, human nature,* or *Manhood,* is to speak of *Divine Good* and *Divine Truth*. Hence, to consider our blessed *Lord's human* as finite would be to consider his *goodness* and *truth* as finite; and as his goodness and truth are revealed only in his sacred *Word*, it would be to consider his *Word* as finite,—that is to say, as possessing only a *creaturely wisdom*. As therefore the action or operation of the Divine *Good* and *Truth* into man, as a *recipient* form of life, produces, through the instrumentality of that form, the whole of *human good* and *truth*, and constitutes their very essence, from which they are truly finite human beings, it follows that *God*, as to his *Divine Good* and *Truth*, is as truly *Infinitely Human*, though always manifested, or brought forth to man's view, under *a finited appearance*. So that the two natures—*Divine* and *Human*—are not, in fact, two different natures, but one and the same in the *glorified Lord Jesus Christ*. The reason of the distinction which we seem to make in them is not on account of any actual difference, but because the Divinity, though *infinite* as to everything affirmed of it, can yet only be *finitely* apprehended by mankind. And as the glorified *Human* of *Jesus Christ*—the Son of God—is the *Divine Human* or *Manhood* of *Jehovah*, therefore in *Jesus Christ* the *Divine* as *Human* presents Himself to us in the manner best suited to inspire creaturely *faith*. "No man has seen God [pure Divinity] at any time; the only begotten Son [or Glorified Human] who is in the bosom of the Father, He has brought Him forth to view." Thus the Father, or essential Divine Spirit, is in the glorified *Human*, and the *Human* in the *Divine*, in One Divine Person. "I and the Father are One." Moreover, a saving faith implies a deliverance from every *false* principle which would ruin the human *understanding*, and from every vicious disposition which would destroy the integrity and innocence of the human *will;* therefore a right *apprehension* of the *Divine Being*, and a true *faith* in Him, are most essential requisites to our salvation.

That *faith* in the *Lord Jesus Christ*, as "God manifest in the flesh," is obviously enjoined in the Gospel, will be seen by a reference to his own words, "He that *believeth* on the *Son* hath everlasting life, and he that *believeth* not on the Son shall not see life, but the wrath of God abideth on him." If the *Son* were not *God*, the want of *faith* in Him would not be attended with the loss of everlasting life; and, as no one can "enter into the kingdom of *God* except he be *born again*," therefore faith *in Him* must be effective of that important change in the human character which is implied in being *born again;* and as that change is confessedly from *natural-* to *spiritual-mindedness*, therefore "the *wrath* of *God*" is said to rest on those who "do not *believe* on the Son,"—on those who have not undergone *this change.* Man's unregenerate nature is in opposition to the Divine Will, and he therefore feels the *Divine Influence*, which in itself is infinite and unchangeable *Love*, as *wrath* upon his unconverted soul. This is what is really meant, in the Scriptures, by the anger and the wrath of God. No such *passions* belong to *Him.* It is the recipient's unchanged heart that gives in all cases this appearance of wrath in God to the beholder. The glorified Jesus, in the character of his *Manhood*, is the Divine Truth, in its universal principle; and therefore it is written, "Whosoever *believeth* on Him shall not perish, but have everlasting life." "Jesus said, I am the resurrection and the life: he that *believeth* on me shall never die." No finite man could, with truth, style himself "the resurrection and the life," nor by his own power preserve from spiritual death all those that *believe on Him.* To have *faith* on Jesus as the Saviour, is to rely on Him for salvation. To *believe* on Him as the *truth*, is to look to Him for internal illumination and instruction. To *believe* that without Him we can do nothing truly good, is to rely on Him for the ability to do whatever He may enjoin us to do; and *to believe* that He has all *power* in *heaven* and in *earth*,—that He knoweth all things,—that by Him were all things made that are made,—that He will always be present with his followers in the regenerate life,—and that even "in the midst of two or three met together in his name, He will also be found,"—implies a confidence in Him, —a reliance on his gracious promises as the Omnipotent, Omniscient, and Omnipresent " *God over all, blessed forever.*"

The apostles, after the resurrection of Jesus, went forth into the world to teach *faith* in the *Lord Jesus Christ*, "*in whom dwelleth all the fullness of the Godhead,*" as the only way of salvation; and that from Him, and by *belief* in Him, all that is constituent of heavenly life is to be obtained. In his name they performed various miracles, and on every occasion directed their hearers to the most full and perfect confidence in Him as the only *One* possessing the power, wisdom, and goodness, to save mankind from the dominion and slavery of sinful desires and of idolatrous and heathen notions. Paul says, "Nevertheless, I live, yet not I, but Christ liveth in me; and the life which I now live in the flesh, I live by faith in Him." This language of *Paul* would be exceedingly ridiculous if *Jesus*, in his *all-glorious Manhood*, were not God, from whom the *all of life* is derived, and by whose almighty power we are continually enabled to *will, understand, think*, and *act*, as finite human beings. Again, "*Paul* testified to the *Jews*, and also to the *Greeks*, repentance towards God, and *Faith* in our *Lord Jesus Christ.*" Repentance towards God implies the turning from all known evil as sin against Him; and *Faith* in our *Lord Jesus*

Christ denotes *faith* in his Divine *Human*, or essential principles of *Manhood*, as the only medium of *salvation*. And again, the same apostle says, "We who are *Jews* by nature, and not sinners of the *Gentiles*, knowing that a man is not justified by the works of the *law*, but by the *Faith of Jesus Christ*, even we have *believed on Jesus Christ*." From this passage it will be evident to our hearers what the apostle meant by justification through the *Faith* of *Jesus*, in opposition to justification by the mere outward keeping of the ceremonial law of Moses. Not that the ceremonial law, when seen in its spiritual character, was opposed to the spirit of *Jesus* and the Gospel, for they are perfectly one in this respect. But the Jews of that age had little or no idea of the spirituality of the law of Moses, or of the *internal* righteousness it required, and consequently they kept it only after an external or outward manner.

From what has been advanced, then, it will be seen that a *saving Faith* is one that is directed to *Jesus Christ*, the *Lord God* and *Saviour*, as to a visible *God*, in whom dwelleth the invisible,—a God manifested, as Paul says, in "his *glorious Body*," or *Manhood*,—as beheld and described by John in the first chapter of Revelation,—a God who can be at once the object of the most sincere *love*, and of the clearest and most certain intelligence of the human understanding; a *Faith* that removes all that vagueness of thought with regard to *God*, which must necessarily exist while the *Divine Being* is supposed to be an incomprehensible something, diffused throughout the Universe like some *ethereal* principle, to whom we can no more rationally ascribe the attributes and properties of a *Divine Mind*, than we can suppose the *electric fluid* to *will, think*, and voluntarily to *act*. We cannot think of a *principle* without its appropriate *subject;* we are not able to think, as the Episcopalians would have us, of a *God* "without body, parts, or passions," neither can we, with the Athenians of old, worship " *an unknown God*," with any saving effect. Every *affection* and *thought* must have an *object*, mentally *tangible* and spiritually *visible*. In every conception of *love* we have an idea of a *being* that *loves*, and in every thought of *wisdom* we have an idea of a being who *thinks* and is intellectually wise ; but of *love* and *wisdom*, as mere *floating*, aerial particles or abstractions, we have no idea, nor indeed can we have, because, as such, they do not exist. *God*, therefore, in presenting Himself to *human thought* and *affection* in the *Human form*, renders Himself to his people both mentally tangible and spiritually visible,—a God whom they can love, worship, and adore.

Peter, in his official character as an apostle, represented Faith in the *Lord God* the *Saviour ;* and *when he confessed that Jesus was the Christ, the Son of the Living God*, he was called a rock, and to him, as the emblem of *that faith*, were given the keys by which to open heaven, and it was added, that whatsoever he or it should bind on earth should be bound in heaven, and whatsoever he or it should loose on earth should be loosed in heaven. Peter's acknowledgment of the Lord in his Divine Human or Manhood is "the rock,"—the foundation of all that is true in doctrine and good in practice. It is the rock on which the Church is built,—the hand into which are delivered "the keys of the kingdom." A *key* is the symbol of power. "The keys of the kingdom" are given, not to *Peter* as an individual, but to *spiritual Faith*, for such *a Faith* is the *power* by which heaven is opened *in* and *to* the human soul. Laying aside, then, the idea of *Peter* as a *person*, except so far as he represents *principles*, and keeping in view the power of *Faith* from *love*, the meaning of "the binding and loosing" will be clear and satisfactory to our hearers. *Faith*, when it works by *love*, accomplishes a great work, and whatsoever it *binds* and *looses* on earth is bound and loosed in heaven. But *what* and *where* are the *earth* and *heaven* in which this *binding* and *loosing* take place? In thinking of *earth* and *heaven* we must lift our minds above the ideas of time and space. There is a *heaven* and there is an *earth* in the mind of every one of us. The Lord said to those around Him, " *The kingdom of heaven is within you.*" There is a *region of the mind* which is receptive of *heavenly truth*, and where the Lord's voice is heard, instructing, correcting, or reproving. The apostle describes the conflicting action of the *two regions of the mind* in those who have entered the *regenerate* life, which he calls "the spirit warring against the flesh, and the flesh against the spirit," the two being contrary the one to the other. These *two regions of the human mind*—the *higher* and the *lower*, or internal and external—are in the Bible compared to *heaven* and *earth*. When the regenerating Christian prays, " *Thy will be done on earth as it is in heaven,*" he prays that the *earthly* within him may be brought under the dominion and guidance of the *heavenly*,—that the empire of Divine good, set up in the *higher*, or the *heavenly region*, may descend, and be established in the *lower* region, or in the *earthly*. Every part of the Word relates to *personal regeneration*. The *two* ruling principles of the lower *mental region*, or natural mind, are the *love of self* and the *love of the world*. These stand opposed to the two heavenly principles which ought to rule in and over every one, —we speak of *the love of the Lord*, and *the love of our neighbor*. These are, in fact, the very principles of *heaven*, everything in heaven being constituted of them. But, unless we *bind* or *subdue* the motions and propensities of our *earthly region of mind*, the principles of heaven which we may feel in our *higher* or *spiritual region of mind* cannot come down and rule and exercise dominion in the *earthly region*, or *external mind*. But when we do *bind* or subdue the motions and propensities of our earthly region of mind, the things of heaven are *loosed*, and *descend* to earth. The natural becomes filled with the spiritual. The thoughts, affections, and life are in harmony with the principles of a saving *Faith*. *Heaven* descends to *earth*, and God's tabernacle is with man. These become the fixed principles of life. Thus these principles are said *to be bound on earth*, and also *in heaven*, because *what* we receive into our hearts and lives remains with us forever, and forms our heaven after death, for heaven has its very basis in regeneration. But when any one intellectually perceives *truth*, but does not love it, nor do it, it is not *bound on earth*, and it is not *bound in heaven, for such a man*. Thus we may see that whatever power was conferred on *Peter* was not confined to him exclusively or personally. It is a power offered to *all* who believe and ask for it in a proper manner and in a true and Christian Faith. Faith is a clear and intellectual perception of the truths of the Bible. This gives the mind a settled confidence in the total fulfillment of the Lord's promises, and a dependence on Him for all things. *Faith* without the *life* of *love* and *charity* is a dead *faith*,—a mere blind persuasion of the region of the carnal mind,—a faith which prompts the *unregenerate* rudely to ask of *God* those *heavenly* enjoyments for which their souls have neither *appetite* nor *taste*. But to *believe* even the greatest truths without a *life* corresponding with such a *faith* is of *no avail*. "Thou believest," says the Apostle James, "that there is one God; thou doest well: the devils also *believe* and tremble." But if this *belief* had been all that was requisite for salvation, then had these devils never been devils. It is most important that every one should form just ideas of *faith;* and to enable us all to do so the *Lord* has put into our hands his revealed *Word*, and has accompanied it with this injunction, "Search the Scriptures; in them ye think ye have eternal life, and they are they which testify of *me.*" One great cause of the diversity of *belief*, and of erroneous *faith*, is neglect of obedience to this plain injunction. Instead of searching the Scriptures for themselves, men have in many cases taken for granted what others have said, and have thus forfeited their own mental freedom; but freedom of *will* is that which renders us accountable before God, and this freedom, consequently, cannot be relinquished without criminality. If we would learn from the volume of Inspiration in what true and saving faith consists, we have only to be guided by the Saviour's injunction, and search the Scriptures. There we shall find it recorded, "Thou shalt *love* the Lord thy God with all thy heart, and with all thy soul, and with all thy strength, and with all thy mind, and thy neighbor as thyself. This do, and thou shalt live." What can be plainer than this? This is the Bible's description of true and saving *faith*. It is an epitome of the whole Word of God, for on it "hangs all the law and the prophets."* *Love*, then, may be said to be the *very life* and *soul of faith*. Without this principle of heavenly *Love* there could be no living and true *faith*. The Lord has given us unnumbered proofs of *his love* to us,—the greatest of which, if one may be said to be greater

---

* Love is the fulfilling of the LAW. "He that loveth not, knoweth not God; for God is *love.*" Christianity is *love* embodied in its purest form. The Gospel is a revelation of *love*. And love can be comprehended only by *love*.

than another, is that of his manifestation in the flesh,—his assumption of human nature,—that He might thereby approach to our low state or region of mind, and thus enable us to draw near unto Him, and, by the truths of his Holy Word and Spirit operating on our *wills* and *understandings*, " purify *us* unto *Himself* as a peculiar people, zealous of good works." To *Him*, then, "the only wise God, our Saviour, the author and finisher of our *Faith*," be glory and dominion, now and for evermore. Amen.

DISCOURSE XVI.

SERMON DELIVERED ON THE FIFTIETH ANNIVERSARY OF ORDINATION, AUGUST 11TH, 1861.

MARK xvi. 15.

ONE of the great ends intended by the manifestation of Jesus Christ in the flesh was, that mankind might be more particularly instructed in the things which make for their peace,—that they might be brought from mental darkness to intellectual light, from ignorance to the knowledge of those principles which, illuminating their understandings, influencing their wills, and giving a character to their lives, might prepare them to become participators of the felicities of the kingdom of heaven. More effectually to accomplish this Divine purpose, John the Baptist, as the forerunner of the Lord, came preaching the doctrine of repentance for the remission of sins, as a preparatory measure to man's being benefited by the coming of Christ. Before that event angels also came, and preached or proclaimed to the shepherds on the plains of Bethlehem, "good tidings of great joy, which shall be to all people." Jesus Christ Himself when on earth devoted a large portion of his time to preaching.

He spake as never man spoke, and his sermons, as embodied in the Gospels, have excited the admiration of men and women of refined and pious minds in all ages of the Church. He selected or appointed twelve disciples, and ordained them to preach. And after his resurrection He reimposed the mission of preaching on them, as an all-important part of their future vocation: "Go ye into all the world," said He, "and preach the Gospel to every creature." Hence it is obviously the gracious will of our blessed Lord that the truths of Redemption and Salvation, as well as the other great doctrines of Divine Revelation, should be proclaimed to mankind everywhere. Previous to this commission to the disciples, the means of attaining to a knowledge of the true God had been in a great measure confined to the Jews. They alone were in possession of the oracles of God. The labors of Jesus Christ Himself were principally confined, externally at least, to the lost sheep of the house of Israel; and his disciples were previously prohibited from preaching among the Gentiles. But now the time was fully come when the Gentiles were to be favored with the preaching of the Gospel; when the partition-wall which had separated Israel from all the world should be broken down, and all former distinctions forever cease, that in Jesus Christ there should be neither Greek nor Jew, circumcision nor uncircumcision, barbarian, Scythian, bond nor free, but Christ and the principles of Christianity preached to all people—to every creature throughout the world. The disciples accordingly went forth, preaching the doctrines of Christianity wherever suitable opportunities presented themselves, and fulfilling that department of their mission not only in Judea, but more particularly among the Gentiles throughout the then known world. From the days of the apostles, men have been ordained and introduced into the ministry by the imposition of hands, and have thus assumed, under the authority of the Church, the duties and responsibilities of preachers of the truths of salvation. By such means the will of the Lord has been carried out more or less perfectly, and mankind have been called to repentance and eternal life through their labors in preaching the doctrines of the Word of God.

It is *fifty years* this day since I was ordained into the ministry of the Word of God by the customary imposition of the hands of the appointed minister. It is no ordinary privilege to be admitted to a participation in this great and glorious work of the Lord our God, and, as it were, to be laid under the necessity of cultivating an intimacy with the great principles of the religion of the Bible. Paul magnified his ministry; and well he might, for the wondrous scenes inseparable from the labors of the ministerial office most fully put in requisition all man's intellectual and moral powers. For about a year previous to ordination I had preached to a small congregation, and at their request I consented to be presented as a person suitable to be admitted into the ministerial office. I remember the scene of my inauguration well. Of those who were present at the ceremony, there is but one person now living besides myself. That individual is Brother Wright; he was one of my hearers then, and has been so from that day to this. All others who were witnesses when I bowed my knees before the glorified Lord and Saviour Jesus Christ, as the true God and eternal life, have passed by death from this transitory state of being. A Bible was presented for my acceptance, and a solemn charge given, and I received the great trust and authority from the Lord—by the laying on of the hands of the minister—to teach and to preach the Word, to administer the ordinances of Baptism and the Holy Supper, and to perform all the other duties incumbent upon a minister of the Gospel. To me it was a solemn day, and it was associated with solemn responsibilities. Since that day, it may be said, two generations have passed away. Not one of those to whom I first preached in England, where my ordination took place, is now living, with the exception already stated; and of twenty-eight adult individuals who came to this country with me forty-four years ago, there are only two remaining besides myself. Truly is it written, "One generation goeth, and another cometh, but the earth remaineth forever." I cannot be too thankful that amidst all these changes I have been mercifully preserved, and that I commenced my ministry under a deep impression that I must be a minister of incessant watchfulness and care for the welfare of those intrusted by Providence to my teaching. My mind, even at the outset, was never dazzled either by the prospect of popularity or repose; for thirty-eight years I preached without receiving any pecuniary emolument by way of compensation. This part of my proceeding I would not advise any one hereafter to follow. Ministers cannot live merely on air. Jesus has assured us we cannot faithfully serve two masters,—do our duty as preachers, and be engaged in worldly pursuits,—and He has instructed us that "the laborer is worthy of his hire." In everything but this, if I am not deceived, my work has been my joy, and most my joy when most laborious. I did not enter into the ministry for its wealth, or I might have been differently circumstanced in that respect. I did not enter it as a secular calling, but because I wished to be useful to others in matters of the highest moment for their everlasting interests. Until within the last four years, my sermons, as a general thing, have been extemporaneous. Since then, I have written and delivered two sermons a week, with but a very few exceptions. If I know myself, my aim has always been devoutly to fulfill the ministry I have received in the Divine providence of the Lord Jesus. I am not unaware of my imperfections as a teacher, especially in regard to oratorical abilities. I know also and keenly feel the want of popularity which the practical doctrines I have taught have mostly met with at the hands of the men of the world, and even among the great body of professors of religion. But I have done the best I could, conscientiously and sincerely, for the cause of true religion. That the primitive apostles of Jesus Christ enjoyed many and peculiar privileges during the time in which they were on earth, as the chosen disciples, the devoted friends, and daily companions of their Lord, no one who believes in the truths of the Bible will be disposed to deny. They had the inexpressible happiness of hearing his public discourses, and of listening to his private instructions; they saw his mighty miracles, they heard his beautiful parables, his sublime sermons, and they beheld his meekness and lowliness of heart. The doctrines and spirit of the Christian dispensation they were taught by precept and example; and whenever they understood not the nature of his doctrines, as delivered before the people, He cheerfully explained to them in private and caused them clearly to understand; and these highly favored men, in the fullness of their gratitude and admiration, exclaimed, "Behold the Lamb of God, that taketh away the sin of the world." In the ardency of their affection they declared, "Thou art the Christ, the Son of the living God." Nor need we wonder at this: they had been called to take a part in a new dispensation,—a dispensation of universal benevolence and heaven-born charity. They had been taught the glorious truths of the Gospel, and had been ordained as the first preachers of a faith that went to bring salvation fully before their minds; and they understood and believed,—they obeyed, and lived according to the doctrines they had espoused and the charity they had imbibed. Such were the faithful among the primitive disciples of our blessed Lord; such a few of their privileges, their enjoyments, their co-operation, and their happiness. In after-periods of the Church those entering the ministry have not had any of these external privileges; but yet there is reason to believe that wherever there is sincerity and devotedness of heart, the laborers in the Lord's vineyard are not left comfortless. He is inwardly present, and by the aid and influences of his Spirit, which in all ages of the world are sent forth, He is at all times ready to enlighten, to encourage, and sustain them in their arduous undertaking. Hence the pulpit at all times has had an important influence on the morals of society. The peculiarity of the doctrines I have taught has been one cause of the smallness of the congregation that usually attends in this house. A life and practice in accordance with the knowledge of the truths of Revelation have invariably been enjoined as indispensably necessary to man's happiness; not the hearers of the word, but the doers of the word, are they who find acceptance with the Lord of heaven and earth. "If ye know these things," saith the Lord, "happy are ye if ye do them." Religion has been represented as that which is to be shed into actual and daily life; and this practical requirement has apparently retarded the outward growth of the Church. Mankind, as a general principle, are not only "slow of heart to believe all that the prophets have said," but equally tardy in "laying the axe to the root of the tree," and bringing forth in their lives the fruits of righteousness and true holiness.

From a prayerful exercise of those intellectual and moral faculties with which the Creator has graciously endowed all men, I have seen and taught through the Sacred Scriptures during the last fifty years that there is but one living and true God,—the Creator, Redeemer, and Saviour of the world,—one in essence, one in person,—and that the glorified Jesus Christ is "God over all, blessed forever." The apostle says, "God was in Christ reconciling the world to Himself, not imputing their trespasses to them," nor, as some preachers would have us suppose, reconciling an angry and unforgiving God to sinful, fallen man. He also adds, "All things are of God, who has reconciled US to HIMSELF in Jesus Christ, and has given us the ministry of reconciliation, and has committed unto us the word of reconciliation." "Hear, O Israel, the Lord thy God is one Lord." And says Paul, "In Jesus Christ dwelleth all the fullness of the Godhead bodily." It therefore inevitably follows that if "all the fullness of the Godhead, or Deity, dwells in Him bodily," there can be but one *person* of the Godhead. Let it not be imagined that with this idea of one person in the Godhead I must not have believed in the Trinity. So far from this being the case, I have at all times preached that, while the Scriptures are explicit on the Unity of the Divine Being, they proclaim with equal clearness to the understanding of men the doctrine of a Divine Trinity, as the great characteristic of the Christian Religion. After the resurrection, Jesus Christ commanded his disciples not only "to preach the Gospel to every creature," but to "baptize all nations in the name of the Father, and of the Son, and of the Holy Spirit." In speaking on this doctrine I have not understood or represented the terms Father, Son, and Holy Spirit as meaning three separate and distinct persons, but rather as expressive of a threefold combination of spirit concentrated in the glorified Lord God and Saviour Jesus Christ. As to his Essential Divine Spirit, He is called, in the figurative language of the Bible, the *Father ;* as to the Divine Human Spirit, or Son of Man, He is called the *Son ;* and as to his Divine sphere,—power of operation or energy by which He redeems and regenerates mankind,—He is called the *Holy Spirit*. The Essential Divine Spirit and the glorified manhood of Christ are one in the all-glorious person of Jesus Christ, comparatively; as in this life the soul and body of finite man are one in every individual of the human race, agreeing precisely with the celebrated Athanasian Creed, "As the reasonable *soul* and *flesh* are one man, so God and man, or *Father* and *Son*, are one Christ;" and that the Holy Spirit is one with the Father and the Son, being the emanated energy or power of operation on all human minds, to enlighten, to sanctify, and to save, is also clearly the doctrine of the Bible, particularly from the circumstance that Jesus Christ, previous to his ascension, "breathed on his disciples, and said, Receive ye the Holy Spirit."

Another doctrine I have felt in duty bound to preach for the instruction of my hearers, is that of Redemption by Jesus Christ. If it be true that there is only one Divine Being upon the throne of heaven, and if there is in reality no such feeling as anger or wrath, nor a principle of vindictive justice, in the bosom of the God of the Bible, it is esteemed impossible that the popular teaching, which ascribes to our merciful and heavenly Father such unworthy passions and so odious a principle, can have its foundation in the Sacred Scriptures, when they are correctly understood. Redemption consisted in the assumption of human nature, and its actual recovery, deliverance, and ransom from the dominion of the powers of darkness by the Omnipotent hand of Jehovah Himself, manifest in the flesh. The Bible teaches most clearly that when mankind had fallen from the state of integrity in which they were while dwelling in the Garden of Eden, if they were to be saved, it became necessary that means should be provided for that end. But their restoration could only be effected by a Divine power. He who was the Creator of man could alone become his Redeemer and Saviour, and therefore, in the fullness of time, in his love for fallen man, and in his unbounded mercy, He condescended to assume the nature of man, with all its propensities and proclivities to evil,— to take upon Himself that very nature which needed to be redeemed, and in and through this assumed human nature or manhood, He progressively wrought out deliverance and Redemption for his people,—a Redemption and restoration which no other being in heaven or on earth was capable of effecting. The whole prophetic testimony concurs in teaching that it was Jehovah Himself who came into the world, in the person of Jesus Christ, to accomplish the work of Redemption. This He effected by subduing the powers of darkness, and thus opening up a new way for the salvation of the human family. "Thus saith Jehovah, the King of Israel, and his Redeemer the Lord of hosts, I am the First, and I am the Last, and beside me there is no God." Yet our blessed Lord in the Gospel declares that this work was accomplished by Himself, for He says to his disciples, "Now is the judgment of this world; now shall the prince of this world be cast out." "The Prince of this world is judged." "Be of good cheer, I have overcome the world." In these and other similar expressions, by the world, and the Prince of this world, are implied the whole Powers of Darkness or hell; and by the victory obtained over them is denoted the great work of Redemption and glorification of his Humanity, which opened the way, and led to the deliverance, restoration, security, and final salvation of the faithful of his people in all periods of the Church. From the time I first entered on the duties of the ministry I have taught that the Bible is a revelation of the will of God to mankind. I have advocated its Divine authenticity, its spirituality, and its plenary Inspiration. But time will not permit me to go into an exposition of the all-varied and important doctrines of the Christian system I have preached for the past *fifty years*. Besides what has been already adverted to, I have preached the doctrines of Repentance and the *Remission of Sins;* of man's *Free Will* in things regarding his highest, his spiritual interests, as well as in the temporal things of his outward or natural life. I have not failed to teach the *At-one-ment*, and the doctrine of the *Resurrection* from the dead: a resurrection not of the natural and corruptible body deposited in the grave, but of what the apostle calls the spiritual body. "There is," he says, "a natural body, and there is a spiritual body." At death "a natural body is sown," or committed to the silent grave, never to be reassumed, "and a spiritual body is raised,"—raised, and thenceforward it becomes an inhabitant of the spiritual world. I have maintained that there is a Divine Providence, or a government of the Lord's infinite Love and Wisdom, which has for its end the salvation of mankind and the formation of a heaven out of the human family; and that in all its operations this providence has respect to what is spiritual and eternal. Its laws are twofold,— those of appointment, and those of permission. The doctrines also of Baptism, The Holy Supper, Charity, Faith, and Good Works,—in brief, I have preached all the doctrines of the various Christian denominations, though I have associated and taught very different ideas—respecting many of them—from those of other religious persuasions. On all subjects, and on all occasions, however, I have endeavored to preach the truths of the Christian Church, and to present the Sabbath as a day of worship and of religious instruction; and in this preaching I have gone three times through the Bible, speaking from every chapter in regular rotation. One thing more: I concur with the Apostle Paul, that "It is good neither to eat flesh, nor to drink wine;" "to be temperate in all things," —to strive to subdue the carnal mind, the selfish propensities, and what he calls "the deeds of the body." These sentiments I have preached, and have practiced accordingly, for the last fifty-two years. I have represented them as moral and religious duties.

But I must conclude. The half-century is gone,—gone like the word just spoken, for good or for evil, never to be recalled,—gone as yesterday has gone. Yet why do I say they are gone? Nothing is gone, whose influence remains with man or woman. The Sabbaths, the prayers, the praises, the weeks, the months, the whole half-century, that seem to us to have passed away, live still,—live in the presence and universe of our heavenly Father. Such have been the religious principles I have taught for more than fifty years. They lay, according to my apprehension, a foundation for purer Christian attainments and a more intellectual form of godliness. They are calculated—if adopted into practical life—to renew and to regenerate man's whole nature. Practical religion, with love to God and charity to man, will sweeten all the hours, the years, and the scenes of human life. The esteem of our friends in such case will be sincere; our children will be found traveling with us heavenward by our side. We also shall continue to grow in grace and in spiritual knowledge. The Church will be nurtured, and multiply in numbers. Cheerfulness and gratitude to God will crown our worship; a conscious sense of a Christian spirit, and of progress in the regenerate life, will strengthen our good purposes, and the fruits of love, scattered along our pathway, will be to our souls vital and evident proofs that the Lord our God is ever with us. To Him—"The true God and Eternal Life"—be glory, now and forever. Amen.

DISCOURSE XVII.

THE JUBILEE—BEING A HISTORICAL SKETCH OF THE BIBLE-CHRISTIAN CHURCH—JUNE 12TH, 1859.

Isaiah lxi. 1, 2, 3.

From the earliest periods of the history of the Church, mankind seem to have deemed certain events and occurrences in the world worthy of a particular commemoration; and that the custom has received the Divine approbation is particularly indicated in the institution of the Passover,—a festival that was to be observed through all the generations of the people of Israel, in commemoration of their deliverance from the oppressions and bondage of the Egyptians. We do not, indeed, meet with any record of such commemorations having been celebrated during the antediluvian, or Adamic Dispensation, unless we receive the narrative of the offerings of Cain and Abel as tokens of their having received certain blessings from the Lord, their Creator, which they felt called on to acknowledge and commemorate by those acts of religious devotion. They are the first intimation of acts of Divine worship that are recorded. And what are external acts of worship but mere ceremonies, to bring to our remembrance our obligations to the Lord for his goodness towards us, unless indeed they be accompanied and sanctified by the adoration of our hearts? In the Church of which *Noah* was "a preacher of righteousness," his salvation from the deluge, and his coming forth from the ark of his safety, were events which he and his family commemorated by building an altar, and presenting thereon an offering unto the Lord. This is represented as having been acceptable, and to have been responded to by the gracious announcement from the Lord, that "while the earth remaineth, seed-time and harvest, and cold and heat, and summer and winter, and day and night, shall not cease." After the patriarch Abram had been called, and had left the land of his nativity, and had passed into Canaan, the Lord appeared to him, and said, "To thee and to thy posterity will I give this land;" and Abram commemorated this manifestation by there building an altar unto the Lord. The cause of his posterity going down into Egypt is recorded as having been the result of a famine in Canaan; and their being subsequently led up out of that land by the hand of Moses, when the pursuing Egyptians were thrown into the Red Sea, was commemorated by the song of Moses, sung by him and the congregated sons of Israel, and responsively answered by Miriam and the whole camp of Israelitish women. The events of their subsequent history were mostly celebrated in a way intended to keep their occurrence in the memory of the people. Under the Christian dispensation we have a record of the manner in which the heavenly host, and the *Magi*, or wise men of the East, celebrated the nativity of our LORD JESUS CHRIST; and we all know his birth is still annually commemorated throughout Christendom at the season called Christmas. In the after-ages of the Church, numerous circumstances have taken place from time to time, which have called forth the gratitude of true believers in Christianity, and induced them to celebrate such events. Among other things of this nature is that of celebrating the commencement of various Churches by those who are members of their respective bodies, intending by such means to hand down from generation to generation the knowledge of the origin of their denominations and the peculiarities of their faith. The members of the *Bible-Christian Church* participate in this feeling common to humanity, and accordingly we have come together this morning to worship the Lord in his holy sanctuary, and to commemorate devoutly the fiftieth year or the Jubilee of our existence as a distinct body of professing Christians. Fifty years ago, on the 28th of June, 1809, a number of ministers and lay members met together for the first time as a distinct body, to worship the Lord according to their conviction of truth, and they publicly declared that they did not form a *Sectarian Church* under any particular denomination from man; that they simply professed and wished to be *Bible-Christians;* and that though worshiping and teaching religious principles, according to what they conscientiously believed to be in accordance with the revealed Word of God, they felt in perfect union with the sincere livers in all the various denominations of Christians.

We have selected this portion of the Scriptures because it contains an enumeration of many of the blessings which were to be enjoyed by the Israelites on the recurrence of the year of release, or Jubilee year. The particulars of that law, as given by Moses, will be found recorded in the xxv. chapter of Leviticus, 8-13 verse.

In our text (Isaiah lxi. 1, 2, 3) we have a prophecy relative to the coming of the Lord as the promised Messiah, describing his government and its blessings; and we are officially informed that all the temporal benefits which the Israelites experienced as a people from being governed according to the principles of the Mosaic laws, would be spiritually enjoyed by every true believer under the Christian dispensation; and that liberty of thought, freedom to worship God according to the dictates of conscience, and an unrestrained exercise of all the powers of the mind, should be proclaimed unto all lands, and to all the inhabitants thereof, as blessings and privileges secured unto them by the glad tidings of the everlasting Gospel. It appears, from the laws given to the Israelitish Church, that the return of every seventh day was to be observed as a Sabbath, or day of rest; that every seventh year was to be commemorated as a year of release; and that every seven times seven, or fiftieth year, was to be celebrated as a National Jubilee, in which year the Jubilee trumpets were to be sounded, a general release was to take place,— a restoration of inheritance was to be made, and the oppressed, and those that were in bonds, were to go out free. No person can deliberately take into consideration the nature and tendency of these Bible institutions, even when viewed only as legal regulations, and venture to deny either their wisdom, their justice, their benevolence, or the goodness of Jehovah, from whom they were given. The observance of One day in seven, or the Sabbath, was, in fact, an institution not made for the people of Israel only, nor for any particular age or nation, but it was instituted for *mankind*. It is a day in seven intended to promote man's progress in the heavenly life.

The Sabbatic year was to be observed in the manner specified in the law. There were four peculiarities connected with it. The first was thus expressed, "Thou shalt neither sow thy field nor prune thy vineyard." The *second* peculiarity was in relation to the gracious promise of Jehovah given to the Israelites, that on condition of their obedience to his Commandments He would so bestow his blessings upon them that in the sixth year the land should bring forth fruit sufficient for three years.

The *third* peculiarity in regard to the Sabbatic year related to the relinquishment of debts or claims on the estates of others; and the *fourth* provided for the public reading of the law at the feast of tabernacles in each Sabbatic year, or year of release. In addition to these there were *three* other peculiarities which related exclusively to the Jubilee year. The first of these was, that the Jubilee was to be proclaimed throughout the whole land by the sounding of trumpets. The second observance was, that the Jubilee should be a year of general release of persons and property; all who were in slavery or bondage were in that year to go free; even those who in the Sabbatical year had voluntarily relinquished their privilege of going out free, and had had their ears bored in token of this, were all to be set free in the Jubilee year, because then they were to proclaim liberty throughout *all* the land to *all the inhabitants thereof*. The third peculiarity relating to the Jubilee year was, that in it all estates which had been sold at any time within the preceding forty-nine years, were to be returned to their former proprietors, or to the families to which they had originally belonged. By this arrangement it was graciously provided that no family throughout all the tribes of Israel should ever be finally deprived of their family inheritance or homestead,—made wretched and ruined, and doomed to perpetual poverty,— for such was the benevolent provision that no estate or inheritance could be alienated or sold for a longer period than the next coming Jubilee year. The nearer, therefore, the year of Jubilee was, the less was the value of the purchase of an estate, the worth being always regulated by the number of years between the time of purchase and the expiration of the term. Now, all these regulations, and especially those relative to the Jubilee, considered only in a political or social point of view, were particularly favorable to human happiness, and to the advancement of Israelitish society in civilization, freedom, and independence; and when contemplated as the manifested will of God it must be seen how entirely they were calculated to promote their progress in religion, in righteousness, and true holiness. In every aspect, indeed, the Jubilee was a remarkable feature in the Israelitish government. Its requirements were wisely adapted to prevent the more wealthy from becoming the oppressors of the poorer portion of the theocracy, and from holding any individual in perpetual slavery. They also prevented the rich from getting permanent possession of all the lands of other families, either by way of purchase or of grasping usurpation. Neither could pecuniary debts be unduly multiplied under the Jubilee principles of government. Its laws were well adapted to preserve personal liberty, equality of property, the regular order of family inheritances, freedom, religion, and independence among the people of Israel. But it is our duty, my beloved friends, not only to look at these regulations as they applied externally and politically to the government of Israel, but to observe wherein they are intended for the spiritual instruction of all mankind: for the Bible is a religious Book, and its contents are to be religiously interpreted. "All Scripture," says an apostle, "is given for our instruction in righteousness." "God is a Spirit," and as the Word of God—the Bible—necessarily contains not merely details of historical facts, and national institutions, such as were literally adapted to the moral, social, and religious state of the people of Israel, who were emphatically a worldly and natural-minded people, but within its literal and historical statements, or under their cover, heavenly truths full of spirit and life, intended for the spiritual edification of the Church in all ages, will be found. Let us, then, on this occasion, cast ourselves humbly at the feet of our Lord Jesus Christ, "the only Wise God, our Saviour," fervently praying, that as "He opened the understandings" of his primitive disciples, in order that "they might understand the Scriptures," so He will this day open our minds, and enable us to see the adaptability of the Sabbatic and Jubilee laws of the Israelitish dispensation to the promotion of our spiritual and individual instruction, and to our progressive advancement in the life of Christian Regeneration. Then will the Word of the Lord be indeed "a lamp to our feet and a light to lead us in the paths" of righteousness, joy, and peace.

At the time when these laws were revealed, the Israelites were a people who constituted the visible Church of God on earth. In this respect they were not only the predecessors but the representatives of the Church under the Christian dispensation. The Sabbath, which they were commanded to remember and to keep holy, we have observed was not an exclusively Israelitish institution; its origin is traceable to the time of the creation of man, the Creator having thus early manifested his will in respect to its observance. Among the Israelites the Sabbath was to be received as a day of sanctity and holiness. Six days of the week symbolically represented the labors and combats of the Lord Jesus Christ with the powers of darkness, in "destroying the works of the devil," while effecting man's redemption; and the Sabbath typified his victory over them, and the rest, consequently, "remaining to the people of God." The *Sabbath* was the emblem of the accomplishment of the whole work of Redemption by the LORD, when He was manifested in the flesh, and was therefore to be received as a day of essential holiness. But under the Gospel dispensation the Sabbath is made a day of instruction in heavenly and Divine things,—a day of meditation on subjects concerning God, salvation, and eternal life, and a day of worship, adoration, thanksgiving, and praise. The term, in the original tongue, means *rest;* and it is expressive of the state of joy and peace which the regenerate man experiences in his confidence, or his rest in dependence on the Lord. It is, therefore, a day of the highest importance to the spiritual happiness of the whole family of man. But the *Sabbatic* and *Jubilee* years peculiarly pointed out a release from spiritual oppression, and typified the great and Divine work of the Redemption of mankind by our Lord Jesus Christ, and the renewal or regeneration of our whole nature. "Except a man be born again of water and of the Spirit, he cannot enter into the kingdom of God." Through the reception of the truths of Divine revelation from the Lord, and by the influence of his Spirit, we are put in possession of a knowledge of the true principles of salvation. We are successively released from the power of our spiritual foes, and are brought, through repentance, reformation, and regeneration, to that heavenly rest and spiritual freedom of which the Sabbath and the Sabbatical year were the emblems. By the propensities of our fallen nature, and through improper habits, we are in mental bondage and spiritual slavery to sin. Through the knowledge of the truths of the Word of the Lord, and the sanctifying influences of his Spirit, we are delivered from this bondage, emancipated from this spiritual slavery, and brought into the enjoyment of "the liberty which belongs to the children of God." Through our disobedience and many transgressions we have forfeited all rightful claim to a title to a possession in the heavenly Canaan; but by his Word and Spirit, operating on our hearts and lives, we become born from above,—new creatures,—regenerated,—and heirs of the kingdom of heaven, for that kingdom is open to all true believers; and with all such there is the experimental conviction that the Church and the kingdom of heaven are really within their souls. After this progressive order, then,—released from our spiritual adversaries,—the foes of our own households,—restored to spiritual liberty, united in spirit with the heavenly family,—angels, and the spirits of the just made perfect,—reconciled and *at-one* with our heavenly Father, and, through being thus "transformed into the image and likeness of the LORD," re-entitled to our inheritance in the heavenly Canaan, we may enjoy our Jubilee in the Church on earth,—urge on our way rejoicing; every day, by our conversation and example, proclaiming liberty throughout all the land to all the inhabitants thereof, and thus announcing to all around *the acceptable year of the Lord*. Then, when, in the merciful providence of the Lord, we are removed from our earthly tabernacles, we shall enter into the Paradise of our Great Redeemer, and participate in the joys and rejoicings of an endless Jubilee in the everlasting kingdom of the Lord our God. We have nothing of the imposing rituals of the Israelitish Church by means of which to celebrate the Jubilee of the visible and outward existence of the Bible-Christian Church; but we feel it to be a matter of duty to God, and to our brethren in the religious world, to make acknowledgment of his goodness during the past fifty years in blessing the efforts of his servants, who have faithfully labored, according to their respective capacities, and in their relative spheres of life, in this new department of their Lord's vineyard, and publicly to solicit a continuation of his goodness and loving kindness through the coming future. For *forty-two years* we have been endeavoring to build up a Bible-Christian Church in the City of Brotherly Love. The result is known to many of our hearers: we have not rapidly increased in numbers, as have done many other denominations around us, but there is a reason sufficiently powerful to be found in the required discipline of the Church to account for the paucity of our numbers: *abstinence from the flesh of animals as food,* and *a total abstinence from all kinds of intoxicating beverages,* not simply on account of health, not merely as a physiological injunction, nor yet as a mere moral requirement, but *as a religious duty.*

These principles of *discipline* are *stumbling-blocks* in the estimation of many, and prevent numbers from becoming members of the Bible-Christian Church. We had not been more than two or three weeks resident in this city before we were told, if we would lay aside preaching our discipline, we could have a Church and congregation that would afford us a handsome living. How many have said to us at various times, "I would become a member of your Church but for the discipline in regard to eating and drinking"! Most of our members have told the same tale. It is this peculiarity in our discipline which is the great stumbling-stone and rock of offense to the many; this that is the principal barrier to our numerical progress as a religious community. But it will perhaps be said, If this be the doctrine of the Bible, why do not men see it? Why are they not convinced? When our Lord was on earth preaching glad tidings to the meek, binding up the broken-hearted, proclaiming liberty to the captives, and announcing the acceptable year of the Lord, did He not complain of the slowness of men's hearts to believe all the truths that the prophets had told? Need we wonder, then, if "He who spoke as never man spoke," and whose wisdom silenced the cavils of the self-righteous Pharisees, found it needful to mention the slowness of men to be convinced of the truths He taught? Need we wonder that a like tardiness should still be manifested towards the espousal of the *practical* doctrines of our common Christianity? The fact is, men do not want to be convinced of any truths that require *self-denial.* "He that's convinced against his will is of the same opinion still." Notwithstanding these disciplinary obstacles, we have made some progress in numbers. We also own the building in which we are assembled, and the ground on which it stands, in fee-simple, and—what is more than many other churches, that make a more imposing appearance, can say—*we are out of debt.* Have we not cause, then, to rejoice, and to celebrate the first Jubilee of our existence as a Church with gratitude and praise? Every serious and considerate individual, after reading the Bible account of the Sabbatical and Jubilee years, as enjoined on the Israelites, should reflect and turn his thoughts immediately within himself,—should examine his own heart in the presence of the all-seeing God, and should try to ascertain how far he has mentally experienced any of those blessed effects of which the Sabbatical and Jubilee years of the Israelitish Church were the outward emblems. If he do this in faithfulness, he will not be long in discovering that nothing can be more beautiful, elevating, and harmonious, nor tend more to the happiness of mankind, than that progressive influence of pure and spiritual religion on the human mind, arising from a life according to its principles. This will not fail to lead to the possession of that inward rest and mental enjoyment shadowed forth by the Jubilee of a former dispensation.

Do we, then, beloved, wish to attain to the happy enjoyment of these gradual, but certain, renewals of our fallen and sinful natures?—of those truthful principles and heavenly states of peace,—joy and rejoicing? Let us lose no time in taking upon us the yoke of our Lord Jesus Christ, and following Him in the regeneration. Let us ever live according to the principles of our faith, obey the teachings and adhere to the discipline of the Bible-Christian Church. And then the Spirit of the glorious Lord and Saviour Jesus Christ, the true God and eternal life, will assuredly be unto us a *sun* and a *shield*, will work in us to will and to do, according to his own Divine order, until at length we are, by his gracious and compassionate aid, entirely emancipated from the spiritual bondage of sin, and restored to the possession of a title for the attainment of a heavenly inheritance in the kingdom, and rejoice in the unending Jubilee of " Our Father in the heavens." Amen.

THE END.

LIST OF PUBLICATIONS

OF

J. B. LIPPINCOTT & CO.

PHILADELPHIA.

Will be sent by mail, post paid, on receipt of the price.

The Albert N'Yanza. Great Basin of the Nile, and Explorations of the Nile Sources. By Sir Samuel White Baker, M. A., F. R. G. S., &c. With Maps and numerous Illustrations, from sketches by Mr. Baker. New edition. Crown 8vo. Extra cloth, $3.

"It is one of the most interesting and instructive books of travel ever issued; and this edition, at a reduced price, will bring it within the reach of many who have not before seen it."—*Boston Journal.*

"One of the most fascinating, and certainly not the least important, books of travel published during the century." *Boston Eve. Transcript.*

The Nile Tributaries of Abyssinia, and the Sword Hunters of the Hamran Arabs. By Sir Samuel White Baker, M. A., F. R. G. S., &c. With Maps and numerous Illustrations, from original sketches by the Author. New edition. Crown 8vo. Extra cloth, $2.75.

"We have rarely met with a descriptive work so well conceived and so attractively written as Baker's Abyssinia, and we cordially recommend it to public patronage . . . It is beautifully illustrated."—*N. O Times.*

Eight Years' Wandering in Ceylon. By Sir Samuel White Baker, M. A., F. R. G. S., &c. With Illustrations. 16mo. Extra cloth, $1.50.

"Mr. Baker's description of life in Ceylon, of sport, of the cultivation of the soil, of its birds and beasts and insects and reptiles, of its wild forests and dense jungles, of its palm trees and its betel nuts and intoxicating drugs, will be found very interesting. The book is well written and beautifully printed."—*Balt. Gazette.*

"Notwithstanding the volume abounds with sporting accounts, the natural history of Ceylon is well and carefully described, and the curiosities of the famed island are not neglected. It is a valuable addition to the works on the East Indies."—*Phila Lutheran Observer.*

PUBLICATIONS OF J. B. LIPPINCOTT & CO.

The American Beaver and his Works. By Lewis H. MORGAN, author of "The League of the Iroquois." Handsomely illustrated with twenty-three full-page Lithographs and numerous Wood-Cuts. One vol. 8vo. Tinted paper. Cloth extra, $5.

"The book may be pronounced an expansive and standard work on the American beaver, and a valuable contribution to science."—*N. Y. Herald.*

"The book is an octavo of three hundred and thirty pages, on very thick paper, handsomely bound and abundantly illustrated with maps and diagrams. It is a complete scientific, practical, historical and descriptive treatise on the subject of which it treats, and will form a standard for those who are seeking knowledge in this department of animal life. . . . By the publication of this book, Messrs. J. B. Lippincott & Co., of Philadelphia, have really done a service to science which we trust will be well rewarded"—*Boston Even. Traveler.*

The Autobiography of Dr. Benjamin Franklin. The first and only complete edition of Franklin's Memoirs. Printed from the original MS. With Notes and an Introduction. Edited by the HON. JOHN BIGELOW, late Minister of the United States to France. With Portrait from a line Engraving on Steel. Large 12mo. Toned paper. Fine cloth, beveled boards, $2.50.

"The discovery of the original autograph of Benjamin Franklin's characteristic narrative of his own life was one of the fortunate events of Mr. Bigelow's diplomatic career. It has given him the opportunity of producing a volume of rare bibliographical interest, and performing a valuable service to the cause of letters. He has engaged in his task with the enthusiasm of an American scholar, and completed it in a manner highly creditable to his judgment and industry."—*The New York Tribune.*

"Every one who has at heart the honor of the nation, the interests of American literature and the fame of Franklin will thank the author for so requisite a national service, and applaud the manner and method of its fulfillment."—*Boston Even. Transcript*

The Dervishes. History of the Dervishes; or, Oriental Spiritualism. By JOHN P. BROWN, Interpreter of the American Legation at Constantinople. With twenty-four Illustrations. One vol. crown 8vo. Tinted paper. Cloth, $3.50.

"In this volume are the fruits of long years of study and investigation, with a great deal of personal observation. It treats, in an exhaustive manner, of the belief and principles of the Dervishes.

. . . On the whole, this is a thoroughly original work, which cannot fail to become a book of reference."—*The Philada. Press.*

New America. By Wm. Hepworth Dixon. Fourth edition. Crown 8vo. With Illustrations. Tinted paper. Extra cloth, $2.75.

"In this graphic volume Mr. Dixon sketches American men and women sharply, vigorously and truthfully, under every aspect."—*Dublin University Magazine*

Cottage Piety Exemplified. By the author of "Union to Christ," "Love to God," etc. 16mo. Extra cloth. $1.25.

"A very interesting sketch."—*N. Y. Observer.*

Stories for Sundays, Illustrating the Catechism. By the author of "Little Henry and his Bearer." Revised and edited by A. CLEVELAND COXE, Bishop of Western New York, and author of "Thoughts on the Services," etc. 12mo. Illustrated. Tinted paper. Extra cloth. $1.75. FINE EDITION. Printed within red lines. Extra cloth, gilt edges. $2.50.

"We are glad to see this charming book in such a handsome dress. *This* was one of our few Sunday books when we were a school-boy. Sunday books are more plentiful now, but we doubt whether there is any improvement on Mrs. Sherwood's sterling stories for the young."—*Lutheran Observer.*

"The typography is attractive, and the stories illustrated by pictures which render them yet more likely to interest the young people for wh se religious improvement they are designed."—*N. Y. Evening Post.*

An Index to the Principal Works in Every Department of Religious Literature. Embracing nearly Seventy Thousand Citations, Alphabetically Arranged under Two Thousand Heads. By HOWARD MALCOM, D. D., LL.D. SECOND EDITION. With Addenda to 1870. 8vo. Extra cloth. $4.

"A work of immense labor, such as no one could prepare who had not the years allotted to the lifetime of man. We know of no work of the kind which can compare with it in value."—*Portland Zion's Advocate.*

"The value of such a book can hardly be overestimated. It is a noble contribution to literature. It meets an urgent need, and long after Dr. Malcom shall have left the world many an earnest pen-worker will thank him, with heartfelt benedictions on his name, for help and service rendered."—*Boston Watchman and Reflector.*

The Geological Evidences of the Antiquity of Man, with Remarks on the Origin of Species by Variation. By SIR CHARLES LYELL, F.R.S., author of "Principles of Geology," etc. Illustrated by wood-cuts. Second American, from the latest London Edition. 8vo. Extra cloth. *$3.*

This work treats of one of the most interesting scientific subjects of the day, and will be examined with interest, as well by those who favor its deductions as by those who condemn them.

The Student's Manual of Oriental History. A Manual of the Ancient History of the East, to the Commencement of the Median Wars. By FRANCOIS LENORMANT, Sub-Librarian of the Imperial Institute of France, and E. CHEVALLIER, Member of the Royal Asiatic Society, London. 2 vols. 12mo. Fine cloth. $5.50.

"The best proof of the immense results accomplished in the various departments of philology is to be found in M. Francois Lenormant's admirable *Handbook of Ancient History.*"—*London Athenæum.*

Preparation for Death. Translated from the Italian of Alphonso, Bishop of S. Agatha. By Rev. ORBY SHIPLEY, M. A. Square crown 8vo. Tinted paper. Extra cloth, red edges. $1.75.

"But at the same time many of the pages of this book teem with rich spiritual matter, and many of the prayers may be well studied as models."—*Presbyterian Banner.*

"As to the contents, their merits have long since been settled, deeply and lovingly, in all hearts whose needs and tastes make welcome the precious ore outpoured for us through the long ages by those who have dug earnestly in the exhaustless mine of communion with God."—*Charleston Courier.*

Mizpah. Friends at Prayer. Containing a Prayer or Meditation for Each Day in the Year. By LAFAYETTE C. LOOMIS. 12mo. Beautifully printed on superfine tinted paper, within red lines. Fine cloth. $2. Extra cloth, gilt edges. $2.50.

"A beautifully printed volume with colored border. The plan of the work consists in 'an evening meditation' for each day of the year; with appropriate Scripture references for morning and evening. The meditations are well and piously written, and will, we doubt not, accomplish great good."—*The Lutheran Observer.*

Blunt's Key to the Holy Bible. A Key to the Knowledge and Use of the Holy Bible. By J. H. BLUNT, M. A., author of "Household Theology," etc. 16mo. Extra cloth. $1.

"Is a compact history of Holy Scripture, showing how, when and by whom it was written, with what purpose, what was its writers' inspiration, how it is to be interpreted, and what are the Apocrypha of the Old and New Testaments. There is an Appendix of peculiar Bible words, with their meanings, and a good Index. ... On the whole, this is a singularly well-executed work, of great value in many respects."—*The Philada. Press.*

Pulpit Germs. Plans for Sermons. By Rev. W. W. WYTHE. 12mo. Tinted paper. Extra cloth. $1.50.

"This book is intended as an aid to clergymen in the preparation of their sermons—not as a labor-saving apparatus for drones, but as an incentive to study. It contains 455 texts, upon each of which the leading heads or skeletons of a discourse are supplied with occasional subdivisions under such heads. The utility of the work is obvious."—*San Francisco Times.*

"The book is unquestionably the best and most unexceptionable of its kind we have met with."—*The Prot. Churchman.*

Evidences of Natural and Revealed Theology. By CHAS. E. LORD. 8vo. Toned paper. Extra cloth. $3.50.

"This volume bears the marks of careful study and clear thinking. ... The book is a calm, serious and valuable contribution to the theological literature of the age."—*N. Y. Observer.*

"Dr. Lord is a calm, clear and careful writer, and this volume is a valuable contribution to theological literature."

"... As a summary treatise upon natural and revealed theology, or as a manual for use in schools and higher institutions of learning, this book has few, if any, superiors. It will therefore be welcome to the general reader of religious works and useful to the cause of education."—*N. Y. Times.*

The Christian Worker; A Call to the Laity. By REV. C. F. BEACH. 16mo. Cloth. $1.

Moral Reforms, Suggested in a Pastoral Letter.
With remarks on Practical Religion. By RT. REV. A. CLEVELAND COXE, Bishop of Western New York, and author of "Thoughts on the Services, etc. 12mo. Cloth. $1.

"This volume will be universally welcomed as a fuller and freer discussion of some of the more practical subjects of Christian life and duty, touched upon in he Bishop's Lenten Pastoral and that of the House of Bishops...

"The book must have a large circulation, for its style and matter will make any one who begins it read it through."—*Utica Gospel Messenger.*

Heart Breathings; or, The Soul's Desire Expressed in Earnestness. A Series of Prayers, Meditations and Selections for the "Home Circle." By S. P. GODWIN. 18mo. Tinted paper. Fine cloth. 75 cents.

"A truly precious little volume, which will doubtless aid the devotions and cheer the way of many a Christian pilgrim."—*Protestant Churchman.*

True Protestant Ritualism. Being a Review of a book entitled "The Law of Ritualism." By the REV. CHARLES H. HALL, D. D., Rector of the Church of the Epiphany, Washington, D. C. 16mo. Cloth. $1.50.

"Dr. Hall has contributed one of the most comprehensive and comprehensible arguments upon the subject which has yet been written. It is well worth the careful perusal of all who are interested in this vexed question."—*Philada. Even. Bulletin.*

Divisions in the Society of Friends. By Thomas H. SPEAKMAN. 16mo. Fine cloth. 63 cents.

"The essay under notice furnishes in a compact form the reasons for the separation of the Society into different organizations."—*Balt. Gazette.*

Life of Philip Doddridge, D. D. With Notices of some of his Contemporaries, and Specimens of his Style. By D. H. HARSHA, M. A., author of "The Star of Bethlehem," etc. NEW EDITION. 12mo. Tinted paper. Extra cloth. $1.50.

"Doddridge is one of the purest and most elevated characters in English religious literature. An American minister, attracted by its excellence, made it a study, and reproduces it in the narrative here given. The work is fairly well executed, and the result is a valuable piece of Christian biography—a book the reading of which will give present pleasure and permanent spiritual advantage to any one who may be able to appreciate it."—*N. Y. Christian Advocate.*

The Threefold Grace of the Holy Trinity. By JOHN H. EGAR, B. D. 12mo. Toned paper. Extra cloth. $1.5c.

"It is, in our opinion, one of the ablest and most original contributions to American scientific theology which have been made in our day, and we shall be disappointed if that is not the judgment of the best judges."—*The Amer. Churchman.*

Words in Season. A Manual of Instruction,
Comfort and Devotion for Family Reading and Private Use. By Rev. Henry B. Browning, M. A. 16mo. Toned paper. Extra cloth. $1.

"*Words in Season* is the title of a beautiful little volume of practical religious counsels of instruction, comfort and devotion for family reading and private use. It appears to be truly evangelical, and to be calculated, in style and spirit, to do the good at which it aims."—*Boston Congregationalist.*

"*Words in Season*, a thoughtful, sweet-toned manual for family reading and hours of devotion, prepared by an English minister of the Established Church. Spiritual souls will read it with comfort and strengthening."—*Chicago Advance.*
"A very good book."—*N. Y. Liberal Christian.*

The Scriptural Doctrine of Hades. Comprising an Inquiry into the State of the Righteous and Wicked Dead between Death and the General Judgment, and demonstrating from the Bible that the Atonement was neither made on the Cross nor yet in this World. By Rev. George Bartle, D. D., Principal of Walton College, Liverpool. 12mo. Cloth. $1.50.

The New View of Hell. By B. F. Barrett. 12mo. Extra cloth. $1.25.

"A really valuable contribution to the world's stock of religious ideas. . . . . The book, taken as a whole, is of great interest."—*New York Sun.*
"Contains much that is grotesque and visionary, with much that is profoundly true, and much that is exceedingly suggestive."—*New York Independent.*
"There is not a Christian man or woman in the world who would not be benefited by the reading of this book."—*Westfield News Letter.*

Our Children in Heaven. By William H. Holcombe, M. D., author of "The Sexes," etc. 12mo. Tinted paper. Extra cloth. $1.75.

"Its sweet pathos and comforting sympathy at once warm and interest us."—*Albany Journal.*
"It is written in the most devout spirit, and will interest even those who reject its doctrines."—*Buffalo Express.*

The Sexes: Here and Hereafter. By William H. Holcombe, M. D., author of "Our Children in Heaven," etc. 12mo. Tinted paper. Extra cloth. $1.50.

"Whatever one may think of the doctrines of this book, it would be impossible to deny that it breathes a pure and elevated spirit, and has many thoughts which will commend themselves sympathetically to the followers of all Christian faiths."—*The Independent, N. Y.*

In Both Worlds. By Wm. H. Holcombe, M. D., author of "Our Children in Heaven," "The Sexes: Here and Hereafter," etc., etc. 12mo. Tinted paper. Extra cloth. $1.75.

"While likely to prove of the deepest and most thrilling interest to all whose minds are elevated above materiality and the grosser elements of nature, it is in no sense irreverent."—*Boston Evening Traveler.*

www.ingramcontent.com/pod-product-compliance
Lightning Source LLC
Chambersburg PA
CBHW032144230426
43672CB00011B/2440